NOEL KINGSBURY
gardens

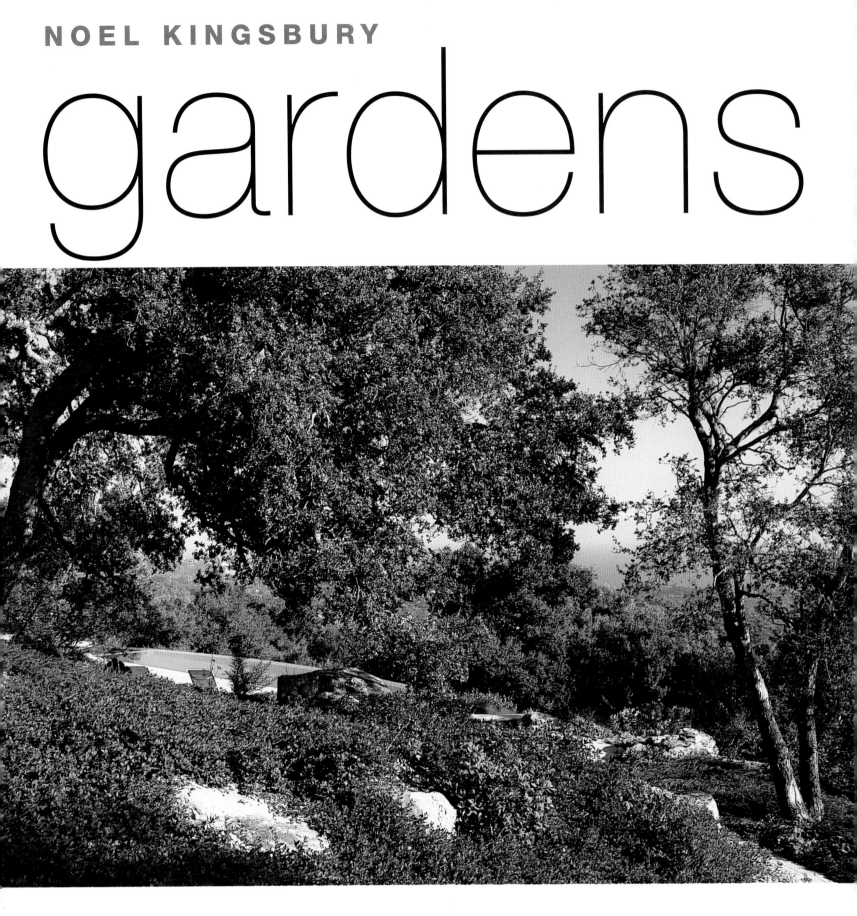

photography by NICOLA BROWNE

by design

TIMBER PRESS
Portland, Oregon

contents

foreword

In this book Noel Kingsbury has developed interesting and extremely useful themes on garden design and planting styles. With a strong emphasis on his own well-developed ideas on design principles, he has cleverly interwoven the thoughts of many of the best modern practitioners in his text.

He has chosen his team for their particular skills. Some deal with planning and surveying, terracing and hard surfaces, others with colour harmonies and/or colour combinations, some with garden architecture and division of space, others with sustainability and management. In "Structural Planting" Piet Oudolf outlines his use of plant shapes, solid or light and airy, to emphasise his flowing lines, while Nori and Sandra Pope delve deeply into the meaning of colour co-ordination and succession through the garden season, with Carol Klein emphasising colour combinations.

Recognising that plants and their environment are not always the main strength of some garden architects, Noel Kingsbury has also asked for contributions to the book from those who are principally renowned for their knowledge of plant habitats, plant needs and wildlife. Beth Chatto, as he points out, is our English "guru", mother of the idea of matching plants to habitat, while Isabelle Greene, a well-known California landscape architect, expands on her respect for rock-placement and native plants in and around Santa Barbara. There are also many new ideas using new materials and new plants, as well as tried and tested favourites.

As a result this is a very successful book. It is also unusual in that much of the information, admirably displayed in writing, pictures and

plans, is aimed at garden owners who take a serious interest, not only in the planning and implementation of plans, but in the meaning of the garden in much broader terms. The designers are there to encourage and suggest but never to dominate the aspiring home gardener. Instead the arrangement of the book encourages a progression of understanding, literally new avenues for the mind to explore. In the end a garden is a personal refuge and that is what Kingsbury wants to convey. But he also reminds you that the garden, even as a sanctuary for an individual, owes a duty to the environment in which it is set. Working with the existing site and not against it, using vernacular materials, considering your neighbours, working out harmonies between "wild" and "tamed" nature, are as vital as more practical decisions.

This is much more than a "how-to" reference book: it looks at principles of design in considerable depth. It deserves to be read from cover to cover, as the information unfolds to reach a final crescendo with mixed borders – the Popes again – and pages on vegetables and exotics. Although Noel Kingsbury is firmly in control, he allows the contributors to express their own philosophies and the reader is enriched by their individuality. As the end of the book is reached the reader can feel that he or she has been on an illuminating and exciting journey, chaperoned by thoughtful and skilful guides, who have not only taught "practicalities" but have illuminated the deeper meaning of the garden.

Penelope Hobhouse, 2005

introduction

In the not-too-distant past, only the very wealthy employed garden designers. Now it seems that there are garden designers practising everywhere, with a wide social mix of clients. There are innumerable television programmes, magazine articles, and books on the subject. Not only, it seems, are we all being encouraged to have our gardens designed professionally, some people might even feel under pressure to do so!

Can you design your own garden? Of course you can – everybody used to. Many people have got an enormous amount of pleasure out of doing so, and probably never even thought of themselves as designers. With garden design now such a high profile profession, it would be a shame if garden owners felt that they could not undertake the job themselves. Which is where this book comes in.

This is not a "how-to", or a "step-by-step" book on garden design, nor is it aiming to encourage people to do without designers (that would not make me very popular with my colleagues, who have so generously allowed me to interview them). Instead, it is intended to offer a series of expert insights into the garden design process. Firstly, offering ideas and tips from leading designers that will help you to design your own garden. Secondly, trying to clarify what the design process is, so that if you are thinking of employing a designer, then you will have a better idea of what it is that they do and will be able to establish a successful and productive working relationship.

The range of subject matter and the choice of designers for this book is inevitably a personal, maybe even an idiosyncratic one, although all the major "topics" which make up the field of garden design are represented, with material on every stage of the design process. One personal bias is

that there is a lot of material on plants and planting design (the uninitiated may be surprised to learn that this area is the least developed in the garden design profession). I have included some sections on people who are first and foremost gardeners, rather than designers, in the belief that they have particular skills and a strong sense of vision in their use of plants.

For the most part, I have tried to emphasize innovative and contemporary design over the traditional, but at the same time taken care to avoid the gimmicky and the pretentious. New approaches to designing gardens, new materials and new plants make the world of garden design an exciting and rapidly-changing one. I hope to convey some of that sense of excitement in the pages to come. I have also tried to place stress on sustainability (that is, the use of materials and techniques that minimize negative impacts on the wider environment and promote bio-diversity), recognizing that, in a world increasingly dominated by urban sprawl and industrial farming, gardens have a vitally important role to play in providing a home for wildlife.

Some of the designers in this book are very well-known, indeed our list includes some practitioners who are undoubtedly amongst the best and most innovative in the world. Others are much less famous, but all have unique insights into garden design from which we can learn. Hopefully readers will be inspired by them to develop ideas and insights of their own. Garden design, as with any creative process, is not simply about learning techniques but developing a way of looking at the world and thinking imaginatively and sensitively about it. It is about *being* "a designer" as well as doing the work.

Noel Kingsbury, 2005

above, left to right The author's own garden acts as something of an experimental playground. The exotic-looking foliage of *Sanguisorba caucasica* adds a sense of definition to beds of perennials; a blue painted Moorish-style arch acts as a focal point in a very informal garden; and a "sawtooth" yew hedge makes a distinctive touch.

one: planning

the garden

the garden in

its setting

Every garden exists in a specific locality, with views *out* of it and views *into* it. Here we look at some of the issues that affect how gardens can achieve a good and harmonious relationship to their surroundings, including buildings, views out over the wider landscape and the local environment. Gardens also exist in relationship to their owners and those who use them (arguably this is the most essential relationship of all), so we also look at sources of inspiration, how to think about how the garden relates to you personally, and how to put the knowledge of what you desire to practical use.

● **looking for inspiration**
Other people's gardens may be the best place to learn about what you want.

● **mind gardens**
All of us carry a garden in the mind, thinks Julie Moir Messervy. We need to discover its outlines before we start to shape the earth.

● **linking house and garden**
James van Sweden looks at integrating house and garden design.

● **the wider landscape**
John Brookes considers the relationship of gardens to the local environment.

looking for inspiration NOEL KINGSBURY

Most people who garden are inspired by the gardens of others. This may not be the reason

why they garden in the first place, but it is often the most important factor in the choice of

particular design features in their gardens.

below Well-established borders such as this can teach us a lot about plant combination: colour, form and texture.

Reading books or magazine articles about gardening, or watching television programmes, can only teach or inspire you up to a certain point. Nothing beats getting out into a garden, feeling the grass beneath your feet, being able to turn round and see it through 360°, to appreciate its surroundings, to smell the fragrances. But enjoying a beautiful garden is one thing, it's quite another to understand why you enjoy it, and then to go on to use your inspiration practically in your own designs. That's why I'm devoting several pages to this topic, to provide a kind of mental tool kit so that you can get the most out of visiting gardens.

right Visiting gardens with distinct habitats, such as deep shade, can be both instructive and an inspiration.

above Contemporary solutions for small spaces can be particularly inspirational.

right Gardens and houses can be intimately involved – this balcony has been built to make the most of views over the garden.

Visiting gardens

Gardens tend to come in two categories: the smaller, private ones and the big, famous and regularly visited. I am going to concentrate on the private gardens that open to the public (often for charity) because they tend to be much more helpful. Usually designed and maintained by the owners, they offer ideas that are more achievable for the domestic gardener. I'm not discounting the grander kind, but remember that they are expertly maintained by professionals and are among the least useful for our purposes because they can be difficult to relate to more modest gardens. They do, though, provide an excellent array of interesting plants which can be grown in other designs and settings, and there's no doubt that seeing the achievements of Vita Sackville-West at Sissinghurst in Kent, and Beth Chatto at her gardens in Essex, is inspirational.

When visiting a garden, try and leave with at least five or six good ideas. First, examine the design and layout, then the selection and combination of plants, and finally the use of particular features. Also note how and why other gardens fail, and make sure that you avoid the same mistakes or see how they could be put right and then try them out at home.

above Formality and geometry do not have to be "classical" or old-fashioned.

below "Less is more" is a great design motto, for small gardens particularly.

Looking at the whole garden

There is clearly a lot to learn from a garden with similarities to your own in terms of size, shape, aspect, location (e.g. is it urban and enclosed, or rural with open views?), climate and soil type. And a garden facing similar problems (e.g. with dry shade and a north-facing slope) can teach you most of all. Which is why you must thoroughly understand your own garden before comparing it with others (know the soil type and how much sun it gets through the year). Looking at other gardens is also an excellent opportunity to view a range of features and decide whether you really want them, and how they will fit your design.

What to look for:

◆ Small gardens How has the owner/designer made the most of a small space? Are the boundaries hidden or an obvious part of the design?

◆ Divisions Nearly all gardens divide space in different ways. The garden's rooms may be large or small, but which do you prefer? Some divisions are partial, e.g. with a knee-high hedge, but will that work for you?

◆ Outward views If a garden has a good view, how has it been tackled? Does the view dominate the garden or is it restricted, being visible from only a particular place or angle?

◆ Views in the garden What do you find yourself looking at? Many medium-sized gardens can be made to feel bigger by dividing them up with axes cutting across, with focal points at the end. Others are more open and accessible, encouraging the eye to sweep across.

• **Paths** Do you feel that the first path invites you into the garden on a journey? And how is this achieved? Are the paths wide enough or too wide?

• **Border sizes** Check the width of the borders – should yours be bigger or smaller? And will they enable you to show off your plants, create a varied, year-round display and provide access (especially to plants at the back) for maintenance and cutting flowers?

• **Shapes** Look at the shapes of ponds, borders, stretches of lawn, areas of paving and decking. Do they use straight lines, sweeping curves, or sudden, angular changes of direction?

• **Informality and/or formality** Deciding how much you need of each is a key question. Examining the former, it's easy to let your eye coast over an apparently undifferentiated stretch of flowers but carefully examine the detail and colour combinations, and the subtle use of, for example, clipped hedges, or topiary cut into abstract shapes in a formal garden.

Materials, features and plants

Visiting other gardens is a good way of seeing how materials are used in different, often unexpected ways. A satisfying find is the clever use of cheap or re-cycled material, e.g. old roofing tiles as paving, or discarded timber on a pergola. And unusual features, such as obelisks, archways and sculptures, can also be a source of first-rate ideas. But the plants invariably come first, and it's vital that you check:

• **Plant size** Will the plants spread too much in your garden? With attractive trees, find out when they were planted so that you know how quickly they grow.

• **Conditions** Are the plants you want to grow in sun or shade? Is the soil moist or dry?

• **Combinations** Look for striking plant combinations, especially ones that might be effective in a confined space.

Finally, garden visits are not only about gathering ideas, they also show what is possible. Making it happen in your garden is up to you. In the rest of this book we look at how, with expert advice, you can do this. And one day your garden too will be an inspiration to others.

above Existing features and semi-natural landscapes are often best left alone. "Knowing when to stop" is one of the skills that marks out many great designers from their more run-of-the-mill fellows.

right A wall or hedge will create a clear line between landscape and domestic space – here, kept low, it allows this woodland to remain an essential visual part of this terrace. Good hedges or other boundaries alongside woodland also help to keep hungry deer out of the garden.

mind gardens JULIE MOIR MESSERVY

Julie Moir Messervy (a garden and landscape designer based in North America) has

a unique approach to garden design, which draws on insights from psychology and

eastern spiritual traditions. "Within each of us lies a garden," she says.

Our minds store a series of images derived from our lifetime's experiences. "But often," Julie suggests, "these images are not pictures but feelings evoked by particular places. Childhood experiences, in particular, lay down key imprints in our minds. And our first job," she stresses, "is to identify this wealth of atmospheric and visual material (which constitutes the "inward garden") before using it to help construct a real garden."

To help her clients clarify the features of their inward garden, Julie has identified seven archetypal landscapes or features; places that correspond to a child's progressively more adventurous exploration of the world.

• **The Sea** Perhaps recalling the experience of the womb, the sea evokes a feeling of immersion.

Make use of a deep woodland or vast, open landscape, particularly one which experiences marked weather conditions, e.g. mists or fog.

• **The Cave** Tight spaces offer protection, safety and a feeling of snugness, with a limited view of the world.

Make use of summerhouses and grottoes where you can retreat and hide away.

• **The Harbour** A place of safety and a vantage point, harbours offer security and a base from which to explore.

Make use of tree glades, backed benches, enclosing hedges and garden rooms.

above "What's around the corner?" is the question that instantly comes to mind – mystery is a vital part of our experience of the garden.

left Trees and shrubs can create a sense of enclosure and protection, but there is also a need to get the right balance to avoid the sense of being overshadowed.

left Elevated sitting areas allow us to be part of the normally unreachable tree canopy. They also offer the opportunity of admiring the garden from above – which may often be the best vantage point.

above Climbers can do wonders softening hard urban surfaces.

right Many people find that a view to the outside is a vital part of an enclosed space.

opposite This Japanese-style garden creates a clear and uncluttered space in front of the house.

◆ **The Promontory** Offering views and a route back to safety, the promontory is a superb vantage point.

Make use of balconies, belvederes, high-level terracing, or vantages at the edge of the site.

◆ **The Island** Symbolizing separation from the world, the island evokes a feeling of independence and security.

Make use of a picnic blanket, chaise longue, or terrace that seems to "float" on the lawn, a specimen tree or lone bench.

◆ **The Mountain** The ultimate vantage point and place of solitude, the mountain can also be an excellent defensive position.

Make use of "mounts" (mounds made of earth) and high places with 360° views – the place in the garden where the whole area can be seen.

◆ **The Sky** Dreams of flying often symbolize confidence and freedom.

Make use of a design which frames the view of the sky or a reflecting pool which brings the heavens down to our picture plane.

Certain existing garden features may clearly suggest some of these archetypes, and if they are important to you, then start developing them. For example, an obvious promontory with a spectacular view can be enhanced by adding a terrace made of decking to create a central feature, and a harbour with a backdrop of mature trees can be enhanced with a foreground of shrubs. But if your desired archetype does not have a corresponding feature in the garden, you might choose to create one. So, an enclosed garden can be given a promontory with views by planting in appropriate places, creating an attractive base which doubles as a viewing position.

Though Julie's basic idea may seem slightly unusual, it does provide a useful way of seeing how a garden can be upgraded, and given a wide range of features which provide variety and interest that is personal to you. A flat garden where everything can be seen at once, without any nooks and crannies, quickly becomes dull. Using one or more of these seven archetypes or features is an excellent way of enhancing an unimaginative garden.

linking house and garden JAMES VAN SWEDEN

Houses and gardens are inextricably linked, with the key distinction that the design of the house almost inevitably comes first. Consequently this often results in the design of the garden being a response to that of the house. A strong design however will give the impression of the house and garden having an integral unity and of having grown up together.

Those with houses that are recognizably of a particular historic period are sometimes tempted to try to achieve this sense of unity by building a garden of the same period. The results are often charming but they lack originality. More daring, and perhaps ultimately offering greater rewards, is to play with contrast, using contemporary elements around a period house for example.

James van Sweden's key word for the house-garden relationship is "marriage". James is one of the most influential garden designers in the US today; with his colleague, Wolfgang Oehme, he has dramatically changed the way that people see gardens, both public and private. Key to the partnership's style is sensitivity to the site, attention to detail and in particular, the use of generous planting.

James argues that house and garden should form parts of an inseparable whole, with the house "looking like it grew out of the site". But what happens if the house has little in the way of outstanding features, or is downright unattractive? The role of a garden must then be to mask its faults as far as possible. Climbers, either trained directly onto the wall or over a pergola, can mask an unattractive surface and help blur the boundary between building and garden. Low walls, terraces and decking can also help root a house in its surroundings. With a beautiful house, the garden's role is more subtle, acting as a frame. The two must work in harmony.

Having trained as an architect, it is not surprising that James looks at, and discusses, gardens using the language of buildings. It's certainly a useful way to start thinking about outdoor spaces. He suggests that paving, lawns and soil can be thought of as the floor, that hedges, fences and plants are the walls, and that overhead trees or pergolas are the ceiling.

To make outdoor rooms effectively link with, and echo, the house, he tries to give them the same proportions as those inside. But he goes one stage further. He reinforces the link by placing the outside dining area, for example, near the kitchen, with the garden sitting area being adjacent to the living room. He then strengthens the house-garden relationship by identifying those themes that give a house its character, and recreating them in the garden.

above Rustic paving and large plants create a contrast with an elegantly proportioned house.

> ❝ *small garden spaces can be treated as outdoor extensions of the house, especially if they are given a strong sense of geometry* ❞

left Terraces create an "outside room" which is both a domestic and a garden space.

right James van
Sweden's own house
is encouraged to blend
into its surroundings
through wild-style
perennial planting.

right James van
Sweden's own house
is encouraged to blend
into its surroundings
through wild-style
perennial planting.

The first step is to use similar materials or colours, carefully selecting garden stone or slate with the same hue as the building. In the case of brick this might mean tracking down old recycled bricks; architectural salvage yards can be an invaluable treasure-trove. If the interior banisters are made from a particular kind of wood, or are shaped in a specific style, then mirror this in the railings around a terrace. But the most dramatic way of achieving a house-garden link is by using flooring materials which guarantee continuity. With stone and bare wooden floors this is easy, in the latter case by using wooden decking which is similar in colour and plank width to the floorboards.

below Decking board-
walks connect the main
house to a guest annex
through the garden.

James stresses that "I rely as much as possible on the architecture of the house to inspire my garden design." This is particularly true of the proportions, with the scale of the garden features appropriate to those in the house. He is equally adamant that the strong architectural framework should be laid out first, before deciding which plants to use. If this architectural framework successfully relates to the house, then there can be enormous scope for a variety of different planting styles, creating the opportunity to be flexible and adventurous with planting. He concludes on a surprising, but telling note: "very informal, even wild planting, only works when it is given a design with a strong backbone."

right The emptiness and simplicity of the landscape around James' house has been echoed by the clean lines of this decking terrace. Such landscapes cry out for simple garden furniture with the minimum of detail.

the wider landscape JOHN BROOKES

Every garden exists in a specific locality. John Brookes believes that a knowledge
of and sympathy to the local environment and growing conditions is paramount
to achieving a successful garden design.

John Brookes has built his reputation as one of the world's leading designers by keeping
his gardens clear and simple, and by staying loyal to the principles of the twentieth century
modern movement in the arts. Having worked in a very wide range of countries and climate
zones he has become increasingly interested in how gardens relate to their surroundings.
He is one of the few who is prepared to voice concerns and criticisms about the direction
that the garden industry is taking. "Every garden centre," he says, "seems to sell the same:
concrete slabs, lamp posts and urns and, worst of all, the same limited range of plants,
irrespective of whether they are suited to local conditions." For the last few years his prime
concern has been the role of the garden in creating a sense of place, a sense he says we
are in danger of losing to universal standardization. He argues that gardens should be far
more individual, relating to the local environment.

He stresses how Britain, and by extension other countries and geographical regions,
has enormous local variations in topography, soil types, flora, vernacular buildings and
gardening traditions. Local materials – for example, clay, flints, chestnuts and reeds – were

left and above Rural landscapes are easily damaged by houses and gardens that stand out too
much. This garden limits this through having only a small area of borders around the house but
plenty of lawn, water and meadow that act as a sympathetic foreground to the surroundings.

above Trees and plenty of quite wild vegetation at the outer edges of a garden help blur and soften boundaries.

> *design outside is to do with line and space and can be interpreted in natural materials in a minimal and modernist way* "

once used to build houses, giving each region a distinctive look. "Now," he says, "the mindless homogenization of horti-business means we are in danger of losing all this. We should use local materials and stop introducing alien colours and textures into the garden". Furthermore, local materials help root the garden in its surroundings, and provide a continuation with regional history and traditions, while benefiting local skills and manufacturing.

In practical terms this means, first of all, using a selection of native plants in the garden to develop a sense of regional identity. And John doesn't just mean using one here and one there, in small groups in the border, but growing them as they appear in the wild, giving them room to spread by seed and sucker out. He is worried that because wholesale nurseries sell the same plants across vast geographical distances, there is a great danger that all gardens will end up looking the same and that regional differences will be lost. "Take the trouble to find out what grows locally," he adds, "and then give gardens a backbone of these native plants."

One big, additional advantage is that natives will be well suited to the local soil and climate. Why go to the expense and trouble of importing plants into an area with

left Gates can be a psychological marker between the area dominated by the house and domesticity, and the greater wildness of the garden.

REGIONAL CONSTRUCTION MATERIALS

- **Slate and stone for paths and walls** Local stone is often used for traditional buildings, and can be one of the most important factors in giving a particular region its distinctive character. In some areas, dry-stone walling is a major part of the landscape.

- **Locally quarried gravel for paths** Gravel, or crushed stone, is one of the most frequently used materials for paths in gardens and gravel gardens. Using a stone not found locally can look surprisingly out of place. Local materials are often cheaper.

- **Wood** Local timber yards often produce distinctive types of wood, such as hazel withies, willow wands, chestnut palings and cedar shingles. Think how they can be used in the garden – to construct garden buildings, furniture, low retaining walls (around raised beds, for example), pergolas and archways.

- **Cob and rammed earth** Traditional building materials for garden walls and houses in some areas, where the soil is slightly sticky and can be used, after mixing with straw, as a building material. They are heavy and bulky, but very cheap. When used by skilled craftsmen using traditional methods the results can be very distinctive.

- **Fencing materials** Reed, willow, split wood and palings have been traditionally used for fencing, often following a local design or construction technique. Try to find a local craftsman to build a fence using traditional skills.

---

distinctive or difficult soil, or a particular climate, when they will struggle, never really succeeding, or demand an enormous amount of help to make them perform well? A second bonus is that they introduce a note of the wild into the garden – John is extremely keen that we stop being "control freaks". He is not alone in pointing out how gardens are increasingly important as nature reserves, and that together they can cover a surprising amount of ground. But his argument does not stop there. "Beneath these ideas," he stresses, "there still needs to be a strong, even modernist design." Gardens should have clear underlying themes and structures. One way of doing this is to use materials in such a way as to show off their intrinsic beauty. "Design outside," says John, "is to do with line and space and can be interpreted in natural materials in a minimal and modernist way perfectly well. It is new materials which can jar in a landscape."

With so many houses all around the world now being built in natural or semi-natural environments, it is imperative that designers show more sensitivity to their surroundings. Ideally house and garden should be practically invisible to someone 2 kilometres (1¼ miles) away – this way we can both live surrrounded by beautiful landscapes and blend into them too.

working with space

Managing space is one of the key aspects of garden design, yet it is one with which many garden owners find it difficult to get to grips. Fundamental is the need to break up space, so that not everything is visible at once and that discrete areas with their own character are created. The result not only has to be aesthetically pleasing, but should also solve practical problems, such as screening. How this is done is a very personal matter, with some preferring relatively formal and geometric solutions, whereas others react quite strongly against such a route, favouring softer and more organic shapes.

open spaces
Julie Moir Messervy considers the importance of the calm centre.

difficult spaces
Jill Billington encourages us to think "outside the box" in odd-shaped gardens.

formal and geometric design
George Carter argues for the timeless virtues of classical geometry.

twisting formality
Piet Oudolf gives the classic a contemporary twist.

shaping borders
John Brookes looks at the relationship between borders, the plants in them and the wider garden context.

plotting paths
Gardens have to be explored to be appreciated and used. Julie Moir Messervy takes us on a journey.

open spaces JULIE MOIR MESSERVY

Having trained in Japan as a garden maker, Julie Moir Messervy is well aware of the significance of the void in the garden, which in many eastern philosophies is regarded to be as important as the tangible.

"Open spaces are important in gardens," she says, "because they provide a horizontal area, as does water, offering a calm, still background for adjacent plantings." Alternatively, they can be a feature in their own right if they are "dynamic and visual". The difference between the two is like that between "wall-to-wall carpet and an oriental rug," she adds, the former being a "muted background against which other elements stand out," the latter being "a feature as important as the furniture".

In gardens where the planting is important, rest for the eyes is vital, and areas of lawn are almost essential when it comes to providing this visual breathing space. And the best way to highlight a lawn is by surrounding it with shrubs and perennials. Julie is pro-lawn, unlike several contemporary designers, and while she clearly loves meadows and long grass, is somewhat sceptical of those who recommend using only them. "A meadow effect has too much texture and is too busy when what is required is tranquility." Or, to use her analogy, the meadow is an oriental rug when you may really need "a void and a place of repose".

In North America, gardens are very different to those elsewhere in the world. Many houses are surrounded by lawn but there are no clear boundaries between properties, and it is very difficult to establish Julie's framed, tranquil kind of space. In such situations

right Simplicity of design encourages us to appreciate detail.

far right In this design by Steve Martino, the flat and featureless expanse of grass allows us to better appreciate the shape and texture of the surrounding walls and planting.

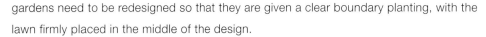

gardens need to be redesigned so that they are given a clear boundary planting, with the lawn firmly placed in the middle of the design.

To create a more enclosed and secluded area, she proposes a dell, an area featuring extended beds of grasses or moss, or ivy or ferns, surrounded by trees or taller vegetation. Such places are most likely to be found where a house has been built in a forest, and where there are few opportunities to create large open spaces. Such dells are often dominated by one plant species, which adds to the sense of tranquility. Ferns are Julie's particular favourite. Many other effective ground-cover plants, such as *epimediums*, *vinca* and *geraniums*, are also shade lovers. While none have the same grace and lightness of touch as ferns, they can be immensely useful where dry soil is a problem. The result will be low-maintenance (almost inevitably less so than grass), and a restful atmosphere. Ground-cover plants can often be combined with spring-flowering bulbs for a burst of early-season colour, the bulb shoots poking up through the matt of foliage.

Grasses probably provide the best ground cover for open areas. Various varieties of creeping thymes are sometimes used (e.g. forms of *Thymus serpyllum*), although they are not quite as tranquil, especially when in flower. Gravel is also a possibility, and plays an important part in Japanese gardens; it too creates a sense of void, pulling together the rest of the garden. Wildflower meadows are increasingly fashionable, and can be an alternative to conventional lawns, although Julie stresses that they do not always look good all-year round, and they do need lot of management in the first few years.

Unlike lawn or gravel, a wildflower meadow will be, at least when in flower, a dynamic design element in its own right, and may even claim the limelight, making the surrounding plants take the role of supporting cast. A good compromise is to plant a lawn with spring bulbs and other early-flowering plants, which can be mown from early summer on. This gives colour and interest at a time of year when the surrounding garden has little to offer, and thereafter assumes the role of tranquil, wall-to-wall greenery.

Left and above In Taoist philosophy, absence is as important as presence. The emptiness of such spaces is a vital complement to the visual complexity of plantings and other garden features. Raked sand is a good Japanese-style alternative to grass for creating such open spaces.

difficult spaces JILL BILLINGTON

Some of the trickiest problems when designing a garden concern awkward

spaces. What do you do with a tight, shady corner? Or a garden with an

irregular outline? You could start by talking to Jill Billington who has been

a designer for 25 years, having previously been a sculptor.

above A very architectural response to an awkwardly shaped site, which makes the most of the longest axis in the garden.

Below Hedging conceals the relatively shallow depth of this garden, instead focusing the eye on a longer diagonal view to a corner, as well as encouraging the viewer to get out and see what lies behind the hedges.

Also a mother, Jill says that having children made her an accomplished multi-tasker and her work is characterised by a problem-solving approach which features lateral thinking and multi-functional solutions. She is renowned for her imaginative designs for London gardens, where plot sizes are often restricted, shapes awkward and growing conditions for plants less than perfect. She clearly relishes describing how "I once designed a garden for a client who turned out to be a big underworld figure with two rottweilers and an alsation. I used lots of prickly things, hollies and *berberis*, to keep the dogs out of the main part of the garden and it seemed to work."

She says that most garden design problems concern space, how we look at it and move around in it. Jill's gift is to cut through the obvious, imagining different ways of using space. She does this through a variety of methods, one of the most basic being the re-orientation of sight lines, i.e. the direction in which the eye gazes. This can often be

left Architectural spaces create "rooms", effectively enclosing the field of vision and making the garden into a space with its own strong sense of identity.

EXAMPLE A

new houses

new trees

trellis

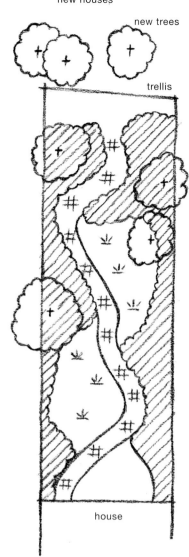

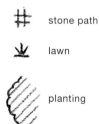

house

achieved by creating paths because we have a strong tendency to follow them with our eyes, even if we don't walk on them. In the following examples we get a clear picture of how Jill tackles a variety of problems in small town gardens. This ranges from planting trees on other people's land to creating unexpected changes of direction.

Example A The view at the end of this long, narrow garden is a new block of flats. Jill's solution was to offer to plant birch trees for the owner of the land on which the flats stood, so that they screened out the flats from the house and garden. A few more birch trees were then planted at the rear of the garden, creating the impression of a grove, linking the outside and the inside of the design. Masses of evergreens, particularly bamboos, which take up little horizontal space, screen the sides. The rectangular shape was thoroughly disguised by creating two areas of grass with organic shapes, while a diagonal path helps suggest that the end of the garden is actually around the corner.

Example B Narrow gardens pose some of the greatest design challenges. Jill's answer here was to force anyone walking down it to keep changing direction "so that at every turn you enter a different space," so making the garden feel much wider. Immediately outside the house is a paved area with pond and water plants occupying one corner. A trellis covered in climbers separates this area from the next, which is reached through an arch. The middle area is paved and includes chairs, tables and plants in containers, while another trellis and arch section off a third, more informal area with a small lawn and shrub planting.

EXAMPLE B

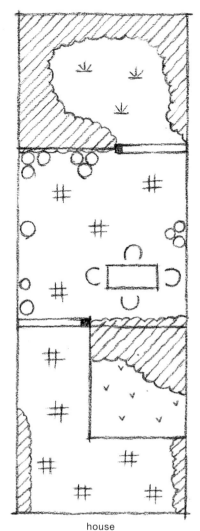

house

Key to Example A

\# stone path

🌿 lawn

🌳 planting

Example C "Perhaps the greatest challenge of all," reckons Jill, "are shallow gardens, wide with little depth." This plan shows how she tackled this problem in the garden pictured on pages 38-39, by creating access routes into the main body of the garden to follow indirect routes, parallel to the house. The direct routes are blocked by a pool parallel to the house, and by hedges and other shrubby planting. The planting also obstructs much of the direct view from the house into the garden. To gain access to, and explore, the garden requires a journey. What was once a shallow and instantly visible space is now broken into smaller, complex, intriguing units.

Example D Square gardens mean that everything can be seen at once. One solution, which draws upon the Islamic garden tradition, divides it up very formally, creating interest through subdivision and geometry. Another solution is to do the complete opposite, and break up the rigidity of the geometry with an almost random planting scheme, while another is to use plants to create a division across the garden, hiding the back of the garden. This turns it into two units, and forces the eye to explore the design diagonally.

Key to Example B

🌿 lawn

\# paving

🍃 containers

🌳 planting

∨ ∨ ∨ water

EXAMPLE C

Key to Example C

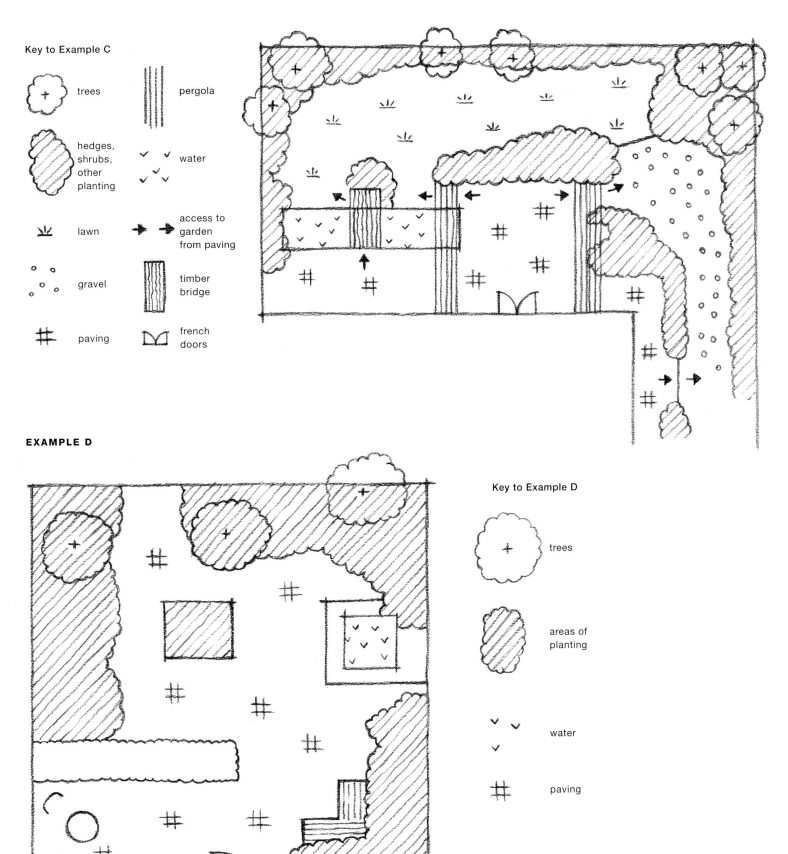

trees

pergola

hedges, shrubs, other planting

water

lawn

access to garden from paving

gravel

timber bridge

paving

french doors

EXAMPLE D

Key to Example D

trees

areas of planting

water

paving

formality and symmetry GEORGE CARTER

Many people have a negative attitude towards the formal garden style, associating it with rigidity and a perceived anti-naturalism. Yet the experience of walking around historical baroque-era gardens and parks is soothing – after all it is scientifically established that the colour green makes us feel relaxed, and green is the predominant element in formal gardens. There is also something very restful about order and regularity, the repetition of key elements imparting a sense of unity and integrity.

top An "eyecatcher" (here a stone urn surrounded with an archway) acts as a focal point at the end of a view.

above The classical language of obelisks and other architectural features still has great resonance.

> *symmetry only works if you can see it contrasted with the organic, which is why you need softening elements, such as foliage*

George Carter's work as a garden designer begins where the early 18th century left off. Essentially his style is "neo-baroque", in the tradition of classical European formality that was prevalent before garden and landscape design was seduced by attempts to copy or evoke nature. "I don't see it as backward looking," he states, and, going on to discuss the relationship between modernist architecture and landscape, "I can never understand why Le Corbusier didn't think that an 18th century landscape was the best backdrop for his work."

The garden as extension of architecture

George takes the view that "you can't divorce the garden from the house, the garden is an extension of the architecture". In particular he stresses how formality is an ideal solution for town gardens, "you can create an outdoor room with walls and a floor". The geometry of clipped hedges, and of the garden plan itself, creates an obvious link with the house.

Key to George's design philosophy is a belief that "what makes gardens interesting is spatial organisation, the materials are secondary". Whether a garden is small or large, the way it is organized is key to how we experience it: is it so open or simple in layout that most of it can be seen at once, or is it broken up into smaller areas (often called "rooms") so that you move from one space to another, as in a house? "You can only divide up a long thin space a limited number of ways," says George, and implicit in this statement is that those ways more or less have to be geometric. Garden owners then, because of the shape of their plots, often have geometry forced upon them. Perhaps it is better to "go with the flow" and work with this geometry, rather than trying to deny its existence?

For those new to designing gardens, formality has one supreme practical advantage, for as George points out, "it is easy to use simple strong structures that are derived from geometry". Much of his work, and many classical formal gardens, appears at first sight to be symmetrical, but he says that although you do need elements of it in the garden, in practice no site actually lends itself to perfect symmetry.

Providing a framework

Drawing upon the work of the 18th century garden and landscape designer Humphry Repton, George suggests that "it is helpful to see things in terms of pictures, with a foreground forming a frame, a middle distance and a background". Foreground planting can be achieved by tree planting, or in a town garden by wall shrubs, or by pots or troughs that can be seen silhouetted against grass. With clear foreground framing, the viewer will get a sense of distance and perspective and will be drawn into seeing the rest of the garden as a picture, something to be looked at and appreciated with a conscious effort and interest, rather than simply registered – like wallpaper.

"You need a reason to walk around a garden," says George, "and geometric organisation can provide this". He contrasts geometry with the situation he sometimes finds in gardens where "everything is "bitty", and there is a disjointed quality … where a framework has to be imposed". Formal organisation can provide a useful framework for the whole garden; indeed this is something that George feels is one of the most important things that he often provides for his clients. "I provide people with a frame, and they can improve on it, they can diversify it."

above Symmetry and a limited plant palette create an atmosphere which is calm, cool and contemplative. The use of silvery *Helichrysum italicum* inside the box enclosures creates contrast and additional visual interest.

right Lighting can be used to great effect to highlight architectural features.

opposite Houses with simple clean lines are greatly enhanced by classically formal gardens.

This use of classical formality as a framework gets to the nub of the argument about whether formality is anti-natural or not. Many designers would argue that once you have a strong framework, all sorts of much more informal planting can then take place within it, and the resulting "creative tension" between the loose planting and the formal skeleton can be immensely satisfying. Many of the greatest gardens have just this quality. But getting the formal design right is the first stage and the key to success.

Few sites are in fact ideal for creating totally symmetrical or geometric gardens – life is never that convenient! A strong outline however will "carry" a variety of deviations from the straight and narrow. A formal approach is particularly useful for larger areas of flat ground, creating perspective and interest. Sloping gardens are not excluded though – many of the great Italian gardens are built on very steep ground.

twisting formality **PIET OUDOLF**

Piet Oudolf is a Dutch garden designer who is a leading proponent of a contemporary style that makes great use of perennials and ornamental grasses. However, he is also very imaginative in using what could be called "contemporary formality", that is the use of clipped shrubs in a modernist idiom.

Piet is particularly good at showing why formal axes in the garden do not have to conform to the traditional, perpendicular pattern. He has shown how it is possible to give classical formality a twist and create something more contemporary and daring, or "wonky baroque", as the garden and art historian Sir Roy Strong puts it.

The best place to understand "wonky baroque" is in Piet's own garden. The first part features a strong diagonal path, and the second a central axial one. Unlike the central axes of classical formality, with which other axes or features meet at right angles, this one has a staggered row of yew columns on either side, and runs through two asymmetric elliptical beds, filled with low ground-cover plants. It is an example of zig-zag symmetry, and it encourages visitors to look from side to side instead of straight ahead. The design incorporates a sense of balance because features are similarly weighted on each side, but the predictable aspect of conventional symmetry is avoided. Whereas classical formality,

right In classical formal schemes, a central axis unifies the space, with subsidiary axes leading off it at right angles. It is all part of an ideological structuring and ordering of space, symbolising man's power over nature.

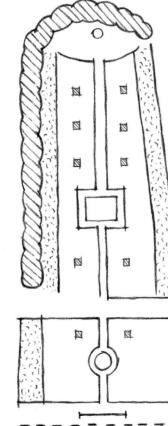

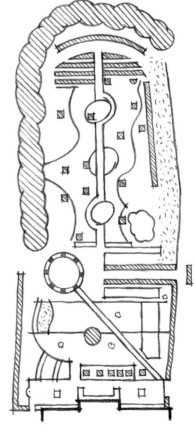

left In Piet Oudolf's garden the viewer is encouraged to view the garden less as an orderly scheme of neatly repeated blocks than as a development analagous to a piece of music, whose rhythm is generated by the structural elements used: the yew and the elliptical borders.

with its dependence on right angles and an all-important focal point at the end of an axis, tends to get to the point too quickly, and is thus quite limited in smaller spaces, this approach makes the viewer slow down and appreciate what is happening on both sides.

The garden at Bury Court, in Hampshire, was Piet's first commission in Britain and deals with a large square area by giving its main path and axis a diagonal thrust, which leads the eye out of the garden to a view over the surrounding countryside. The central area is filled with a large lawn, while extensive borders of perennials and further paths force the visitor to start inspecting other areas.

Piet has shown how diagonals and staggered symmetry can work as well as traditional straight axes – something to think about perhaps for small gardens, where classical lines can make a space feel smaller. For example, small blocks of box in a town garden might be used to create a staggered effect, interspersed with other, looser, planting, or the main axis could be developed on a diagonal, which of course has the advantage that it is the longest possible axis in a square or rectangular garden. The concept of twisting formality is a new one, with many exciting possibilities, open to exploration by any who dare to be different!

above Looking down the main axis of the Oudolf garden. Elliptical beds and staggered yew columns create a powerful sense of rhythm. Blocking the axis with planting prevents the eye running to the end too quickly. Note that there is no terminal "focal point".

shaping borders JOHN BROOKES

Borders come in all shapes and sizes, but usually follow a backdrop (a hedge, wall or fence) and are often strip-like in shape. It has been a priority for many modern designers to break away from this formulaic pattern. John Brookes' own garden in Sussex, southern England, does this dramatically, with sweeping curves and organically shaped borders amongst areas of both short-cut lawn and longer meadow grass.

above Curvy "organic" shaped borders are complemented particularly well by strong uprights – such as these foxgloves and mulleins (*digitalis* and *verbascum* species).

below The huge leaves of *Petasites japonicus* echo the shape of this pool.

John's border sizes are just the right scale for his style of massed planting, while the shapes are consistent with the fact that there are no traditional, clipped geometric shapes anywhere in the garden. "The period and style of the house, and the location, should guide the shapes of the borders," he says. "For example, if a house is immaculately formal inside, then there should be greater formality outside." Although he adds, "there is the precedent of the 18th century house, in its parkland setting, with no formality at all."

One of the fundamental rules of garden design is that where there is a gradient between levels of formality, there should be greater formality (which may be symmetrical or not) around the house, and more looseness further away, especially in rural locations. The level of formality, thinks John, is a very personal matter, "some people" he suggests, "like to feel that they are in control. For them, clear lines and edging, for example with box, is a good way of achieving this."

How big should a border be?

• Many garden borders are simply too narrow. Try to be generous – 2 m (6½ ft) gives you scope for most perennials, 3 m (10 ft) for small to medium shrubs and lots of perennials.
• Spring-flowering perennials and bulbs are small and compact and fit well into borders that have to be narrow.
• Summer-flowering perennials tend to be larger and are often upright-growing which means they have "bare legs" so need shorter plants in front. They are best in a border that is at least 2 to 3 m (6½ to 10 ft) wide.
• If there is only limited space for a deep border, consider using a wavy edge, or organic curving shapes. This will give you some deeper areas.

On a more general note, John adds that "plant masses are an important part of design. They should work with the scale and proportion of the borders." In practice, this means that large and bulky plants such as many shrubs can overwhelm small borders, and that large borders can be let down by plants that are too small. Tall, narrow plants, or "exclamation marks", however, offer size and impact without adding bulk, which makes them very useful. Good examples include species of *verbascum* and *digitalis* (the mullein and foxglove groups), as they are only 30 cm (12 in) across at the base and yet can be 1.5–2.5 m (5–8 ft) high, depending on the species. John thinks that lots of gardeners use too many varieties. He suggests that when designing borders you "do a planting design and then take out half the plant varieties and double up on the remainder".

As plants grow the relationship between them changes, particularly in borders, and so does the relationship to the border in which they are planted and the rest of the garden. It is imagining this change at the design stage which is one of the real challenges of garden design. John thinks "you are creating a piece of sculpture carved from vegetation, and unlike other materials it may take years to mature." One day plants may well get too large, but that should not put you off from getting at least six years of good value from them, so long, he concludes, "as you are brave enough to dig them out. I love taking the odd thing out – you get a whole new perspective."

below Large masses, such as this clipped box, and the terracotta urn, form strong focal points around which swirl richly-planted borders. The yellow flower in the foreground is *Asphodoline lutea*.

plotting paths JULIE MOIR MESSERVY

If anyone thinks that a path is simply a way of getting quickly from the back door to the potting shed,

they haven't met Julie Moir Messervy. She has an interesting view on the function of paths which she

thinks add to the spiritual sense of a garden.

above Paths in this garden are a means of access, as well as being a complement to other surfaces.

She states, "the single most useful metaphor that I know for the composing of elements of a landscape into a coherent and interesting whole is "the journey". A good journey," she adds, "alters the psyche, refreshes the soul and reinvigorates the senses." The key elements are the start and finish, the pace, and the choices one has to make en route.

"The path is a way of choreographing an interesting journey through space," she says, before making a distinction between two kinds of journey: "stroll journeys" and "mind journeys". The former is the physical one, and the latter a mental one, full of the thoughts and feelings experienced when we stop and look at a scene. In other words, she stresses that when thinking about paths we must remember that they don't just take us from A to B but also offer stopping places where we can pause, look and contemplate. Julie points out that "your job as a designer is to compose a journey through the garden, and to plan it so that it evokes the feelings you want to convey, and to give order to the various garden elements so that they appear as an aesthetic whole".

The garden journey

For Julie, a journey through a garden needs four ingredients – a departure point, a destination point, a linking path and events along the way. She describes a departure point as "a threshold between two realms: the outer world and the garden … the beginning of the garden experience." A gate or archway can be an effective start, or indeed anything else that forces you to go through a barrier of some kind. A destination point (and there can be several in a garden) is a place where there is a clear invitation to begin a "mind journey", a place to sit or at least stop and look, either at a view within the garden or beyond it. There has to be some suggestion that you have "arrived". If you include several destination points Julie suggests that "they are hidden from each other, with each one offering a whole, fresh experience". The journey between a departure and destination point offers the opportunity for a change of style; she suggests that the former "relates to the architecture of the house" while the latter can be quite different, and more rustic and natural in feel.

While paths are the means by which you explore the garden, it is important to remember that they do have a dynamic of their own. Julie says that when she designs a garden she thinks of the paths as streams, and imagines how the water would flow; "wide and straight walks are like canals, curving paths are like meandering streams, while steps are waterfalls, and terraces are pools or reservoirs." She adds, "paths can be smooth or turbulent, purposeful or curvy."

left The surface upon which we walk should be of interest – here designer Julie Toll has used railway sleepers to create pattern and a sense of direction.

Changes of direction make effective invitations to stop or at least pause and look, and the way ahead should not be too obvious. One of the key principles of garden design is that there should be enticing mysteries around each corner, leading you on. Curves and meanders are particularly useful in this respect. The design of the paths plays an important role in how people are "directed" along; a wide, straight path leads somewhere in a very obvious way, whereas irregularly winding stones signify a more private, solitary path. With longer paths you can create a sense of anticipation. In the absence of a spectacular view at the destination, this is met by breaking up a long path with frequent, lesser features of interest, or "events", along the way which provide

above Very low ground-covers such as creeping thymes can be used to create an effective surround to stepping stones.

a pause for thought. These events include ornaments, feature plants, views and vistas which can be near or far, without any obvious route towards them.

Julie adds that when walking along a path we experience the garden on each side as a series of changing stimuli; if there are too many changes then the result may be confusing and over-stimulating. Julie solution is "constancy in change", the idea being that as you move along a path, one element will change but the others stay constant. For example, while a path might lead you from a cottage-style garden to a more formal area, the bricks remain the same. She adds that continuous elements, such as paths, hedges and fences, can play an important role in maintaining this element of constancy, linking one part of a garden with another. And so can the repetition of particular plants.

Japanese garden designers believe that the surface of paths should vary, so that the feet have an experience of the garden too – some surfaces are quicker to walk on than others, and it is possible to slow down the progress of the garden viewer by using paths that need more attention to negotiate (by using challenging materials to walk on for example). Varying the material of paths helps to "change the pace", and can be used as another means of differentiating one garden space from another.

right In the Toronto Music Garden, vegetation hides paths, which can be used to great effect in gardens of all sizes, creating the illusion of continuous planting.

below Main paths should be broad, as seen here in the Toronto Music Garden, making it clear which way we should go.

garden types

and styles

Creating a successful garden involves recognizing certain "facts on the ground" – garden designers only rarely have a blank slate on which to work. First and foremost a gardener has to work within the boundaries of the garden and to work around existing features. Next in importance is the need to create a relationship between the house and the garden – which can be a particular challenge where contemporary architecture is concerned. A skilful designer can turn challenges or problems into opportunities. Good design is not just about coming up with an original idea but about responding to the type of site and developing a creative dialogue with it.

town gardens
Sue Berger and Helen Phillips make the most of small gardens in urban areas.

wildflower meadows
Julie Toll shows how meadows are not just a home for wildlife, but potentially a major visual element too.

contemporary gardens
Dan Pearson looks at how gardens can work well with contemporary architecture.

old gardens
Existing features offer the possibility of seamlessly blending old and new – Dan Pearson has some useful guidelines.

town gardens SUE BERGER AND HELEN PHILLIPS

Small urban gardens can be the trickiest kind for designers. You need a clear head and some good guidelines. Sue Berger and Helen Phillips specialize in town gardening and say that "drama and romance" best sum up their approach to design.

above Focal points such as sculpture add interest to intensely used areas.

While they are delighted that many urban dwellers want exuberant flowers and growth, they stress that town gardens need a good design. Being so small with relatively few plants, the ones which they do include must perform over a long period. There isn't room for plants that have one good month and eleven nondescript months. "Aim to make one third of the planting evergreen," is Sue's message.

Like many contemporary designers, they begin by trying to persuade their clients to reduce or give up their lawns. "A small lawn has to look immaculate," Sue says, "and it's difficult to keep it looking consistently good, so we suggest alternatives that don't need constant maintenance. But it is always the men who want to keep the grass." The alternatives often involve a formal use of evergreens, such as a central parterre, "which looks good in a city environment, and reduces work as it only needs a clip once a year," says Sue. Box is the most useful plant for such formal plantings, being compact,

below Open space in town gardens needs to be big enough to fit a decent-sized dining table but intimate enough for a small one too.

easy to shape and vigorous if well fed. But while parterres are often thought of as being excessively formal, Sue and Helen use them as a frame for looser-growing, flowering herbaceous plants. They often fill the spaces between the box with just two varieties, one earlier and one later flowering. (Note: in some areas, the disease "box blight" can wreck box hedges or features which use the dwarf variety *Buxus sempervirens* "Suffruticosa". Use ordinary box instead, or if a really low hedge is wanted, try *Buxus microphylla* or the Japanese holly relative *Ilex crenata*.)

Evergreens are one of their key elements, especially used to divide up the garden, creating areas or rooms. "Small children particularly enjoy this aspect," Sue adds, "as it gives them places to hide and provides places for imaginative play … and the rooms make the garden look longer and bigger. It is important that you never see the whole garden at once." Yew and beech (which when kept clipped as a hedge keeps its attractive, dead beige leaves through winter) or sometimes hornbeam, are used to create the walls while rosemary can be used to make a low-growing hedge. Rosemary is rarely used for hedging, as it has a rather awkward branching habit, but Sue and Helen have found that if it is pruned hard back for three years and then allowed to grow, it makes much more solid growth.

Elsewhere in the garden, there is also a role for evergreens as medium-sized, rounded border shrubs where they create a sense of weight and permanence: Mexican orange blossom (*Choisya ternata*) and Honey spurge (*Euphorbia mellifera*) are very useful, both having fragrant flowers. Sue adds "we use the bamboo *Phyllostachys aurea* in many of our designs. It's a very undemanding plant, thriving in impoverished ground, and suits both

above Two pollarded lime trees have been used to frame an axis which forms the backbone for the whole of this city garden.

TREES FOR TOWN GARDENS

- *Amelanchier*
- *Betula*
- *Catalpa* (perhaps kept pollarded, i.e. cut back every few years, either to head height, or to ground level)
- *Clerodendron trichotomum*
- Crab apple (*Malus*)
- Magnolia e.g. *Magnolia x soulangeana*
- *Prunus subhirtella* 'Autumnalis'
- *Prunus* 'Taihaku'

ancient and modern architecture." A quite different effect is created by clipping evergreens, such as bay, into cones, balls or pyramids. Sue thinks that, "they create vertical interest and an eccentric look. They also fit into parterres, providing evergreen leaves at a high level."

Seating areas

Outdoor seating areas can take up a substantial proportion of a town garden, and Sue adds that "our clients always underestimate the space needed – we always allow for a trestle table and eight chairs. When calculating space, actually go into the dining room and measure how much space such furniture can take, including the space needed for pushing chairs back; make sure that diners can get up without chairs toppling into borders."

above Many urban gardens are viewed from above as much as at eye level – a variety of foliage textures contributes enormously to their visual interest.

left Sitting areas need to be both sheltered but also have sufficient light and a prospect.

above Here a "rebar" pergola supports climbers. It is vital that the views from windows are not blocked by growing foliage.

Many people like to have outdoor seating areas underneath some kind of structure where there's dappled shade, which explains why such structures are another key element of Sue and Helen's work. "But because we like the plants to do the talking," Sue adds, "we prefer to use materials such as steel re-inforcing bars (rebar), which are inconspicuous when covered by growth, as well as being immensely robust. Although heavy and difficult to manage, they will last for 50 years." Rebar structures support a considerable weight of climbers, but take up little space and don't block views or dominate the garden.

Planting

Walls can be a dominant element in urban gardens, but they do offer plenty of scope for climbers, such as roses and clematis, *Clematis armandii* being one of their favourites as it has very good evergreen foliage, and Helen says that *Hydrangea petiolaris* "is superb for creating living walls, growing up to 5 m (16 ft) high, and will survive in complete shade." Within the framework created by such evergreens and other structural plants, Sue and Helen like to use heavily scented Mediterranean plants. Favourites include cistus, santolina, sedum, lavender, sage, helichrysum, artemesia and rosemary. These are mostly green/grey and silver leaved plants that spread and join up to make a compact

---

CLIMBERS FOR PERGOLAS AND ARCHWAYS

- *Clematis armandii*
- *Lonicera*
- *Rosa banksii* 'Lutea', and *R.* 'Félicité Parmentier', 'Tour de Malakoff', 'Tuscany Superba', 'William Lobb'
- *Solanum crispum* or, in sheltered spots, *Solanum jasminoides*
- *Vitis vinifera* (grapevine)

---

right Pleaching is a way of training trees which creates a "hedge on stilts", so that a wall of foliage is created from about 2 m (6 ft) above ground, with bare trunks below. This creates some privacy while providing space at the base for new plants.

left Warm walls are ideal places for seats, especially for the cooler times of the year.

PLANTS FOR CONTAINERS

- *Agapanthus* being slightly tender they do well in town gardens. Tidy and attractive, they have broad, strap-shaped leaves and mid-summer flowers in various shades of blue, including some stunning true blues, e.g. *A. campanulatus*.
- *Buxus sempervirens* box is especially effective if trimmed into balls, which look best in extra tall "Long Tom" pots.
- *Diascia* slightly tender perennials available in a range of pinks and pink-reds, flower all summer and trail attractively over the side of containers.
- *Lilium* any lilies are good in containers, the fabulously scented *L.regale* is particularly popular.
- *Teucrium fruticosum* a Mediterranean shrub with dark green leaves, silver-grey underneath, with mid-blue flowers in summer.
- *Rosmarinus officianalis* especially trailing varieties, e.g. *Prostratus* group and "Severn Sea".
- *Tulipa* tulips always look good in containers, especially if combined with plants which have complementary flower or leaf colours.

---

under-planting for old roses, their other source of scent in the garden. They add, "we also like the tension achieved by planting strong shapes to break up the horizontal plain. Clumps of the dark cerise *Knautia macedonica* and the deep purple drumstick heads of ornamental alliums are regularly used to punctuate the flat heads of santolina and sedum. Such beds need to be a minimum of 1.5m (4 ft) deep to get a good variety of texture and form."

Finally, Sue and Helen recommend using containers. In many urban gardens, there may be little or no soil, in which case pots and tubs play an extremely important role. Containers can be moved around letting you highlight the plants when they are at their best. Evergreens, such as box, clipped into balls, are particularly effective.

Urban gardens might initially provide a range of problems but the potential is huge. One particular reason is the opportunity sheltered town gardens give you to grow tender species that might suffer winter damage in suburban or country gardens. Sue and Helen suggest "the lovely jasmine-scented trachelospermums or lavender-coloured *Abutilon vitifolium*".

PLANTS FOR SHADE

- *Epimedium* particularly in combination with *Alchemilla mollis*
- *Erythronium*
- *Euphorbia amygdaloides* var. *robbiae*
- *Euphorbia characias* subsp. *wulfenii*
- Ferns especially *Polystichium setiferum*
- *Helleborus*
- *Iris foetidissima*
- *Luzula*
- *Pulmonaria*
- *Sarcococca*

wildflower meadows **JULIE TOLL**

After a series of highly regarded Chelsea Flower Show gardens featuring recreations of

wildflower habitats, Julie Toll's name is inextricably linked with meadows and wild species,

although in fact they are only part of her work.

above Wild orchids
will often appear
spontaneously in
established meadows –
Nature's seal of approval
on your efforts.

Most wildflowers are a good deal less strong growing than the accompanying grasses, and are rapidly displaced by them on fertile or moist soils. So a site that might be regarded by most gardeners as all but hopeless – with thin, dry, infertile, calcareous soil and even crushed building rubble – will, in fact, offer the meadow gardener the best prospect. It's ideal for a wide variety of wildflowers and slower-growing, fine-textured grasses. "If you haven't got low fertility soil," warns Julie, "it will be difficult and you may end up with just grasses, although removing the clippings from mowing every year will slowly reduce the fertility."

But for those determined to give it a try, meadows are a source of endless fascination, with different wildflower species tending to dominate from one year to another, and more species appearing spontaneously as the years go by. The arrival of orchids is regarded

left This early summer
meadow is typical
for northern Europe,
and includes ox-eye
daisies (*Leucanthemum
vulgaris*) and yellow
Lady's bedstraw
(*Galium verum*).

above Pools, with
accompanying waterside
vegetation, are a
wonderful companion
to meadows.

by many as Nature's final seal of approval. Wildflower meadows are places of great beauty with myriad spots of colour dotted across a wispy carpet of grasses, with every breath of air blowing waves across the surface.

The dominant feature of meadows through much of the year, though, is the long grass. So it is crucially important that a meadow is incorporated into a garden in such a way as to make it obvious that it is intended, and isn't just a patch that has gone to waste. One way of giving them some sense of structure is by mowing short, neat paths through the grass. They can be very romantic and present all sorts of creative opportunities; you can change the layout of the paths every time the grass is mown, or mow patterns, a maze or labyrinth. It is even possible to mow a grid, with the grass and wildflowers left in square blocks.

In country gardens, meadows are often used in the outer reaches so that they form a transition zone between the more conventionally ordered parts of the garden and the landscape beyond. However, where they are more tightly integrated into the garden, perhaps even replacing lawn, Julie believes that edging the meadow with a mown strip is important for creating the intentional look. This strip can offer a very attractive place to walk, allowing the meadow to be seen and appreciated without actually being walked on. Where borders adjoin the meadow this strip is essential, but it can also play a part in a rather neat optical illusion; as you walk away the gap between the two vanishes and the border and meadow appear to be seamlessly linked.

Alternatively you can have what Julie calls a "flowering lawn" where grass, short and rosette-forming wildflowers are encouraged to grow. "You can either let a weedy lawn

right Mown paths are the most effective, as well as the most romantic, way of gaining access to meadows. Their pattern can be changed every year.

grow and flower," she says, "or you can sow a mixture of slower-growing grasses with seed of daisy, bird's foot trefoil, speedwell, plantains and self-heal."

Flowering lawns are ideal for smaller gardens or situations where a meadow may look untidy. They have an innate flexibility as the species survive regular close mowing and can be mown monthly. Don't begin cutting until the flowering has finished, as this gives plants time to scatter their seed. The lawn can be kept quite short and then, whenever you want flowers, stop mowing, and within four weeks there they are.

Another possibility is maintaining a flowering lawn primarily as a spring feature with bulbs such as crocuses and small-growing daffodils, followed by daisies; then, after the bulb foliage has died down, the grass can be kept mown short for the rest of the year. In the right situation, cowslips and primroses can be included in flowering lawns, the former requiring dry sunny locations, and the latter light shade or cool humid areas. But again, to allow them to spread, never mow the lawn until after the plants have set seed.

Meadow species vary from region to region, and in North America it is more useful to think instead of prairie as being the equivalent habitat. Seed mixtures appropriate to the site and to your region should be used for the best results. Over time nature will add species, resulting in increasing bio-diversity.

above Hemp agrimony (*Eupatorium cannabinum*) is a lush mid to late summer flowering perennial which favours lightly shaded or slightly moist sites. It is more of a hedgerow or woodland edge plant than a meadow species, and therefore useful in helping to make the transition between meadow and woodland. It is a very good butterfly plant.

contemporary gardens **DAN PEARSON**

Dan Pearson is a designer known for his contemporary naturalistic style. When it comes to designing gardens against modern buildings, he takes the view that "less is more. You mustn't compete when working with architecture, you must complement the building."

above The bold foliage of *Euphorbia mellifera* contrasts well with grasses.

Most would agree that modern buildings and naturalistic planting work well together, the hard lines and clear forms of the architecture being contrasted with the softness and simplicity of nature-inspired planting. "The landscape around such buildings," Dan says, "must be quiet and calm." For one particular project in London, illustrated here, he has used a grove of birches to screen a contemporary house from the road, partly for privacy but also to help integrate the property into a neighbourhood where all the other houses are much older. He adds that he and the client wanted to create "not so much a garden as an environment".

Birch trees were used to form a grove because they cast only very light shade but, in time, Dan says that he hopes to coppice some of them so that they become multi-stem specimens, "creating a sense of multiple generations". The ground-layer planting beneath the birches is

below Birch trees are ideal for under-planting, as they cast only a light shade.

made up of a restricted number of woodland species. Crucial to creating this atmosphere of simplicity are, firstly, sticking to a limited number of species, and secondly, planting them in a naturalistic style, blending them into a mosaic and avoiding formulaic, single-species blocks. At the rear of the house, there is a more severe style of planting where again a restricted palette of plants is used to edge a rectangular area of lawn. They include a willow (*Salix alba* "Argentea") which will eventually be pollarded so that its new twiggy growth or wands throw dramatic shadows across the lawn.

With any planting design, but particularly with the more unconventional kind, Dan stresses how important it is that the client and designer communicate well and don't hold back if something is worrying them. They need to keep communicating as the garden develops. Management, he adds, is a key part of the process – with a design such as this one, he expects to be involved until everything in the garden has matured, which may be several years.

below Bold architecture requires simple, unfussy planting solutions. Here bulbs and woodland perennials are used to underplant the birches.

Creating gardens around contemporary architecture

• The simple shapes used by much contemporary architecture are best complemented by minimalist plantings with large masses of just a few well chosen species.

• Foliage is often a better partner for modern architecture than flowers.

• Contemporary architecture can seem very stark in the winter. Perennials or grasses that retain their winter skeletons or trees with a sculptural outline can be an effective softening influence.

• Massed foliage offers contrast to large expanses of hard material such as cement.

• Large and bold leaves often look very good with geometric architecture.

• Self-clinging climbers are ideal for those modern buildings which have large areas of bare wall, as they retain the structure of the building whilst softening its outline.

old gardens DAN PEARSON

Few garden designers get to start with a blank canvas. One of a designer's first jobs when upgrading any garden is to look at the existing features, the borders, walls, shrubs and trees, deciding how much to keep.

above Details of old surfaces such as this can be an important part of ground-level interest.

These issues are particularly important when tackling an old garden. It may even have a special atmosphere which needs to be enhanced, retained, or changed.

One reason why it can be difficult to respond well to an old garden is that the atmosphere can seem very oppressive. This is usually due to old established trees, which have grown to become over-large and domineering. Yet, cutting them down can seem like a drastic step. Dan Pearson also dislikes cutting down old trees and stresses, "there has to be a very good reason for doing so." He describes how he once had a large weeping willow felled in his own garden because "it completely blocked out the sun, and the root system was enormous." Leaving it clearly was not possible. In many cases, though, he suggests a compromise because old trees do have many virtues, chiefly that wonderful

below Getting a balance between maturity and wildness contributes much to a garden's atmosphere.

left Features such as old walls can be a vital part of a garden design. Choose plants to complement them – and not hide them!

below Existing walls and the remains of old buildings are often associated with rubble in the soil, leaving a legacy of alkaline and dry soil conditions. Good plant selection will be needed – these bearded irises are amongst the many that will thrive.

sense of maturity. Always try calling in a tree surgeon, he adds, to see if you can improve the shape of the tree or reduce the number of branches to let in more light.

Hedges often have a valuable functional or aesthetic purpose, but they too can pose problems. "The fast-growing kind, like *leylandii*, can pose terrible problems if they aren't regularly cut back, but I prefer to avoid any trouble whatsoever by replacing them with something slower growing, such as yew (*Taxus baccata*) or beech (*Fagus sylvatica*) that will be less work in years to come and look better." Old yew or beech hedges should be cherished though, and if they have become ungainly, misshapen and tangled over the years, they can be cut back hard into old wood to generate new, fresh growth.

One of the main benefits of old gardens is that many have attractively aged brick and stone. Such features need to be retained and highlighted. In one garden Dan designed, he even found that he was "developing a colour scheme for a planting plan based on the grey, khaki, orange and lime-green lichens growing on a limestone wall."

When working with older gardens, you must spend as much time in them as possible before committing yourself to a particular couse of action; visiting at different times, in different conditions, will help you capture the "sense of place". Once you have experienced the different moods of the garden, you will be in a much better position to make bold decisions. You will also understand what "works" both visually and functionally, and of course what does not. With such experience behind you, you will be in a strong position to make large-scale changes with confidence.

the design process

Good garden design unites the intuitive and the creative with the hard-headed and the practical, and it is perhaps this combination that makes it such a rewarding activity. Here we consider some of the larger practical issues you need to get to grips with, which are also intimately related to more "artistic" issues, specifically how to bring together your patch of land, your dreams and your ability to make them happen. Garden design is a collaborative process, between you, your environment and the other people you have chosen to work with.

● **simple surveying techniques**
A simple means of making plans – the starting point of any design.

● **understanding your environment**
Observing what the garden has to offer as a growing environment is fundamental to achieving a garden that works both visually and horticulturally.

● **the planning process**
Karena Batstone introduces us to some tricks of the trade which she uses to think creatively about garden spaces.

● **using a designer**
As increasing numbers of people employ a professional designer, Lesley Rosser discusses how they can be used most effectively.

simple surveying techniques NOEL KINGSBURY

Garden designers use a variety of surveying techniques to draw up an accurate site plan. However, it is most unlikely that the amateur gardener would need or want to go to the lengths that professionals do when drawing up a plan. But if you do call in a professional, even for a specific job, such as paving, he or she will almost certainly want to do their own measuring.

above Main axes in gardens are useful to use as a baseline. Offset lines are used to measure distances from features which you want to map.

A basic plan drawn by you will always be very useful because it records the development of the garden, and can be used in later years to work out, for example, how much topsoil and grass seed you might need, and can help you calculate the size and potential impact of large features, such as ponds and trees.

Many people feel intimidated by plans and measurements. Yet there is one simple surveying technique which you can easily do yourself, and which is extremely useful for a variety of purposes. You just need a long, flexible tape measure and a steel tape measure, with a clipboard and paper. Chose an axis from which to take measurements, the obvious one being a line running longitudinally down the centre of the garden. This is the line that your flexible tape should be placed along. Or, if there is one straight boundary that dominates the garden, the flexible tape can be laid against this.

Once your flexible tape is in position, go to the garden feature that you wish to map out. Using the steel tape, lay it at a right angle to the garden feature and the flexible tape and measure the distance from the feature to the flexible tape measure. Also record how far along the flexible tape the steel measure falls. This will give you two co-ordinates. Back at your desk, the axial line can be drawn on a piece of paper, and features drawn to scale by their relation to that axial line. For small gardens a scale of 1:50 for metric measurements works well, and 1:100 for larger.

If the garden design is in any way complex, it is best to use several pieces of large paper to record your measurements, as trying to fit too much detail onto one sheet can get very confusing (40-60 cm [16-24 in] long is as large as is practicable to handle outside). I suggest one sheet for the boundaries, another for the borders and trees, and another for the artificial features. When measuring trees, take care to record not just the location of the trunk but of the outermost branches of the canopy too, allowing you to keep a record of the shade cast. .

One of the great things about garden design is that accurate measurement is not quite as important as in many other "do-it-yourself" activities. Dealing as it does with living things and complex environments it simply cannot be. Accuracy is most important for "hard" landscaping projects such as laying paving or for building garden structures of any kind. Anything involving planting however always has to make allowances for the fact that plants will never grow in ways that are entirely predictable. Your plan can be quite rough, as in the example opposite.

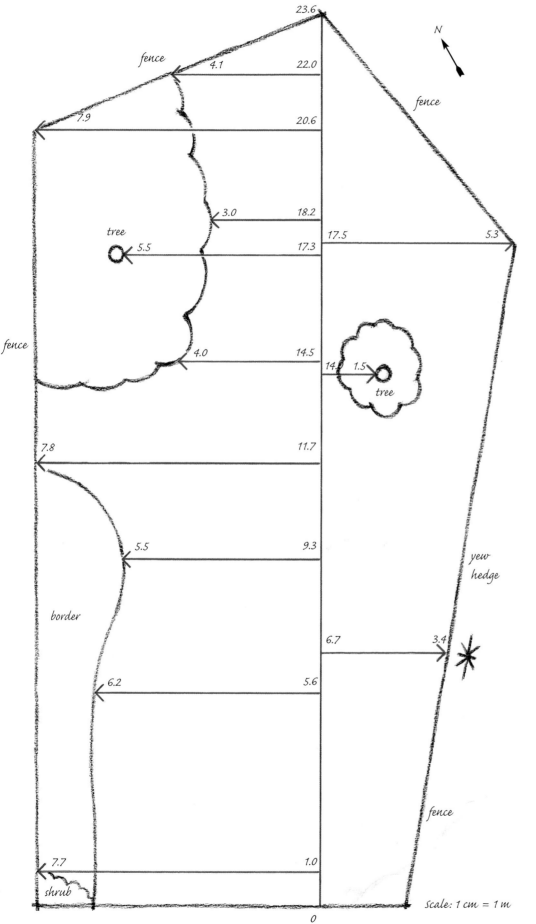

Scale: 1 cm = 1 m

GARDEN SURVEY

This is a simplified example of a survey of a garden. The red line is the axial line laid along the ground, the blue lines are "offset" lines which describe the distance from the axial line to the position of the feature being mapped. For example, starting on the left, the first measurement is 1.0, ie. one metre from the start (indicated by 0), from this an offset line reaches to 7.7 m (bottom-left hand corner) which indicates both the canopy of a shrub in a corner of the garden and the distance to a fence. The next one, 5.6, indicates the width of a border, 6.2m from the axial line; further along, 9.3, is the distance to the widest point the border reaches – 5.5 m. And so on.

Other points mapped include:

• the end of a border

• the edge of the canopy of a large tree

• the trunk of a tree

• corners of the garden

• the position at which a fence gives way to a hedge.

Finally, at the top, 23.6 indicates the distance to the end of the garden.

Note: a plan should always feature the scale, which is most easily indicated by what distance on the ground is equal to a unit of measurement on the plan – in this case, 1 cm = 1 m. Never mix your measurements – always work in *either* metric *or* imperial. An indication of the direction of North is also useful.

understanding your environment **NOEL KINGSBURY**

Although you can call in a garden designer at any time, there are plenty of tasks that you can do yourself.

You will always have a big advantage over any hired help because it is *your* garden, and you know it better than

anyone else, and that applies to the soil, drainage, local weather conditions, and the degrees of sun and shade.

above *Astilbe* and ferns are very happy in damp soil and shady conditions – here they create a lush and luxuriant effect.

At least, you will understand your garden if you have lived there for some time. Which is why one well-known gardener once suggested that you shouldn't do anything to a new garden for at least a year – letting you get to know the site before making any decisions. That will help make sure that you avoid any expensive mistakes, e.g. putting seating areas in a windy site, or borders where the ground dries out or gets flooded. Wait and watch.

Soil

Plants are the core of the garden, and are completely dependent upon the quality of the soil. Yet soil types and conditions can vary enormously across a garden, particularly in urban or suburban areas, where it is not just geology but history that dictates what the plants have to grow in. Here are nine simple ways to learn about the soil in your garden:

1 Get a spade and start digging, to two spits depth (one spit is the depth of a spade). Repeat the exercise at intervals over the area of the garden that you want to work on.

right A large clump of crocosmia and a fig tree here make the most of a warm and sheltered wall. It is important to exploit such favourable micro-climates.

2 If you encounter solid rock or large quantities of stones you have thin soil, which will limit the growth of plants that like deep fertile soils, such as roses, fruit trees and large perennials. However, low-growing perennials, and many trees and shrubs, may thrive here.

3 Water If the hole fills up with water which won't drain away, has sticky grey patches or smells bad, then there may be a drainage problem (see "moisture and drought", page 76).

4 Topsoil and subsoil Try to distinguish between the topsoil (darker) and the subsoil (paler, often yellow or red). If there is less topsoil than one spit then there may well be problems growing plants, such as annuals or large perennials, which need high fertility.

5 Variation in conditions Next, see if there is a major variation in conditions between one part of the garden and another.

6 Examine the topsoil Take out a handful of topsoil and examine it. Does it feel gritty, or sandy, or sticky?

7 Clay Next, add water to it. If it is possible to mould it into shapes it is a clay soil. Clay soils are hard to work, but very good for roses and many perennials.

8 Sandy soil If the soil stays loose it is likely to be sandy. Sandy conditions are suitable for many smaller perennials and grasses – and often rhododendrons and heathers.

9 Soil types Finally, add some soil to a jar of water, stir, and then allow to settle. Material that immediately falls to the bottom is sand or grit, that which floats is organic matter, while that which stays in suspension for a long time, as a dark mass, is silt and clay. This test helps you to assess your soil.

above Roof gardens are not easy places – they are liable to be hot and exposed. Drought-tolerant plants are a must if regular watering cannot be guaranteed, so cacti and succulents seem an obvious answer – although only if they can be protected during the winter. Wind damage is also a possibility.

Moisture and drought

Plants need water, but they can have too much of it. Just how much they get depends on many factors, the condition of the soil being one. Often it takes more than a year to really appreciate which are the driest and wettest parts of the garden. Identifying areas that have extreme conditions is crucial when it comes to selecting plants that will survive, and sometimes for planning of major garden features. Here is what to look out for:

• After periods of prolonged rain, are there any areas with standing water?

• During droughts are there areas of lawn that go yellow before others, or particular parts of the garden where plants start to look drought-stressed before others? Sunny banks are the first places to look.

An area where poor drainage is a problem might be the best place to build a bog garden and accompanying pond, which is certainly an easier solution than laying drains. Such areas should not be used for hard features, such as walls or paving, because you might end up with localized flooding. Digging up wet slopes can also result in additional problems, with water seeping into the trench or hole.

above Coastal conditions are demanding, but the tough evergreen foliage of many salt- and exposure-tolerant plants is often attractive. Many Mediterranean climate species are also suitable.

If you have a hot, dry spot, it may be the ideal place for a seating area, but may well need to be surrounded by drought-tolerant plants. Choosing appropriate plants is generally a cheaper option than trying to alter the soil.

Microclimate

Understanding the microclimate is vital when you are selecting the best places for various features. When siting a seating area, bear in mind that an area which gets sun in spring, autumn and winter, must also have shelter from prevailing winds in order to be any good. A wall or slope at the rear will store and reflect back heat. If there is little shelter from the wind, consider where to plant a hedge, but remember that the hedge itself will cast shade. For a summer seating area, the best place is one that gets evening light. In regions where the daytime summer temperatures are too hot to sit outside, choose an area that is shady during the hottest part of the day, or where a structure can be built, such as a pergola, that will provide protection from the sun.

When siting borders, areas prone to wind and frost are best avoided because they can easily damage plants. The fall of light and shade is a particularly crucial issue – take photographs of a new garden regularly to keep a record which will help you at the planning stage, and ask the neighbours about their experiences.

Trees

Buying a property with trees or a large hedge, or with trees next door, means that you will inevitably be affected by shade. It's even worse when you don't know how much more, or how fast, they will grow. And many gardens, particularly suburban ones, are often planted with inappropriately large species. The following points should help you clarify matters.

• When trees are a concern, ask a tree surgeon, or better still, someone from a nursery specializing in trees, to come and advise how they will grow and spread out.

• Try to think 10 or 20 years ahead. How big will the trees be then? If they are definitely going to be a problem, then think laterally about solutions, e.g. if a view is especially important and the growth of a neighbouring tree or hedge threatens it, consider moving the main viewpoint if you can.

• If the tree is yours, and the likely growth will seriously impair your enjoyment of the garden, consider having it felled. If it is deciduous, consider pollarding (cutting it back to 1.8 m [6 ft] high every year, for example) which will limit its growth. It is best to ask a tree surgeon for advice.

• You will save a great deal of money, aggravation, and damage to the garden if you act sooner rather than later. Arguably, for the good of the environment, you have a responsibility to replace any trees which are cut down with something smaller or narrower.

above Waterside plants are characteristically lush and often very vigorous. Only a few will be needed to fill out quite a lot of space. Once established they will need little maintenance.

the planning process **KARENA BATSTONE**

"You have to imagine yourself in the client's garden," says Karena Batstone, outlining the way she develops

designs, "to ensure that the experiences provided by the garden will meet the needs of those who will be using it."

One of the ways she does this is to use models and a variety of exercises to encourage the free flow of ideas and

to try to evaluate how those ideas might work in practice.

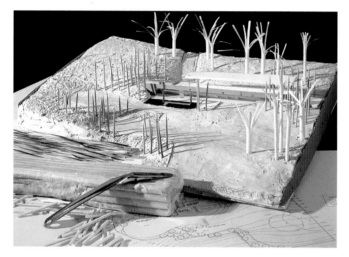

above Models are a good way of getting to grips with gardens, particularly if they can be made to an approximate scale. For example, they can enable you to see how mature trees might work. A light source, such as a torch, can be used to simulate the effect of the sun, and resulting shadows.

Karena's work, which takes her to a wide variety of both urban and rural properties, balances a hard-headed sense of the practical with a terrific sense of excitement about the visual and tactile qualities of the materials she works with. Increasingly well-known for her clear and uncluttered contemporary style, and her enthusiasm for new materials, she can be relied upon to practise what she preaches. "On my first visit to a new site," she says, "I like to spend some time on my own getting to know the land and its qualities. I always search out the loveliest part of the garden, though this may change with the time of day and the seasons."

Karena stresses the importance of light, of how the atmosphere of a garden can change dramatically as the sun moves, highlighting, backlighting or silhouetting different elements. She notes good places for planting trees, checking that they will cast welcome shade, and that their trunks and branches will throw attractive shadows in the low winter sun. She also notes where large ponds can be placed so that they don't cause glare in the summer sun. Discussing individual elements, she stresses how vital it is to think not only about the form and shape but also how its colour and texture will affect the "subtle play of light in the garden".

Models

Karena uses plasticine models to help her think about her designs. Plasticine is easy to work with, and its surface can be textured with a variety of implements to represent grass or paving, for example. Light and shadow is created by shining a light from the side, representing the sun passing over the garden from east to west. Straws are useful for modelling trees, as cutting them at one end enables them to be splayed out to represent branches. Alternatively, use matchsticks or toothpicks.

The plan is the central point and focus of any garden designer's work. Many non-professionals cannot "read" plans as people have very different ways of thinking about space. And many amateur gardeners create extremely successful gardens without using plans at all. However, where accurate measurements are needed, for hard landscaping or decking for instance, then the use of plans is vital – at least for the construction itself.

Plans do not have to be accurate scale drawings to be useful. They can also be used to "brainstorm", to loosen up the mind to think creatively and laterally. The mental

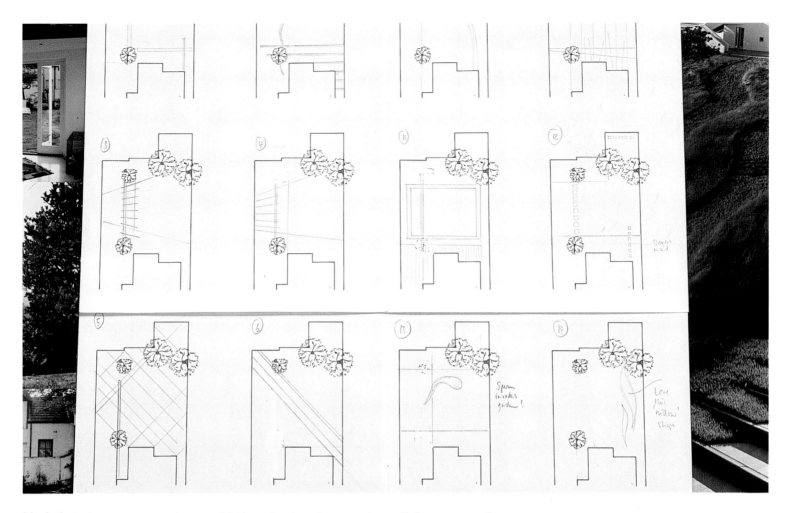

block that stops many people even thinking of using plans can be partially overcome if plans are used in this creative, but non-quantitative way. Karena prints as many as 10–20 outline plans and uses them to explore form and composition, producing a series of drawings of different ideas, each drawing having a strong dominant feature. When no more ideas come forward, she starts the process of elimination, working to produce a shortlist.

Such plans help ensure the different parts of the garden relate to each other. She adds, "I think of a garden from the house outwards, and always try to blend the two – functionally and aesthetically – by aligning new garden forms with the outside walls and corners of the house, and with the edges of doors and windows."

Photographs of the site are also a valuable tool. They can be copied on a scanner and printer, and be sketched over to see if new features can be added. Alternatively, Karena sometimes uses tracing paper to overlay a photograph, sketching on possible garden changes. This process is particularly useful for seeing how high various features have to be, such as trees and hedges, when viewed from particular angles.

Thinking and planning techniques such as these can be used by anyone. They encourage garden owners to think their way round problems and possibilities; and doing so in media such as models and abstract plans can be very helpful – in establishing a sense of distance from the reality of the site, the mind is encouraged to work in a different way, making it easier to encourage leaps of the imagination and hopefully resulting in a more original and successful garden design.

INSPIRATION

Ideas often come to people at odd moments – as the brain tends to think creatively at a sub-conscious level. Keep a small notebook and pencil handy at all times to scribble down ideas as they come to you. And don't just look at gardens for inspiration – many other environments can suggest ideas. Creative people find that the best ideas come to them when they are least expecting them!

using a designer **LESLEY ROSSER**

The first meeting between a potential client and a designer is crucial. It is vital that both parties feel comfortable and confident with each other. Lesley Rosser is a very experienced designer who has largely worked with rural gardens in south-west England; creating exciting but easily-managed planting is very much her forte.

"A good designer," Lesley says, "tries to get inside the mind of a client" but since most clients know relatively little about gardens and find it difficult to describe what they like, or want, she finds pictures invaluable. "I always take a pile of books," she says, "and then we sit around a table, talking about what they like and the range of possibilities. Getting their reactions is very important, and the more definite they are, the more successful the eventual design."

The designer will then survey the garden, and provide some plans. These may be actual plans or something more artistic, with a series of pictures illustrating potential garden features or plants. When the client is happy and the designer feels that they are in

above and below Your garden is *yours*, a personal space to enjoy. A good designer will do their best to put themselves in your shoes and respond to your needs.

left At Splatts Cottages in the front garden Lesley suggested a very minimalist treatment of box balls in a cross shape, inspired by a feature on the house. The owner said he'd never have thought of doing that himself, but he loves it because it is so simple and so effective. An outsider to the garden is perhaps more likely to have those leaps of imagination that really make people say "wow".

CHECKLIST FOR A FIRST MEETING WITH A GARDEN DESIGNER

- Borrow library books on garden design or famous gardens, and get a feel for the subject and the different atmospheres and styles.
- Make a list of features that you want, e.g. a seating area, children's area, pond, etc. Use photographs of gardens that you have liked and visited to illustrate such elements.
- Make a list of your hates, and make sure that the designer knows what they are.
- Think about who the garden is to be for, and what differing, or even conflicting needs it may have: elderly relatives, young children, dogs, growing vegetables.
- Gardens are rarely a blank slate. What is there in the garden that you definitely want to keep? Or definitely want to get rid of?
- Make a note of the views which you want to keep, improve, or lose.
- Study how the sun moves across the garden, preferably over six months. It may be important to know where the last sun of the day can be found in summer, or where the warmest spot is in winter.
- Think about the micro-climate: which areas are the coldest, windiest and hottest, etc?
- Try to pinpoint the different kinds of soil in your garden, the waterlogged patches and fast-drying, etc.

agreement, the designer will then produce precise plans for the hard landscaping and plants. Various options are now possible:

◆ The designer offers a design-and-build service, seeing through the entire project. This is the ideal situation as the designer knows exactly what's planned, and if anything needs to be changed you can immediately discuss it.

◆ The designer brings in the contractors, with whom he/she may or may not have worked before. A good designer and an aware client will keep a close eye on progress to ensure that the plans are adhered to. Or the client puts the work out to tender, selecting a contractor, but employing the designer to supervise. Or the client pays the designer for his/her work and selects a contractor, and supervises the work. Or the client actually does all or some of the work.

• The client rejects the overall plan, but keeps some elements. In this case the designer is being used more as a consultant. This can work particularly well where the client has some garden knowledge or is confident about his/her abilities in some areas, but wants advice on others.

Lesley stresses that, "When the designer has little or no involvement during the construction and planting phases the job may run less smoothly, and the chances of an unpredictable outcome might be higher." She adds that she sometimes wonders "why a garden designer was engaged in the first instance when clients working with contractors make changes in a design, leading to the undoing of the whole garden."

Advantages of employing a designer

Even if a designer is not employed to carry out the whole job, he/she can be immensely useful:

• Designers can help source a far wider range of materials than a client, through builders merchants and specialist suppliers.

• Designers will be able to locate a wide range of plants, often far wider than is possible from a garden centre. These should be supplied more cheaply too, especially if large numbers are needed.

above One of the first rules of garden design is that everything should *not* be visible at first sight: paths in particular should lead off, asking you to follow them.

• "A garden is only as good as its maintenance," Lesley adds. A designer will be able to advise on plant aftercare and maintenance. He/she should also be able to provide a client with a schedule describing what needs doing and when. Alternatively, Lesley likes to walk around the garden describing the different maintenance procedures. Clients should expect post-installation support from designers, and be able to ask questions as the garden develops.

• All committed designers will want to see the garden through to completion. Choose a designer experienced in doing this because he/she will be able to hone the quality of both the workmanship and the finished garden. The client might consider that any extra expense offsets the worries and expense if things start to go wrong during construction.

• A designer can tell you what is *not* possible (and, conversely, what *is* possible). Knowledge and experience count. This is particularly important where plants are concerned – but if the planting aspect is especially complex, ensure you employ a designer who has a wide plant knowledge.

right Professional help is invaluable for the planning and construction of features where accurate detailing is important, such as this pool.

two: furnishing

the garden

practicalities

and surfaces

A garden is a collection of surfaces. Selecting surfaces appropriate to the site, the look and the function of the garden and its different areas is a key early decision. Whether they are going to be planted or hard land-scaped (paving, decking, etc.) is the first choice, and beyond this, there are more choices to be made. Practical considerations are often the most important, but given the huge range of materials we now have available, it is possible to create elegant solutions to practical problems that are also visually striking, and which enrich the wider environment.

working with light CATHERINE HEATHERINGTON

Garden designers need to be acutely aware of the importance of light: its strength and composition, from where and how it comes into the garden, and what it does when it gets there. Catherine Heatherington works in London, where gardens and light levels are almost inevitably constrained by walls and fences.

Catherine Heatherington was brought up in East Anglia, where she remembers "expanses of reed beds and the open feel of an agrarian landscape". Her experience of working as a designer in London is very different as most clients want to block out views and gain privacy. But though these two experiences might seem miles apart, they share an interest in, and have made her acutely aware of, the importance of light and how it affects a garden.

"Looking at the sky is part of the experience of designing in cities," says Catherine, "although the opportunity to make use of it can be limited. Sometimes it's possible to make a feature out of the sky reflected in water, and you can use shadows in various ways."

Like many modern designers, Catherine is fond of using strong, sculptural plants, but she goes one step further because she uses them to cast shadows. She lists Japanese maples, grasses and bamboos as being especially good subjects, "particularly in the morning when low-angled sunshine casts plant shadows on a wall". Plain surfaces, like a smoothly rendered wall, are best for shadows and exploring the "different effects they have at different times of the year and day".

Walls are one of the most obvious distinguishing marks of Catherine's work; geometric flat blocks break up and sometimes dominate her gardens. But whereas a rough surface, such as stone or brick, always keeps its own personality under a wide variety of different

above Careful siting of lights can bring out features which are practically invisible in "normal" daylight conditions, such as the "grain" of stone and subtle changes in level and texture. Endlessly fascinating abstract patterns can be the result.

left Lighting can be used to create both patterns on surfaces – which depend very much on the texture of the material – and dramatic shadows. Small objects, well-lit, can be hugely magnified.

right The interplay of water and light can be particularly dramatic.

USING LIGHTING IN GARDENS

- Make a clear distinction between functional lighting, i.e. the lights used to illuminate paths and eating areas, and ornamental lighting.

- Put the functional and ornamental lights onto different circuits so that when the garden is not being used, only the ornamental lighting is seen.

- It is possible to have several different lighting effects in a garden, but you won't want them all on at once – put each one of them on a different circuit.

- "Less is more" is very appropriate – often the best effects are minimal.

- Few light fittings are attractive, so hide them.

- Lighting trees can be particularly striking, e.g. when ground-level up-lighters illuminate the bark of silver birches, highlight branch patterns or throw their shadows against a wall.

- Lights are particularly effective when aimed at a single sculptural object, so that it becomes a focal point.

- Think how planting, lights and hard surfaces might interact. What would make an effective shadow? Where should it be cast? How will shadows look on a particular surface? Pencil beams are very narrow beams of light and can be used to highlight particular features or point up a wall, creating stripes of light.

- If there is water, think how it can be lit to create interesting effects, or how underwater lighting might affect its appearance.

- Be aware that light pollution is a major issue. Ensure that your lights do not shine upwards more than necessary to minimize their contribution to the glow over built-up areas, which reduces views of the stars, and do not let them shine into neighbouring gardens. Also switch them off at night so that they don't upset nocturnal wildlife.

lighting conditions, a flat surface does not, instead changing colour and luminosity dramatically, registering shadows with an accuracy impossible on a rough surface. Catherine names the Mexican architect, Luis Barragan, famous for the strong colouring of exterior walls and the creation of minimalist but strongly-characterful spaces, as one of her influences, although she would never consider using his vivid colours on walls in the often weak light of England.

Catherine adds that night-lighting can transform a garden, creating atmosphere and drama, and can "bring the outside into the house, especially in winter". In fact, she uses lighting to create all sorts of dramatic and unusual effects. For example, in one of the gardens featured here, Catherine used underwater lights to cast "moving psychedelic patterns on the surrounding walls". In another, she set a light over slate paving. In daylight the surface looks perfectly smooth, but at night the horizontal beam of light highlights every minute change in relief.

"I like contrast," Catherine stresses, and that's precisely what she creates at night when the lights thrust certain features at us, hiding others in the darkness. Such lighting makes certain aspects of the garden's geometry appear more starkly, emphasizes shapes, and makes colours all but disappear. Night lighting can almost transform the garden into an abstraction. Don't underestimate its use.

above Shadows of moving vegetation create a constant abstract lightshow.

above Recesses can be highlighted with appropriate hidden lighting.

left Choosing plants on the basis of the shadows they throw is a whole new dimension in plant selection.

right Subtle underwater lights can create some of the most exciting effects of all.

changes in level KARENA BATSTONE

Few gardens are totally flat, and most have a slope of some kind (whether artificial or natural). But instead of seeing it as a problem, learn how to utilize this change of level.

The first thing you will probably need is a path going up or down the slope, simply as access to the end of the garden. This can be achieved either by digging into the slope to create a path or steps, or by constructing above-ground stairs or decking.

◆ Decking platforms are often the easiest and most cost-effective way of evening-out changes in gradient.

◆ Decking is supported on "posts" which ideally should be set into concrete. Installing these involves much less earth-moving than digging into a slope to create a level path. This can be a huge advantage if the ground is rocky or difficult to work.

◆ Where there is only a small gradient to be overcome, decking can be used as an alternative to steps – using the decking to create wide shallow steps (*see diagram 2*). In theory a ramp with a very shallow gradient could be used, but Karena favours the use of a steel grating pathway – which offers a better "non-slip" solution.

◆ Decking areas on steep slopes which are projected out can be used to create additional space underneath, which could be used for storage or a play space for children, for example.

If slopes are being dug into, Karena strongly advises never removing any material off-site. If soil that is dug out can be re-used elsewhere in the garden, not only are transport costs (and environmental costs) kept down, but it is more likely that the end result will look more natural.

As an alternative to digging into the slope, Karena favours using decking which is slightly raised above ground level. Decking can also be used to create occasional, wider lookout points, which can give dramatic views, although they will create large gaps beneath which need to be carefully obscured, perhaps with shrubs. Stairs are the third option, and can give the feeling that you are hovering above the planting below.

above This "hidden edge" pool is a clever way of creating a barrier without obstructing the view.

below Decking areas halfway down invite stopping and looking.

Slopes can also be very sculptural," says Karena, "and cutting into them is like carving stone. I love the way that you get different views at different levels, and how the atmosphere changes at the different points where you stop, turn and look. Correctly positioning these turning places is very important." Also note how you can position a path so that, as you walk up to the highest point, you get a close view of the tree canopy. But don't forget that while you can look out from the top of the slope, your neighbours might well be able to look in.

The banks to the side of the path offer excellent scope for planting. The kind of planting depends partly on the direction of a slope – if the main view is downhill, then plants which look good from above are needed, for example those with bold, upwardly held leaves such as hostas, rheums or macleaya species, whereas if the main view is uphill, towards the sun, you can dramatically backlight perennials and grasses – and the latter are often more effective when placed in positions where they are backlit. Steep slopes facing the sun might need drought-tolerant species, such as Mediterranean sub-shrubs like lavender and *cistus*. If you have a garden with a very steep slope, however, when standing at the top you might end up looking out over the garden and not at it. Karena's solution is to use vertical elements which help grab the eye, a principle applied in many Italian gardens where the pencil-thin cypress *Cupressus sempervirens* is used extensively.

right For accessing changes in level, nothing beats stone steps for durability and efficiency in using space.

left Two different ways of dealing with slopes:
1 Steps, which occupy a small area.
2 Steps extended to form a series of decking platforms.

Diagram 1

Diagram 2

slopes ISABELLE GREENE

As living density increases, so more people find themselves with houses

and gardens on slopes. The key decision when faced with a slope is whether

to terrace or live with it.

Sloping gardens are an increasing phenomenon – housing developers often flatten off a bit of rising ground, putting a house on top leaving the owner to create a garden on a slope, possibly with a very steep gradient and poor, exposed subsoil.

above These narrow terraces full of dramatic succulent plants have been created as an alternative to a conventional retaining wall.

There are not many options available to you if you have steep slope – terracing off flat areas or working with it. Many garden designers caution against using terracing, which is all too often very visually obtrusive and poor on sustainability – especially if concrete is used. It is also a highly expensive option and if you do it yourself, involves a lot of very hard work, shifting soil and installing retaining walls. Its only advantage is to ensure that there are plenty of level areas in the garden that are easier to traverse and work on. Whatever you do, especially in areas that are earthquake-prone, the advice of a structural or soil engineer should be sought.

left Stones found on site have been incorporated into this hillside garden.

left "Hidden edge" pools provide the ultimate in
swimming experiences – the ability to be in the water
and be on the edge of a fantastic view at the same
time. Water which spills over the edge is caught
in a drain at a lower level. However they need to be
designed so that they impact on the local environment
as little as possible.

Isabelle Greene is a designer based in southern California who has a deep understanding of the land, the geology and the flora of her region. She always prefers to work with the site instead of imposing dramatic changes on it. "I try to rearrange the site to avoid creating steep drop-offs," she says. "For example, driveways and paths can often be given an extra curve or zig-zag to minimize cutting into the ground."

Steep slopes are particularly prone to erosion, caused by hard rainfall washing away soil particles. "Cover them with plants" is Isabelle's answer, advising people to "use woody, low, evergreen shrubs with a fibrous-rooting system." Ceanothus are a very useful group of shrubs for dry climates. Some commercial landscape contractors have perhaps given such shrubs a bad name through over-use, but domestic gardeners will have access to a wider range of species, and can be more creative. Isabelle suggests we observe the growth habits of mature shrubs before deciding which ones to buy. Some have a dense, tight, mounding effect such as lavenders or hebes, whereas others have a more wispy, free-flowing habit.

Finally, if a retaining wall is needed, remember to use local rocks if possible, rather than concrete. Not only will the effect be more naturalistic and practical, but planting spaces will be created in the gaps between the rocks, which can create a softening effect when established.

right Existing trees have been preserved on this site, to minimise disruption to the environment, and paths given broad curving sweeps to reduce the number of steps.

boundaries LESLEY ROSSER

All gardens have boundaries, yet they are often the most neglected part of the garden. There is scope for a wide range of effects – don't be neutral about them – either make the most of them or hide them completely.

Designer Lesley Rosser thinks that in many, if not most, medium-sized gardens it's actually best to hide boundaries. "I like a central area, with plenty of distance between that and the boundaries giving a planting space so that you can't see the edge." But in small gardens it is usually impossible to hide the boundary and here, she thinks, "it is best to make a statement using natural materials that are good to look at, or make a feature using climbers."

Country gardens tend to be a different matter because the need isn't so much to exclude the neighbours as to provide glimpses of the outside world. But that very openness means that you might then need screening or a windbreak. "Clients always get very worried when I mention these two," she says, "as they think they are going to lose the view, but a framed view is often better than an open panorama." And boundaries such as hedges, fences or walls can be so designed as to attract the eye to the best part of the view, or they can have peepholes cut in them so that although views are restricted, they are unexpected and dramatic when you do see them.

Fences and walls in country gardens are best built out of local materials to help the garden meld into the landscape. Different regions use different local materials, hence the predominance of dry-stone walls in rocky, upland districts. A vast array of different materials are now available, but whereas brick or imported stone can look out of place in some locations, natural materials, such as willow, reed, bamboo and heather, are more likely to fit in. They are often available in rolls (a bit like wallpaper), and can be fixed to posts and supported by horizontal wires.

above Walls can be covered in fast-growing ivy – especially useful if they are made of unattractive materials, or you simply feel you are surrounded by too many hard surfaces.

below Traditional dry stone walling is durable and, where traditional, ties a property into its surroundings.

> ❝ *a framed view is often better than an open panorama* ❞

Lesley points out that some of these natural panels are like net curtains because they are semi-opaque, and they filter the wind instead of blocking it, making them more likely to survive storms than solid fencing panels which are liable to end up half-way across town after a wild and windy night. The panels' life-span is not particularly long, often no more than five years, but Lesley advises that they can be preserved by an annual spraying of linseed oil mixed with white spirit. A short lifespan won't be a problem, though, if the screening material is intended as a temporary measure, for example providing shelter for a young hedge.

Garden owners often feel the need for such windbreaks, either to protect the plants or provide a sheltered environment for themselves, yet the sheltering structures or hedges often end up blocking a view. "So why not," suggests Lesley, "create a screened-off area inside the garden rather than around the boundaries?" A seating area can be protected in this way without losing views from the house or the rest of the garden.

The creation of boundaries is a particular priority for owners of new gardens, to create windbreaks and privacy and to develop a sense of differentiation between one part of a garden and another – often these boundaries end up being temporary.

above A variety of natural materials is now available for fencing. These panels are made of willow wands fixed to horizontal wooden supports. This material allows for some visual transparency, as well as air movement – an advantage in windy weather when fences which offer total resistance to wind are vulnerable.

above This boundary is made by a hedge of such looseness that it may not be interpreted as a hedge at all, with views out and a variety of shrubs. Its loose definition serves to hide its function and thus seem less of a boundary than it really is.

Mixed country hedges

A traditional feature between fields in Britain and parts of northern France, the idea is now being applied elsewhere in the world, as ecologically inclined gardeners create plantings that benefit wildlife. Lesley is adamant that a mixed hedge is attractive as a garden feature, but only if a "terribly informal, rustic look" is wanted. The different species grow at different rates and make keeping an even, straight line virtually impossible – it is not suitable for gardens with modernist, clean lines.

A mixed hedge can be grown anywhere though, even where it isn't traditional, and is a good way of including a wide variety of native shrubs (and even trees) in the garden without having to grow them as large, individual features. They are a great bonus for supporting local wildlife. Traditionally, hawthorn is the basis, with about a quarter of the plants from a choice of over a dozen other species. The final choice will depend on your soil type and climate. *Viburnum opulus,* for example, is good for thin alkaline soils, amelanchier and willow species for wet soils, and hornbeam *(Carpinus betulus)* for northern latitudes.

right Beech makes a good solid hedge – this one forms an internal garden division.

HEDGING

- **Beech (*Fagus sylvatica*) and hornbeam (*Carpinus betulus*)** by far the best choices, forming dense growth with elegant leaves. Both are best for formal hedging, i.e. being close-clipped to give a geometric shape.

- **Box (*Buxus sempervirens*) and related species such as the more drought-tolerant *B. microphylla*** rarely used for boundary hedging as it is slow-growing, but it is invaluable for creating the "bones" of a garden, marking internal divisions.

- **Griselinia (*Griselinia littoralis*) and pittosporum (*Pittosporum tenuifolium*)** good in coastal locations where strong winds but not hard frosts are a problem.

- **Hawthorn (*Crataegus monogyna*)** makes an effective, dense thorny hedge if security or excluding animals is important, and establishes quickly. Especially useful for surrounding paddocks and orchards, it needs cutting only every three to five years for an informal look.

- **Holly (*Ilex aquifolium*)** has a good, close texture and is suitable for either clipping as a formal hedge or letting go as a more informal, rounded one.

- **Laurel (*Prunus laurocerasus*)** not good for smaller hedges as the large leaves inevitably get cut in half when being pruned, making it look untidy. Best for larger scale screening.

- **Privet (*Ligustrum vulgare*)** tends to be greedy, starving nearby plants. Also, it grows so fast that it needs clipping more than once a year, and has a tendency to be gappy.

- ***Rosa rugosa*** its cultivars are among the best choices for an informal flowering hedge being very adaptable, robust and forming a dense barrier.

- **Yew *(Taxus baccata)*** is rightfully used extensively, and works well cut into a square or rounded shape. It is faster growing than often thought, making 30 cm (12 in) a year if kept well fed and watered through the summer.

materials for hard surfaces **JAMES VAN SWEDEN**

The materials chosen for the garden floor will shape and define the rest of a garden design.

Practical issues, such as how you will be using the garden, as well as aesthetics must be

considered carefully before any decision is made.

"I usually design paved areas first," says James van Sweden. "They provide the basic structure of the garden; they define how areas are used, and they act as a framework for planting." Hard surfaces, such as terraces, are often where everyone socializes in the garden, while paths provide physical access. Paths also provide a kind of visual access too, as the eyes go ahead of the feet, following paths through the garden, effectively controlling how we look at it. Modern gardeners have an enormous range of different materials to choose from for covering the ground. Choosing one rather than another is the result of balancing utilitarian and aesthetic factors.

JAMES' POINTS TO CONSIDER

- Paving for terraces must be safe. It must be well lit, and smooth, but not so smooth that it might get slippery when wet.
- Paths need to follow routes which will lead people conveniently to where they want to go. If they don't do this, people will find a better route, taking a short cut across lawns, treading the grass down to bare earth.
- Paved surfaces are with you all through the year, and they can cover a lot of ground. You must be absolutely sure you can live with them.
- Terraces, and other paved areas will always look bigger on a plan than they will in real life, where you will be looking at them at an angle, rather than the bird's eye view afforded by a plan. "I err on the big side, when I design," says James.
- When planning a terrace, consider how much it will be used and what for. Assemble furniture, barbecue equipment, etc., and see how much space it requires.
- Tile, cut stone, brick or pavers are geometric, creating an ordered and finished appearance. Fine textures will make small spaces appear larger.
- Randomly placed, irregularly cut stone, has a much more unfinished and "rustic" appearance. Some people find this look distracting and fussy.

left This mixture of slate and stone chippings succeeds in looking very natural. Plants frequently self-sow into such a loose surface, which adds to the natural and spontaneous atmosphere.

below Old wooden railway sleepers (railroad ties) can be very effective in the garden, combining durability with a rough "earthy" look. Nowadays it is even possible to get concrete or recycled plastic imitations – even more durable!

right This is a particularly spectacular example of a hidden-edge pool with an adjacent shelter for barbecues and other events.

below left and right Earth colours work well with an uneven rendered surface, evoking adobe, cob, or other traditional media. They also go well with furniture made from natural materials. What is particularly exciting here is the "window" which frames a dramatic cactus screen – so the natural environment is brought right into the seating area. The other side of this area has a "borrowed landscape" of a distant mountain.

outdoor living spaces STEVE MARTINO

"It gets to 110°F (over 40°C) out here in summer, so shade is pretty essential," says Steve Martino, a designer whose work with desert plants in Phoenix, Arizona has "made people look a lot more closely at what they think of as weeds."

We don't all live in such extreme conditions, but most gardens will experience hot weather at some point during the summer. And the ways of dealing with it are much the same. One of the most distinctive aspects of Steve's work is that he uses locally native species – proven to survive extreme conditions.

The design of an outdoor living space is obviously dependent on the climate; in more temperate zones, shelter from the rain and wind and not the sun may be more appropriate. But certain aspects of choosing sites for outdoor living spaces are universal: closeness to the house, especially the kitchen; attractive views; and perhaps the most important, privacy. "You have to make people feel as though they are in their own sanctuary," Steve adds, "so they can even walk around naked if they like."

> " *colour on a wall is like a piece of furniture* "

Equally important, is the use of attractive boundary or dividing, internal walls, which can also be used to cast shade. One of the most striking features of Steve's work is his use of coloured walls, inspired by the work of Franklin D. Israel. His choice of colours is often strong, and includes deep blues, reds or oranges. Steve urges people to think hard before choosing because "colour on a wall is like a piece of furniture."

Planting also plays an important role in and around living spaces, providing screening, shade, framing views and offering flowers or scent. Climbers are amongst the most useful plants for such situations, especially since many have wonderful scents which are often stronger in the evening. In clear sunlight, highly sculptural plants, such as cacti, can cast dramatic shadows on coloured walls, which is another factor to consider when choosing the paint. And make sure that you use some plants which attract plenty of wildlife – precisely what you use depends very much on what your local wildlife is, although as a general rule, butterflies like flowerheads made up of with masses of tiny flowers and humming-birds prefer tubular flowers.

right Warm climate zones allow for a lot of life to be conducted outside, needing only a shelter from rain. Here a fully equipped eating area benefits from spectacular views.

play areas **KARENA BATSTONE**

Children and adults use the garden in different ways, which do not always combine well. But there are solutions. Karena Batstone says that, "things have to be adaptable and multifunctional, especially if the space is small."

Think about how spaces are going to be used differently as children grow up. Karena recommends using a concrete ramp because it can be visually exciting and is multifunctional, "great for skateboarding, wheelchairs and wheelbarrows".

Water features have to be safe, but Karena is adamant that water is "fantastic for older children to play in", and should not be excluded from gardens. It is only the very young who need to be supervised closely and, as Karena points out, water features can be made safe. Try installing a metal grid just below the water surface, ensuring that both safety and appearance are not compromised. What she calls "convertible features" also work well, for example ponds filled with soil and bog plants or pebbles which can be filled with water again when the children are older.

In one garden she designed, illustrated here, a play area has been built at the highest level so that it is not visible from the terrace immediately outside the house. Children love places that adults can't get to, and such concealment serves both parties well. Areas of decking reached by child-friendly ladders or anything else which deters adults serves the same function. Karena also suggests screening, in the form of hedging or a row of pleached trees, which is particularly useful for concealing larger play equipment such as climbing frames.

Some of the biggest conflicts of use concern lawns, which often dominate the middle of the garden. Karena's answer is to build a special sunken lawn, with a low wall around the perimeter, greatly reducing the risk of balls, pets or children hurtling into surrounding planting, adult seating areas or water features.

Karena also suggests concentrating the planting in one large border which can be positioned where it is least likely to be damaged by over-exuberant play. "But it's important," she adds, "that such planting doesn't appear mean. It needs to be intentional and strong, and ideally should get full sun."

below Elevating play areas is one way of reducing their impact on the rest of the garden.

above A pleached lime hedge helps screen this play area at the end of a town garden. The low wall around the lawn helps to limit play, and accompanying toys, to the grass.

left This pool has a roll-back cover to ensure that no-one falls in when the area is unsupervised. An existing tree has been incorporated into the area, with one branch supporting a swing.

sustainable design ISABELLE VAN GROENINGEN & GABRIELLA PAPE

Isabelle van Groeningen and Gabriella Pape are garden and landscape designers who work in both Britain and Germany, and have been in the forefront of their profession in developing "sustainable" garden design. Isabelle defines the concept of sustainability in their work as "the creation of a garden which will have the least possible impact on the environment".

above This seat, designed by Gaze Burville, is made from sustainably sourced oak cut from managed woodland. This green timber will last for decades without artificial preservatives, and is also practically fireproof!

Making gardens, in particular constructing "hard" features such as paths, paving and decking, involves the use of materials which may have a damaging effect on the region where they are mined or harvested, on the wider environment (through air or water pollution), or which may involve costs when their usefulness is over and they are disposed of.

Isabelle and Gabriella do realize, however, that "the bottom line is how much people can afford". The most sustainable options are rarely the cheapest and sometimes may be considerably more expensive. Nevertheless, ecologically friendly options are becoming increasingly widely available and, as they do so, prices fall.

To create a sustainable garden, they suggest that you:

• Try to avoid pressure-treated timber because it uses persistent, toxic chemicals. There are various alternatives, such as hardwoods (e.g. oak) which naturally resist decay. New methods of protecting wood are being developed which will soon become more readily available, including a process of heat-treating softwood – ask for them.

• Look out for new products on the market made of recycled plastics. Some are designed to replace wood (and can look remarkably like it). Others have a highly distinctive appearance that could suit a contemporary garden design.

• Be aware how transport miles affect the environment. If something has been delivered from thousands of miles away, transporting it to your door will have used up enormous amounts of energy and contributed to CO_2 emissions. Local products not only minimize the problem, but often blend better into the environment.

• Visit reclamation yards for materials. They have stocks of old bricks, tiles, slates and timber, etc. In many cases they are no longer being made and can be used to create an instant period effect. Since stocks change regularly, frequent visits are advisable.

below Seedheads are an important element in the autumn herbaceous garden. Many are a useful food source for birds, some also harbour insect larvae, which in turn can be eaten by insect-eating species. Note the use of broken recycled slates for the path – an inexpensive and very attractive surfacing material, which, unlike gravel or chippings, is relatively weed-proof.

above Decking is intrinsically more eco-friendly than paving or other impermeable surfaces, providing it comes from a sustainably managed and relatively local source.

◆ Note that attractive local stone can be expensive. Re-constituted stone is a lot better than it used to be, and is much cheaper. If ethical practices are important to you, but you want to use imported stone, remember that quarries in some countries use slave labour – ensure your supplier has signed up to a fair-trade policy.

◆ Minimize the use of hard surfaces in the garden because they do not absorb water, and contribute to run-off and flooding. Decking is better than paving, as is traditional gravel and hoggin, where stones are set in a semi-permeable clay.

◆ To minimize environmental impact, the best and cheapest way to is to re-use materials found on site. This will avoid the transport miles involved in taking it away, reduce the pressure on landfill sites, and save you money. Use your imagination – if you don't really like the way the material was originally used, try to think of other ways it could be used and incorporate it into your new design.

rocks and earthenscapes ISABELLE GREEN

"I never met a rock I didn't like," says Isabelle Greene, "they are so permanent and they have a personality of their own." Rocks are often a fundamental aspect of a landscape – make use of them, rather than disposing of them.

Whilst some garden designers have followed the Japanese art of rock placement, Isabelle's inspiration is much more grounded in having been born and bred in southern California. She learned to love its rocky landscapes at a young age.

Making use of rocks that already exist in a garden, or importing them from the local area, ties a garden into a landscape. How these rocks occur locally is a guide as to how they should be used in the garden. A good example is the huge (40 ton [40,640 kg]) rock Isabelle once moved within a property. Many designers might have been tempted to leave it exposed, thinking that the cost of hiring equipment should be recouped through maximum visibility. Instead, like an iceberg, it ended up mostly invisible, but looking as if that is where nature intended it, with a seating area, steps and planting positioned around it.

below This 8 ton (8,128 kg) rock was found on site and re-located in a new position. It now makes a superb backdrop for a sitting and dining area. Paving has been chosen to complement it and the local geology.

A great advantage of rocks as aesthetic elements in the garden is, as Isabelle half-jokingly observes, that "they are low maintenance". They are also a good complement to planting. Isabelle often matches rock shapes with plant shapes, although sometimes she will go for contrast, for example by using straight ornamental grasses.

above Natural rock is a good accompaniment to succulents, complementing their textures and colours.

Earthenscapes

This is a term Isabelle invented for non-living ground cover. It was an idea born during a severe drought, when she had to think of design solutions that involved the minimum of plant life and irrigation. The materials used need to be locally and plentifully available, and ideally re-cycled. Isabelle uses railway sleepers, alternating with gravel of various colours as a background for succulents, and also crushed brick for its warm tones, crushed roof tiles, slates, broken clay pots, and organic materials such as walnut shells.

Although Isabelle is a lover of plants, she explains she is drawn to "the museum-like quality you get" in these earthenscapes where plant use is minimal and where colours can be restricted, almost monochromatic. Cool and restful, such areas have a similar appeal to the classic simplicity of a Japanese garden.

left The construction of houses on slopes often results in hillside being cut into. This staircase was cut from the live native rock. Areas of exposed solid rock can be regarded as an attractive feature, whilst less-attractive areas of weathered material can be planted up with appropriate plants to cover them up and complement the undamaged rock.

creating interest

A garden can have a well-designed basic structure but still be lacking

spark. For some this interest can be achieved purely through planting,

but for others there needs to be a greater use of artifice. Indeed, some

might argue that this aspect of gardening was more important in the

past than today, with many of the great gardens of history relying very

heavily on sculpture, extensive water features and special effects. Today

we may have become too focused on plants and relaxation rather than

stimulation. Here we look at a variety of contemporary approaches.

creating illusions
George Carter looks at ways to make
the garden seem something other than
what it is.

sculpture
Anthony Paul uses gardens as
gallery space.

water in the garden
Anthony Paul argues for a natural look to
garden water features.

**water in the
contemporary garden**
Ted Smyth's bold new slant on one of
the most popular aspects of gardens
through history.

creating illusions **GEORGE CARTER**

Gardens lend themselves to all kinds of effects and optical illusions – they are playgrounds for the senses. George Carter makes great use of illusions; the first thing that a visitor to one of his gardens might notice is two-dimensional structures masquerading as three-dimensional ones.

His illusions are highly effective, combining stylish design and wit. The barns around his house are full of them, in storage or in various states of construction; there is the feeling that you are in the workshops of a maker of theatre stage-sets which, in a way, you are.

"The garden is theatre," claims George. Quite rightly too. Renaissance Italian gardens and the formal French baroque style, to which it gave birth, were theatrical places and not just because of the way they were created but because they were used as stages for balls, masques, plays and firework displays. George's use of painted wooden structures as garden features, in particular his use of *trompe l'oeil* (illusion), is a revival of a long and largely forgotten tradition.

above Even ducks can have a period-style house! This was inspired by artisan mannerist architecture of the 17th century, and though tiny in proportion it tricks the eye into perceiving a greater distance – as though you were looking at a full-size structure from further away.

right Seats and other structures can be made with simple materials and incorporate two-dimensional versions of complex three-dimensional patterns.

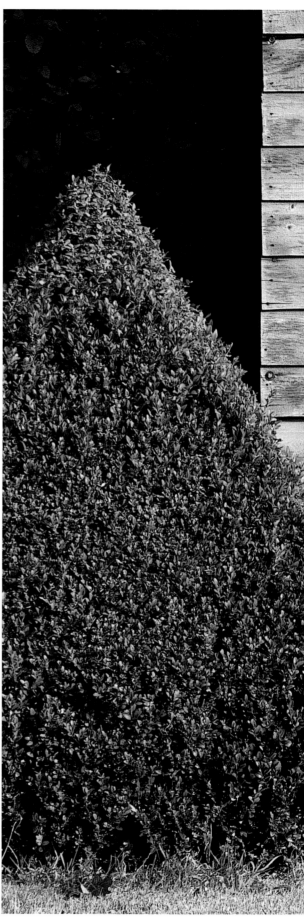

"They are all very basic, simple and cheap," he says. "I like the idea of using inexpensive materials to create good 18th-century effects." He uses plywood or other sheet materials, painted with flat colours: greys, blues and greens. "The colours that, at a distance, imitate the effects of perspective: a blackish-green in the foreground and bluish-green in the distance." Once complete, these sheets can be placed in a variety of key positions in the garden: at the end of a vista for example, or at the back of a border – the less expected the place the stronger will be the effect of the illusion for the viewer. Wood can also be painted with *trompe l'oeil* paint effects to successfully imitate a variety of stone surfaces.

More complex, elegant 3D structures such as pergola-type frameworks can be made using wooden laths that can be used to support climbers such as clematis or sweet peas, a revival of what was known as carpenter's work, which was common in 17th-century gardens. George prefers oak for such permanent unpainted structures as it is so durable, and warns that any painted structure does need a certain amount of maintenance, although modern wood stains can alleviate this problem.

above The urn here functions as an eyecatcher or focal point. Behind it is a two-dimensional trellis designed to look three-dimensional, thus making it seem as if there is more garden beyond.

right This gazebo has definite period appeal and yet is constructed from simple and inexpensive materials.

George's structures, the two-dimensional ones in particular, lend themselves to parties and special events and other temporary uses. In particular, George suggests that "people can seasonally re-arrange them, adding different finials for the posts at different times of the year". Plywood mock-ups can also be used in planning major new structures, such as gate posts; "you can see what they are going to look like before committing yourself," he suggests.

There are plenty of other illusory aspects to garden design besides getting 2-D to look like 3-D. One of the most important roles of illusion in the garden, which Italian and French designers explored with great skill and inventiveness, was in "stretching distances", making gardens seem bigger than they really were, or distant points look further away.

"Illusions that work," George says, "are those that change the scale so that the viewer is made to expect something different." For example, openings in walls can be made smaller than they should be, so that they appear further away. "In addition," he says, "once you have detected a possible illusion, you want to go up and examine it." In other words, such illusions make people explore the garden.

TO CREATE ILLUSIONS THAT "STRETCH THE DISTANCE"

- Change the size of gravel on paths and surfaces, so that the larger size is nearer the main viewpoint and the smaller is at the far end.
- Use grey or blue coloured gravel because it adds to the sense of distance – this also applies to plants.
- Mow areas of grass to make them look bigger.
- Use reflective surfaces because they dissolve boundaries, and are less of a sudden full stop. Mirrors are often used, but galvanized steel will create a softer effect.
- Positioning *trompe l'oeil* and other special effects along the side of a narrow garden creates interest sideways, hence reducing the impact of the overall long and thin effect.

- You can make paths, canal-shaped ponds, and other features that involve parallel lines stretching away from the viewer, appear longer if the sides gradually angle slightly inwards (see below).

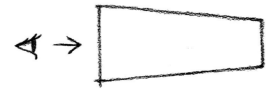

- Use repeating upright elements that are taller at the front, gradually getting shorter in the distance (see below).

- Any element on the ground that is repeated, such as stepping stones, can be placed closer together in the distance (see below).

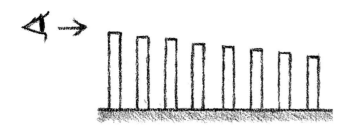

sculpture ANTHONY PAUL

Of all areas of garden making, this is one of the most personal and subjective.

Whatever your taste, however, there are arguably some basic ground rules that

govern the positioning of any sculpture.

Landscape designer Anthony Paul is married to art dealer Hannah Peschar and their garden is open to the public as an outdoor sculpture gallery. "Most people think of siting sculptures at axis points, but it is too obvious," says Anthony, highlighting one of the lessons that many have learnt (albeit subconsciously) from classical formal garden style, and arguably applied too widely. Because classical formality is so dependent on symmetry, axes meeting at right angles and clear straight vistas, it tends to "get to the point too quickly", a particular problem for small gardens. As a consequence there is no sense of discovery. "Sculpture should have an element of mystery," says Anthony, "you need to draw people in, you need hidden places and, especially in a small garden, areas of intimacy."

above This urn echoes the bark of the tree behind, while its base introduces an artistic element into the woodland. *Landscape Urn* by Billy Adams (fired clay).

Left Sculpture can be inventive and fun, but think carefully about work which entertains at first sight, but which may pall with time. *Damselflies* by Paul Amey (plastic/stainless steel).

BEFORE YOU BUY

- Beware of work out of context. This is often the fate of ethnic pieces, and in the case of classical-inspired work can make them into clichés.
- A garden is all too easily overdressed with sculpture. One piece in a minimalist environment can be very effective.
- Don't be afraid to buy art. There is more work at reasonable prices around now than ever before. Take advantage of instalment payment schemes.
- If you can afford to buy a piece, you can afford to commission. Commissioning involves meeting and talking with the artist, and can be an enjoyable and enriching experience.

above Some of the best garden sculpture is easily moveable, making it possible to reposition works with the seasons, thus involving you in constant creative decision making. *Pods* by Mike Savages (copper).

POSITIONING SCULPTURE

- Think creatively about where sculpture should go – less obvious places have an element of surprise.
- Think about how light falls onto the material, glass for example needs to be lit from behind.
- Sculpture doesn't have to be at eye level. Try placing works where they have to be looked down on, or up to.
- Artwork can interact with the landscape, for example by being hung in a tree, or be placed where it can allude to or comment on something in the surroundings.
- Move sculpture around, so that it is displayed effectively during different seasons. Moving works, and the act of choosing new places for them, reconnects you with them, and makes you look at them anew.

left Some sculpture plays with our perceptions, causing those who are unfamiliar with the garden to look again. *Ghost* by David Begbie (wire mesh).

water in the garden ANTHONY PAUL

The popularity of water in the garden seems universal, either as a still pool, or when moving (e.g. as a stream or fountain). For many gardeners it is the most demanding and expensive project, and you've got to know what you are doing to avoid the many pitfalls.

above Large pools need large-growing or vigorous plants to give them scale.

Designer Anthony Paul is renowned for his use of water, in a wide variety of different situations and climates. Few places, he thinks, are totally unsuitable, only perhaps deep shade. However, he warns that water features must always have a context and that, if they are to appear natural, they must be in a place where water might appear naturally. He also warns that everything to do with water has to be done properly, and there is no space for cutting corners or half-measures as leaks are immensely difficult to repair. "If you can't do it properly, don't do it," he adds.

One popular place for water in the garden is next to a seating area, but he argues that paving mustn't abut the water because you can't create an acceptable look to the join. He says that decking is an attractive option as it can overhang the edge of the pool and hide any liner visible at the sides. In his own garden, Anthony has dramatically illustrated the potential of decking by cantilevering a wide area of it out, at about 1 m (3½ ft) above the water level of a large pool directly outside his house, integrating pool, house, seating area and the landscape.

below Water steps are a change from the ubiquitous waterfall and fit more easily into most gardens. They are not for walking on however!

Scale and proportion

"Scale is so important," says Anthony, "and often people make ponds so small that they are overwhelmed by their surroundings." Large pools can easily merge into the rest of the garden by planting of the kind of lush and leafy wetland plants you would expect to find naturally next to water. In a small garden, a pond which is large relative to the size of the garden can also create the illusion that the whole garden is larger than it really is. Scale and relativity are the key issues here; even in a tiny garden, a body of water that is small in absolute terms can appear large if it occupies a key position or is large in proportion to the whole area.

He suggests that large ponds also offer some exciting creative possibilities, such as islands and bridges. "I love Japanese bridges which are fun and interesting. And simplicity is so important, but don't let them look like they come straight out of Monet's garden in France because that has become quite a cliché." He also suggests that a good-sized pond is also "a good way to end a garden" – water always seems to beckon to us to imagine what there is on the other side.

right Leaving waterside borders relatively wild makes the water body look natural and is of great benefit to wildlife.

Anthony also stresses how, for him, the clarity of water is important, although whether it is possible to achieve this depends very much on the type of water body you have. He likes the effect of "water that is crystal clear, like a big aquarium". Pebbles or gravel provide an attractive pond bottom, but if a layer of soil is used in the bottom of the pool in which to grow water plants, then he recommends "covering it with gravel, and keeping fish can keep it clean." He also recommends using gravel to form a beach, "so that there is a place where the water laps against stone". "Too often," he adds, "you see a pond where there is just one type of edge, and a gently angled beach provides extra interest." It is also good for the wildlife, allowing frogs and newts to get out easily, and birds to get in.

Moving water, such as streams or waterfalls, is particularly problematic in gardens because it is so difficult to make it look anything other than contrived. Rills running through paving are different, however, because they don't pretend to be natural, and are particularly welcome in hot climates for their soothing and cooling properties. Anthony also says that he "loves fine rills to water the bog plants, as water can gently leak out of this area".

Other unashamedly artificial water features can also be highly effective, such as the Japanese *Shishi-Odoshi* where water flows from a bamboo pipe. "Moving water," he concludes, "needs to have some noise which draws people to it, but note that the noises can be very different – water hitting stone is a lot more sensual than water hitting water."

119

water in the contemporary garden TED SMYTH

Ted Smyth is a New Zealand designer who is very much his own man, specializing in work that is dramatic, bold and, above all, clear-cut. For those who associate water with water plants and natural environments, Ted has some startling opinions: "I don't use water plants, I've been through all that."

Ted's views on the use of water in contemporary garden-making are hardly surprising given that this is the man who states baldly that, "I pay no homage to the traditions of standard English-based picturesque garden-making." In a Tao-like utterance, he says "water is about what's *not* there, rather than what is there." With their clean lines, absence of distracting elements (such as water plants), reflective surfaces and sheer simplicity, his water features make a strong counterpoint to the solid elements of the surroundings. "I also use a lot of stainless steel," he adds, "because I like its anonymity and purity." Recently he has been including natural materials, such as boulders, to try and capture the essence of nature.

below Water here is one of several elements in an entranceway, and its exact location creates a sense of surprise.

right These dramatic steel structures conceal a waterfall as well as framing and drawing attention to the view.

General principles on designing with water features

◆ **Focal point** A water feature has an extraordinary power to attract attention, which needs to be borne in mind when deciding where to place it. Everyone will automatically gravitate towards the feature, whether you want them to or not.

◆ **Calm** Still water has a great ability to make us feel calm, and any water feature will make us feel cooler. That is why seating areas are so often placed next to water in the garden; they are the ideal places to chill out at the end of the day.

◆ **Life** Water always attracts life, unless it is a completely sterile water feature, ie, purely ornamental with no plantlife. Birds come to drink, insects hover and frogs move in. But ponds that aim to be nature areas need special design features as areas where waterside or marginal plants can grow in soil that is kept constantly moist.

◆ **Drama** Water's ability to reflect the sky brings the drama of sunlight and cloud down to ground level. Dark pools create a sense of mystery. Pools or other water features in unexpected places create surprise.

◆ **Movement** As a dramatic element, moving water is unsurpassable and unique in the garden, adding a tranquil quality.

◆ **Void** Water is an antidote to hard surroundings, a counterpoint to cement, stone, brick and glass. This gives it the ability to soften man-made environments, and to change the appearance of the hard materials that are reflected in them.

above Sculpture and water are often strongly related. Amidst exotic vegetation, both can be usefully simple and calm elements.

right Here the viewer's gaze is taken out as far as it will go, the rill and sculpture forming one arrow to the horizon.

three: planting

the garden

planting principles

For most of us, planting is at the core of what gardens are about. Plants are living things, and understanding their requirements is fundamental to successful planting schemes. Beyond this, visual factors come into play, and here it helps to have a good grasp of some underlying principles about how colours, shapes and textures work together. What "works" though is completely subjective, and the best planting schemes are the result of people being true to themselves and not being swayed by what they think is fashionable. The range of plants available now is wider than at any time in history – inspiration indeed!

plant selection NOEL KINGSBURY

Plant buyers tend to fall into two groups: design orientated people who choose whatever plants look best in the scheme, and more plant focused people who have definite views about the kind of plants they want to include.

The more plant focused are likely to select the right plants when the conditions are challenging. But those who love plants for their own sake often have gardens that are weak in design terms, lacking strong, unifying themes. So, when selecting plants, think about the following factors:

Ecology

It makes sense to choose plants that suit the site, e.g. using drought-tolerant species in dry gardens, and bog plants in wet ones, etc. While most garden plants are very tolerant, they will always have a preference for sun or shade.

Interestingly, plants from particular, difficult environments often have a similar look, with drought-, (eg. lavender) and exposure-tolerant ones, (eg. hebes) often having grey foliage and a tough, wiry texture, while many shade lovers such as hellebores have glossy, evergreen leaves. The plants, in other words, have already done some of the designing for you, establishing a common visual theme which you can incorporate in the design. So, for example, you can match grey grasses with dark slate paving. Having identified the natural aesthetic of those plants best suited to your garden, you may well find yourself developing a real love for them, which is how many great gardens were

above Reedmace (*typha* species) are great plants – but only for those with large ponds, as they are very invasive.

right Silver foliage plants and tussock grasses (this is a species of *pennisetum*) tend to thrive on dry soils, often flourishing where other plants will die. As a general rule anything with physically tough and wiry foliage is good for dry or exposed sites.

left *Lythrum salicaria* 'Blush' and *Echinacea purpurea* 'Rubinglow' both thrive on relatively moist fertile soils. Extra efforts at soil preparation and maybe even irrigation are necessary for healthy perennials on poor or dry sites.

created. Choosing plants that suit the site will also save you time and money because, for example, you won't have to keep watering stressed, thirsty plants in a garden with fast-draining soil in an area of low rainfall.

Design

Look for plants whose shape contributes to a particular design, or whose foliage or flower colour matches your colour scheme. Plants with a very strong form, such as narrow, upright pencil-like trees, make useful theme plants that stamp their powerful personality on the whole garden. Too many different plants with a strong form will, however, create a restless feel. Also avoid impulse buying at the garden centre – plants must not be chosen in isolation but to fit the design and existing range of plants.

Size and numbers

Far too many gardens include young trees that will eventually tower above the neighbourhood, or shrubs that will overwhelm paths and borders. This is perhaps the biggest mistake that many people make, including professional designers. It is therefore important to check the ultimate size of all plants before buying them, especially if you

above California poppy (*Eschscholzia californica*) is an annual which often self-seeds, particularly on light dry soils.

have a small garden. Do some research, and check the information in reference books which is often more detailed than that on plant labels. The spread of plants is equally important, even more so in restricted spaces.

Trees and shrubs can often be used in smaller gardens, though, by cutting them back to the base every few years (i.e. coppicing), or to head height (pollarding), both of which often result in much larger foliage. However, not all species respond well – it's impossible with conifers – but specialist nurserymen will be able to advise.

When planting a new garden or border with young plants which have not yet filled out, there will invariably be gaps between them. The best way to fill these spaces, and create immediate impact, is with other plants, and there is nothing wrong with this provided you don't mind removing them in a few years time when the original ones get bigger. Lower growing perennials, such as species geraniums, are particularly good at filling the gaps between woody plants.

right *Cimicifuga* species need cool woodland conditions, although at higher altitudes they can be grown in full sun.

above *Eryngium alpinum* is one of those plants that looks drought-resistant, but take care – it isn't!

below Pyramidal orchid (*Anacamptis pyramidalis*) is one of many species which do well on dry, limestone soils.

above *Heleniums* are robust plants for fertile moist soils and, like many plants which have originated on the American prairie, are invaluable for late summer and autumn colour. This is *Helenium* 'Moerheim Beauty'.

below *Monardas* are also prairie plants and are particularly useful for August, when there are relatively few other perennial plants in flower.

habitat planting **BETH CHATTO**

"I try to follow Nature," states Beth Chatto. It is emphatic advice from the gardener and writer

who is possibly one of the most influential of all "garden gurus" and mother of the idea of

matching plants to habitat, at least in the English-speaking world.

centre Japanese anemones (*Anemone* x *hybrida* varieties) grow well in light shade, but tend to dominate a habitat over time.

Although she follows it up with a caveat: "but not to copy Her; we cannot do that in the garden." Beth believes that you should "put together plants which have similar needs in a situation for which they are adapted", a philosophy which was surprisingly radical when she began gardening in the 1950s.

Historically, gardeners have tried to change conditions in the garden to suit the kind of plants that they wish to grow, and have tended to regard anything other than perfect loam as "difficult". Since Beth's own garden combines a variety of relatively extreme conditions (wet and dry, open and shaded by trees), her experience has led her towards the full and interesting range of plants that will naturally thrive there. Beth says "choose plants adapted by nature to the conditions you have and they will repay you by flourishing, harmonizing with each other and requiring little attention because they are in the right environment."

Travelling in places with a rich flora has been a real inspiration for Beth, and she and her late husband Andrew made a connection between what they were seeing in places like Corsica, the Swiss Alps and North Africa, with their garden back home. "Perhaps the best way to understand specific plants is by seeing them in their native environment," she

right An ornamental garlic (*Allium pulchellum* 'Album') is one of many bulbs which need a sunny situation.

above Dry, stony soil is no barrier to attractive planting – many suitable species have high quality evergreen foliage.

below Pink Joe Pye weed (*Eupatorium purpureum* subsp. *maculatum*) flourishes amidst a variety of waterside plants in late summer.

PLANTS WITH LARGE, DRAMATIC FOLIAGE FOR SITES ADJACENT TO WATER

- *Arundo donax* very tall reed, to 3 or 4 m (10 or 13 ft)
- *Darmera peltata* large heads of pink flowers in spring and plate-like leaves, spreading to 1 m (3 ft) after 3-4 years
- *Gunnera manicata* huge rhubarb-like leaves, 2 x 3 m (6½ x 10 ft)
- *Gunnera tinctoria* similar but at least half the size, 1 x 2 m (3 x 6½ ft)
- *Iris pseudacorus* 'Variegata' tall, up to 1.2 m (4 ft) sword-shaped leaves, yellow flowers

below The depth that water and waterside plants will grow in varies considerably. The *Pontederia cordata* on the left will only grow at the edge in very shallow water.

says. The best shortcut is a good garden reference book or a quick visual check. So, grey foliage nearly always indicates drought tolerance, and large, soft leaves a need for moist, usually fertile soil, or perhaps shade.

But selecting plants according to their preferred habitat not only creates successful planting but also introduces a particular look. Many shade-loving plants, for example, are evergreen with dark glossy leaves, or have large leaves held horizontally to capture the light. Choosing plants from similar habitats introduces visual consistency. Do note, however, that when choosing plants for shade you must distinguish between moist and dry, the latter conditions often the result of tree roots taking all the available moisture. Beth has found the range of ground covering plants more limited than in areas of heavier rainfall, but despite the low rainfall in her Essex garden those which succeed include vincas, epimediums, symphytum, pachysandra, trachystemon and various cranesbills, ie. hardy geraniums. Late winter/early spring plants which provide colour before the tree canopy closes in include *Galanthus*, species *Narcissus*, *Erythronium* and *Corydalis*.

Many shade-lovers have attractive leaves and plants such as epimediums give a long season of foliage interest. However, a much wider variety of plants is available for damper shade, with anemones for spring, candelabra primulas for early summer, and cimicifugas and Japanese anemones (varieties of *Anemone x hybrida*) for late summer and autumn. Permanent damp shade is ideal for ferns. To find out what sort of shade you have, keep checking through the year. Many plants for damp soil have large, dramatic foliage, enabling gardeners to create a luxuriant, jungle-like style of planting. Some of these plants (called marginals) prefer having their roots in water while others (moisture-loving) require damp, but not waterlogged, soil. Appreciating that there is a gradient from damp soil to permanently wet is an important part of realizing the potential of ground near a natural pond.

above Ferns and spotted leaved pulmonarias flourish in the light shade of woodland edge habitats.

left A variegated *Hosta* 'Gold Standard' brings light to a shaded woodland walk.

PLANTS WITH LUXURIANT FOLIAGE FOR DAMP (NOT WATERLOGGED) SITES

- *Angelica archangelica* very large, biennial cow parsley, to 2.5 m (8 ft)
- *Eupatorium fistulosum* 'Atropurpureum' pink flowers on tall stems, 2.2 x 0.8 m (7½ x 2½ ft)
- *Ligularia* yellow-orange daisy-like flowers in midsummer, mostly 1.5 x 1 m (5 x 3 ft)
- *Miscanthus* tall grasses, mostly 2–2.5 m (6½–8 ft), although there are shorter ones, down to 0.6 m (2 ft), like elegant reeds
- *Rheum palmatum* there are various selections of this ornamental rhubarb, some with red/bronze-flushed leaves, 1.5 x 2 m (5 x 6½ ft) – but they hate any competition

foliage NOEL KINGSBURY

When we look at a garden, most of what we see is leaves. They have a long

season, whereas flowers have only a short one, and for this reason alone

gardeners interested in good design should pay foliage more heed.

That said, the shape, colour and texture of the leaves of most garden plants is actually relatively nondescript, yet the occasional more distinctive leaves can make all the difference, especially at times when there are few flowers. Look out for:

• **Linear foliage** The leaves of irises, hemerocallis, grasses or kniphofias, for example, can make all the difference by providing "punctuation" in a border scheme, helping to break up the flow. But too much in close proximity does not always work.

• **Bold large leaves/distinctively coloured or textured** They stand out and can be used

Below Large leaves are characteristic of many moisture-loving plants. *Darmera peltata* is growing by the water's edge at lower right.

left From the top – *Gunnera manicata*, *Darmera peltata* and *Hosta sieboldiana* in a damp environment.

below A variety of flower head shapes by a small garden pond.

in a similar fashion to linear leaves. However, because they have plenty of impact, placing further back in the garden means that they can "jump forward", foreshortening the view.

• **Fine foliage** It tends to make the view recede, and when planted to the back of a garden makes it seem further away.

• **Textured foliage** Texture is a subtle but important part of a garden's appeal. It is a quality that can be appreciated on two levels, the macro (how the garden looks from a distance) and micro (how it looks from close-up, an aspect which you need to develop by seating places, for example, and when creating schemes for the visually impaired).

In both cases, bold foliage, leaves with lots of variation in shape, and glossy leaves, provide a rich visual texture, for example laurel or *Magnolia grandiflora*. A mass of little leaves, however, results in a dense, rather matt and potentially uninteresting texture, for

left *Geranium pratense* next to the autumnal shades of *Aralia cachemeriana*.

right A variety of *rodgersia* species – a moisture-loving genus noted for its magnificent foliage.

example the light-absorbing leaves of Bronze fennel (*Foeniculum vulgare* 'Purpureum'). To check the effectiveness of foliage, take a black and white photograph of your garden because it will immediately be apparent, even without colour, if it has good visual texture.

• Aromatic foliage A great many plants have aromatic foliage, those from dry habitats especially. This is rarely thought of as a design feature but it can add a whole new, and most delightful, dimension to a garden, and one quite vital for the visually impaired. Think about what the garden would be like if you were blind, and imagine how you might site aromatic foliage plants, putting some in strategic places. Remember too that plant aromas do not necessarily have to be pleasant, which can be quite a talking point.

• Coloured foliage It is particularly appreciated in spring when perennials are just starting to grow, and there may be little in the way of floral interest. Many perennials have strikingly coloured foliage as they emerge from the earth.

In fact, a great many garden plants have non-green foliage, and they fall into three camps: the variegated with cream (or silver); variegated with yellow (or gold), or yellow-tinted; and the dark tinted (with bronze or purple). They can be very useful because they add a sense of punctuation or rhythm, create interesting foliage-based colour combinations or, perhaps most strikingly, create attractive combinations with flowers.

TIPS FOR USING FOLIAGE

• Putting too many variegated or tinted leaves together can become rather fussy.
• Silver or gold variegation is particularly welcome in darker corners, although deep shade should be avoided because the leaves will lose their distinctive colouring.
• Gold variegation is very welcome in winter, particularly in higher latitudes where winters are dark.
• Effective colour combinations can be made by using either a variety of yellow-tinted and gold-variegated foliage plants together, or dark-tinted ones. Some, though, find the former anaemic and the latter oppressive.
• Yellow and gold foliage can be striking with blue and blue-violet flowers, as can dark leaves. Most find the combination of pink flowers and yellow unattractive, but strong pinks and dark leaves can work well.
• Dark foliage is very effective at a distance in a garden, as it merges with the background. It is also particularly effective when used at intervals to create a sense of rhythm.

monochrome borders NORI AND SANDRA POPE

While many have experimented with one-colour borders, Nori and Sandra Pope have raised them to

a high art form at Hadspen Garden in Somerset. Not only does the use of one colour create the

harmony that the couple regard as central to their work, it changes the way we look at plants.

above *Anthemis tinctoria* 'EC Buxton' is a delightful pale shade of yellow – a useful colour, as so many yellow daisies are a darker golden shade.

The eye stops looking for immediate colour variation and instead starts noticing other differences, for example the leaf and flower shapes, and whether they are trumpets, buttons, spires, whorls or panicles.

Most gardeners only have room for a limited number of single-colour borders, and fitting too many into a small space where they can be seen together can ruin the effect. Collecting plants for a single colour border is great fun, and you can scour nurseries and seed catalogues for the latest variation in shade. "There hasn't been a better time to be a gardener," Sandra says, "because there are so many new plants, often with exciting new colours."

Experimenting with new plants is clearly a large part of the joy of gardening at Hadspen. Annuals come high on the list because they usually flower profusely and only last a year, so if the results are unsatisfactory it doesn't matter. And once you have decided what kind of effect you want to create, just start adding shrubs and perennials.

The yellow border at Hadspen is the best established. Nori describes it as "being in the same tone of yellow and high in lime greens," but he points out that "any border is principally green, and because green is made up of yellow and blue, yellow flowers will not clash with their own leaves." Yellow-leaved and yellow-variegated plants are therefore used as well as those with yellow flowers, helping to create a strong background.

right Looking down the double yellow borders at Hadspen. Notice how the different plant shapes really stand out.

left There is plenty of visual interest in this plant combination. The vertical thrust of the lupin (*Lupinus* 'Chandelier') creates a sense of dynamism, but is balanced by the soft shape of the cut-leaved elder (*Sambucus racemosa* 'Plumosa Aurea') and the grassy carex (*Carex elata* 'Aurea'). Amorphous fennel (*Foeniculum vulgare*) provides fill-in between the more defined shapes. Yellow-tinted foliage complements the shade of the flowers.

right The firm shape of *Dahlia* 'David Howard' contrasted with fennel (*Foeniculum vulgare*). *Helenium* 'Chipperfield Orange' is in the background on the right.

Opposite, clockwise from top left *Allium aflatuense* surrounded by *Nepeta* 'Six Hills Giant'; *Lupinus* 'Thunderbird', one of the many smoky flower shades now available; *Nasturtium* 'Red Wonder'; *Gladiolus* 'Ruby'.

below *Dahlia* 'David Howard' and fennel create a subtle harmony.

Other favourites are "uprights" which, Nori says, "give a rhythmic effect", as do repeated blocks of profusely flowering plants, such as argyranthemums. What Nori calls "see-through plants", for example the tall, narrow *Digitalis lutea*, provide glimpses of more solid plants behind.

But the key to the success of the yellow border is that it is not actually all-yellow. Nori explains that "we always try to have 2-3 per cent of blue (the complementary colour to yellow) so that the eye does not fatigue too much from seeing one colour." Blue, in other words, is refreshment.

What is true of yellow is also true of blue – that the plants don't clash with their own foliage – but blue is more interesting as it varies so enormously. "True blue is rarely found in nature," Nori points out, with most so-called blue flowers actually being shades of mauve or purple. Also note that blue's most important characteristic is its tendency to recede, accentuating a sense of distance in the garden.

As for red, a large splash is "sheer impact", Nori adds, yet too much of it can create a deadening impression, especially when combined with too much dark foliage. He suggests combining it with silver or grey foliage for a lighter feeling.

Hadspen was one of the very first gardens to highlight dark plum-coloured shades, including some very unusual near-black flowers, often new seed strains of familiar plants. Plum can create a sense of opulence, although Nori warns that this all too easily tips over into what he calls "Victorian gloom". The most striking effects are dark flowers combined with silver foliage such as *Artemesia* 'Powis Castle'.

There are an enormous number of pink flowers, especially for the early summer period, and it is a colour that is ideal for novices because it is difficult to misuse. But once you have moved beyond the beginner phase, the Popes suggest you add "a sense of theatre with hot pink and magenta". Such a strong colour grabs attention and needs careful placing; if used at the end of a vista it will foreshorten the perspective. Strong colours belong in the foreground, paler tones however recede and so are effective in the distance.

combining colours CAROL KLEIN

Carol Klein is first and foremost a nurserywoman, well-known for her stands at flower shows with skillfully planned and subtle colour combinations. Her flamboyant personal style is part and parcel of the display – sometimes she even achieves a match between her hair dye and a plant on the stand!

above Adjacent plants with different shades of the same colour will focus the eye on the qualities of each. *Achillea* 'Cerise Queen' (rear), *Astilbe* 'Rosy Veil' (middle) and *Stachys officianalis* 'Rosea Superba'.

Starting out with colour

"When combining colours there are many dos and hardly any don'ts," Carol says, "although the whole business is actually very subjective." First of all, "start from what you like – which means identifying what you like, not what happens to be fashionable at the moment. If you start with what you are sure of, you'll achieve results that will encourage you. Your colour sense will develop, and then you can try something else."

Carol thinks that the hardest thing in working with colour is the fourth dimension – time. "It's not flower arranging," she says, "different things happen in different years." Unless you are putting plants together that are already in flower, it can be difficult to predict a final effect. She suggests that you should look around you, see what is in flower at the same time and make notes.

"I love blue and yellow," says Carol, "that's a good one to start off with – it's easy, a lot of people like it, and it is very joyful and optimistic." It is a good combination for both spring and autumn, as during these seasons there is a wide variety of plants with colours in these

> 66 *I love the way different people do different things. This is the most expressive part of planting* 99

below A soft colour and a very strong one often work well together. *Dahlia* 'Bishop of Llandaff' with *Euphorbia schillingii.*

left Pastel shades usually combine well. Here are pale blue *Adenophora liliifolia* with yellow *Helichrysum thianschanicum.*

above *Allium sphaerocephalon* with *Nepeta govaniana.*

left *Allium sphaerocephalon* with *Agastache* 'Firebird' and *Stipa arundinacea.*

ranges: daffodils, pulmonarias and scillas in spring, goldenrods and many other yellow daisy family plants, and asters in autumn.

Leaves

"Whether you like it or not," says Carol, "most plants have leaves, and it is lovely to be able to use them deliberately." Their advantage is their longevity, and the slow pace with which they change, both of which help develop a sense of continuity. Leaf colours often work in concert with their texture and shape and Carol finds that sometimes she puts together greens that are very similar, which tends to create a uniform, but subtly graded background against which differences in colour can be most readily appreciated. At other times she finds herself combining very disparate leaves, which make interesting combinations in themselves.

Foliage can be very useful for picking out and drawing attention to very small areas of colour which might otherwise get missed out. An example is Anchusa 'Lodden Royalist', whose stunning deep blue flowers instantly attract attention. Something planted alongside with very dark foliage, such as *Atriplex hortensis* 'Rubra' or a dark heuchera variety, picks out the dark eye which every anchusa flower has. Without the foliage, most of us might never notice this aspect of the flower. It is this awareness of the many very tiny gradations in colour in plants that makes Carol's eye so special. I shall never forget her pointing out to me the beauty of the dark stems of *Aster divaricatus* many years ago, a plant which at first sight can seem rather dull.

Colour and light

As a general rule, pastel colours work best at higher latitudes where summer light is relatively soft and skies often grey and overcast. For a start, there is a very wide availability of pastels for these climates. In regions with stronger light, pastel colours appear washed out, so bolder colours are needed. Soft flat light, Carol thinks, is good for appreciating fine detail, such as those plants which have vast numbers of small flowers crammed into heads, like gypsophila and cow-parsley family members.

above Red ornamental kale with *Potentilla nepalensis* 'Miss Willmott' – related but with very different colours.

below Similar shades together can be very effective. *Dahlia* 'Le Coco' and *Achillea* 'Great Expectations'.

Carol warns against using white in full sun, as "you can't see it properly", and that white and yellow are best in spring or in shade, where light levels are lower. Blues, and those colours with a lot of blue in them such as mauves and purples, "look so much better in the evening," thinks Carol. "Hesperis (*Hesperis matronalis* – a soft purple fragrant stock relative) takes on a real glow then." She adds, "I love vivid colours first thing in the morning in that very bright early light."

For summer, Carol suggests that quite similar colours can work together well, perhaps because strong light emphasizes the subtle differences between strong colours. An example is magenta *Geranium psilostemon* with dark red *Knautia macedonica* and deep pink rose 'William Lobb'.

Finally, "the direction light comes from can be quite crucial", says Carol. "Think of the grass *Imperator cylindrica* (which has deep red leaves) – it is a different plant when it is backlit, when it can seem almost illuminated." She suggests that this is an example of a plant which can be used in many different ways; a favourite autumnal combination is to use it with golden-yellow *Rudbeckia fulgida* and the pale yellow-flowered, dusky leaved *Crocosmia* 'Solfatare'.

drawing planting plans NOEL KINGSBURY

Designers use planting plans for a number of different reasons. They enable them to think about

juxtapositions of plants, e.g. which colours and shapes should go next to each other, and how plants

relate to surrounding features, such as walls and lawns. Crucially, they are also used to decide how

many plants are needed, particularly when tackling large beds and borders.

below Useful symbols for planting plans.

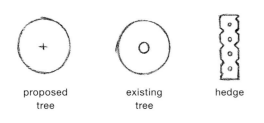

proposed
tree

existing
tree

hedge

below Symbols, each representing a particular plant
variety, are a good way of depicting plants on plans,
although for large schemes, or where a large number
of varieties are used, they can become confusing.

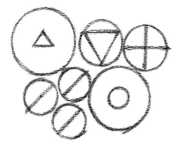

below Alternatively, try abbreviations for plants.
Notice the method used here to indicate multiples
in groups.

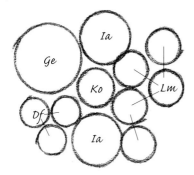

Trees and shrubs are generally shown as individual plants on plans, but it also helps to show perennials and dwarf shrubs as separate items, represented by circles. The diameter of the circle shown on the plan should correspond either to the eventual spread of the plant, or to the spread of the plant after a reasonable number of years – five years is a good rule of thumb.

Many reference books are vague on the matter of spread, giving "indefinite" for some ground-cover perennials, which tells us nothing about how large they will be in a specific given number of years. The staff at specialist nurseries, though, will often be able to give more precise information. In general, expect perennials and ground-cover plants to fill their adjoining gaps after three years. Many shrubs, which become very large with time, can be kept to a diameter of 2-3 m by cutting them to ground level every few years. Nearly all respond well, sending up vigorous and healthy new growth.

If you are making such a plan, compile a list of the plants you want to use, and write down the figure for the spread. Then, use a circle template to draw the symbols to scale on the plan, which will also feature the main structural features (e.g. borders and paths, etc.). This is often best done on tracing paper taped over the plan, enabling you to start again if necessary.

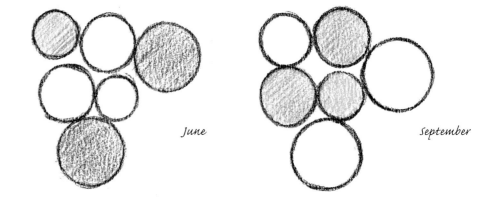

June

September

above Using colours, perhaps for the different times of year, is a good way of tackling plantings. It will help you think about what colours work near each other, when they will be in flower, and how they are distributed across the whole scheme.

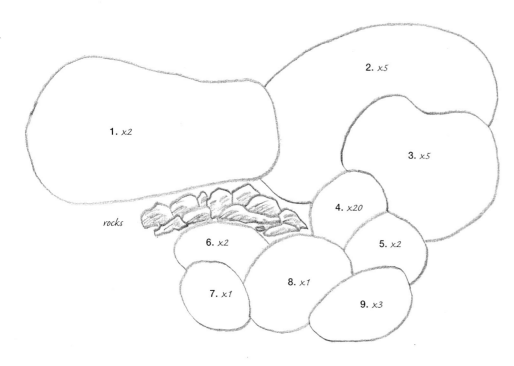

rocks

1. x2

2. x5

3. x5

4. x20

5. x2

6. x2

7. x1

8. x1

9. x3

above and left This border is on a dry and stony site, and shows a good long-season planting for drought-tolerance. The diagram illustrates a more traditional method of drawing a planting plan, which reflects a philosophy whereby varieties are used in groups. The "x3" for example means that three individuals of that variety are to be used.

KEY

1. *Yucca gloriosa*
2. *Phomis italica*
3. *Yucca filimentosa* 'Bright Edge'
4. *Tulipa tarda* (dormant)
5. *Sedum spectabile*
6. *Stipa tenuissima*
7. *Helianthemum* variety
8. *Zauschneria californica*
9. *Bergenia cordifolia*

structural planting

Structure has been regarded as a central element in the garden throughout history. Best thought of as a skeleton or framework, it provides coherence to a garden, as well as continuity through the seasons, and from year to year. Contemporary thoughts on structure are many and varied – we have come on a long way from the endless repetition of clipped evergreen hedges which has given "formality" a bad name in some quarters. Modern designers play with new forms, re-invent old ones and make use of the huge variety offered by natural plant forms.

● **plant shapes**
Piet Oudolf shows how we can use a wide variety of plant shapes to give backbone to border plantings.

● **formal shapes**
Classical formality still has plenty of mileage in it says George Carter.

● **grasses**
Piet Oudolf explains how grasses are one of the best sources of natural structure and continuity.

● **using evergreens**
Jill Billington discusses the virtues of evergreens in providing seasonal continuity to our gardens.

plant shapes **PIET OUDOLF**

Many writers on gardening and amateur gardeners are primarily interested in colour as the main

element in planting design. So talking to Piet Oudolf about his distinctive shape-based style is very

instructive because while he says "I'm not a colour gardener", he actually has very colourful borders.

right Grasses are wonderful for providing a hazy effect, perfect as a backdrop for firmer shapes, such as these cimicifuga seedheads and the leaves of *Darmera peltata.*

below *Miscanthus sinensis* 'Malepartus' combines both boldness and softness.

Piet is not one of those gardeners who only uses structural elements and foliage plants and despises flowers – he clearly loves them. However, most of the plants he uses are wild species, or varieties with the natural proportion and grace of their wild ancestors, which have a larger proportion of leaf to flower, reducing the likelihood of colour clashes. This means that he creates a sense of harmony by balancing and gently contrasting plant shapes and textures; once the shapes are harmonious, it is much easier to assemble a variety of colours.

Flower shapes

In general, flower shapes tend to fall into a number of fairly clear-cut categories, some dramatic, others less so. Too much drama can be visually tiring, but balancing strong shapes (such as spires) with gentler shapes (such as umbels and plumes) does create a sense of balance. Small, round forms (buttons and daisies) can be used as points of definition against larger shapes or less solid forms. Soft, ill-defined flowers can create

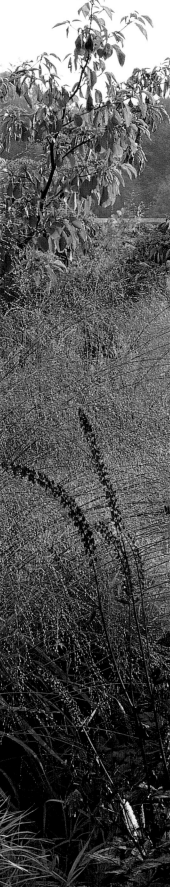

above *Cimicifuga ramosa* 'Atropurpurea' has clear white flower spikes in late summer. Its definitive, confident shape is a useful design element in the border.

below Groups of similarly-sized and shaped flowers make for a naturalistic effect: *Echinacea purpurea*, *Helenium* 'Rubinzwerg', *Angelica gigas*, *Eupatorium maculatum* 'Atropurpureum' and *lavatera*.

links between harder forms, or an form an effective backdrop for smaller, more definite shapes.

◆ Spires Spires and spikes are the most attention-seeking shapes. Very narrow ones grown en masse, such as foxgloves or mulleins, can be spectacular. Other examples include *Cimicifuga*, Willow herb (*Epilobium angustifolium* 'Album'), *Lythrum* and *Veronicastrum virginicum*. More usually though, they are used to give a lift to schemes composed of rounded, more amorphous shapes.

◆ Umbels Flat, plate-like shapes, the opposite of a spire, are restful and help to create a soft, naturalistic feel. Many are members of the *Umbelliferae* family, familiar as roadside wildflowers. Other examples of umbels include *Achillea*, Hemp agrimony (*Eupatorium fistulosum* 'Atropurpureum' var. *purpureum*), Fennel, *Sedum telephium* and *S.spectabile* and its hybrids.

◆ Plumes Fluffy plumes are particularly effective when planted in large groups, but are less clearly defined than spires and umbels. Too many plumes, though, and the border can look a bit of a blur. It's also important to note that some can be one-sided, such as the miscanthus grasses, which end up getting blown in the same direction by the wind. Other good choices include *Filipendula*, *Persicaria polymorpha*, *Solidago* and *Thalictrum*.

above Bold masses work well in larger gardens. In the raised bed is a combination of the grass *Miscanthus* 'Malepartus' and the evergreen sedge *Carex muskingumensis*.

◆ Buttons and Globes These shapes create points of definition and often bright colour. Some have relatively loose heads, such as the astrantias, centaureas and deep red-purple *Knautia macedonica*, others stand stiffly above the foliage, such as the perfectly spherical globes of *Echinops* and drumstick alliums, whereas others (monarda) are neatly arranged, one above the other, as whorls on a distinct stalk. Others have more egg-shaped flower clusters, such as the clovers, *Trifolium*. Many in this group are relatively weatherproof and stand well into winter – monarda and phlomis in particular.

◆ Daisies These combine definition with softness and often bright colours. When vibrant and planted in groups, they can be used to control the overall impact of a border, while dotting a few amongst other shapes creates separate points of impact and a quieter impression. Good choices include asters, *Doronicum*, *Echinacea purpurea*, *Helenium* and sunflowers.

◆ Transparency *Verbena bonariensis* is a good example of a see-though plant. Its tall, vertical stems are so thin and leaves so narrow that it is possible to see through its haze of violet flowers to whatever is growing behind. Some grasses, such as *Stipa gigantea*, share this characteristic, as indeed does anything with tall, leafless stems. The effect has great subtlety and such plants combine well with hard, clearly-defined forms behind. Other good examples include Fennel, *Molinia*, *Sanguisorba* and *Thalictrum*.

formal shapes **GEORGE CARTER**

Clipped trees and shrubs are essential raw material for the formal-garden look,

providing geometry, definition and contrast. However, they can also play an

important role in less formal gardens, contrasting effectively with informality.

above, below and right Clipped trees play an important design role in many settings, adding an orderly touch of green.

In winter, clipped shapes often come into their own, frequently being the only decorative elements in an otherwise hibernating garden. In spring, too, they add structure at a time when there is often a mass of colour but no underlying order.

Garden centres now sell a wide range of pre-shaped or topiarized plants, but you can certainly grow you own and save a lot of money. The range of clipped shapes that are commercially available is generally very limited and traditional; clipping your own is an opportunity to create something much more individual. This also avoids buying clipped trees and shrubs that were grown in countries with different climates and which may not adapt well to new conditions, so suffering a check in growth.

Again, when it comes to hedges, you don't have to stick to conventional shapes. George suggests using a row of stilt-trained trees, essentially a hedge on legs, hornbeam being particularly suitable for this treatment. He adds that you can also try creating vistas,

TREES FOR CLIPPING

- **Cherry laurel (*Prunus laurocerasus*)** elegant, dark foliage which gives a heavy, coarse-grained texture when cut.
- **Hawthorn (*Crataegus monogyna*)** fast growing, forming dense growth with a fine texture. Good for quick results. Underrated.
- **Hornbeam (*Carpinus betulus*)** very good at high latitudes, and can be cut into relatively detailed shapes, such as distinctly narrow hedges. Rather underrated.
- **Holm oak (*Quercus ilex*)** greyer tones to the foliage than other trees suitable for clipping. Good in exposed sites, especially on the coast.
- **Leyland cypress (x *Cupressocyparis leylandii*)** notorious for making annoyingly high hedges, but can be clipped three times a year to stop it getting out of hand. Good for quick results.
- **Phillyrea (*Phillyrea latifolia*)** used in the 18th century, it is now making a come-back. Dark evergreen foliage. Best in a warm, sheltered spot.
- **Yew (*Taxus baccata*)** excellent dense habit and fine foliage give it a "flat" texture, while its dark colour makes it useful as a backdrop.

right The use of defined geometric shapes has an immensely long history in garden design. Evergreen topiary is particularly suited for climates where high summer temperatures make the growing of flowering perennials difficult. Here, the interest is created through shape, rather than differentiating colours.

left Beech is one of the best trees for clipping into hedges and other large geometric shapes. However, hornbeam, seen here, is denser, which makes it possible to have more detail.

the longer the better, and running off in several directions, which simultaneously breaks up the garden into several different areas.

The key considerations for isolated features or hedges is size and shape, but bear in mind also that dark colours make a useful backdrop, while light colours can brighten up dark places. George also stresses the importance of texture, and of distinguishing between the heavy textures of larger-leaved plants and the flatness of the fine-leaved. "Also note the way the light falls," he adds, "with geometric shapes looking particularly good in strong light."

Besides buying or shaping your own plants, also consider those plants with inherent style, for example *hebes* (such as 'Pewter Dome') which make low mounds, and form grey-green hummocks which do not need clipping.

grasses **PIET OUDOLF**

In recent years, there has been an enormous expansion of interest in grasses, largely thanks to designer Piet Oudolf. He particularly values their attractive form, which is held for a long period. Unlike many perennials, grasses tend to remain attractive well into winter, providing important continuity.

above The perennial *Sanguisorba officianalis* 'Red Thunder' caught up in *Molina litoralis* 'Transparent'.

Piet recommends that "grasses are grown with space around them so that you can appreciate their form", but adds that they can be grown in other ways. "They make a different effect when massed, or when grown with perennials, because they harmonize and give a more natural look." Since so many wild or semi-natural habitats are dominated by grasses, you need only include a few in a border to evoke such an atmosphere.

He also recommends using grasses with a strong shape, repeated through a border, to create a bold impression. If planted at regular intervals they create a formal look, but when scattered irregularly create more relaxed rhythms. When one species is used *en masse* it can create a particularly powerful effect.

One practical reason why grasses are such useful garden plants is that they are remarkably tolerant of a wide range of conditions. Most species must have full sunlight but are tolerant of poor soils, occasional drought and exposure, the latter being a particular feature of the small New Zealand sedges with coloured foliage (they are not true grasses but are closely related).

A large, shapely grass, which looks good for most of the year, can also be planted alone, or in a bed beside other smaller plants, letting it dominate its immediate surroundings. Pampas grass (*Cortaderia selloana*) works well provided it isn't crammed into a relatively small space. Other smaller, but still imposing grasses, are often far more

left *Molinia litoralis* 'Transparent' lives up to its name with its see-through quality, yet its size gives it a dramatic air.

above A block planting of *Molinia caerulea* 'Paul Peterson' contrasts with a clipped box. Grasses used in such plantings need to be tidy all year round.

right A variety of grasses add interest to late autumn borders. Most will look good well into the winter – one of their great virtues for the designer.

above A "meadow" of *Deschampsia* 'Goldtau' makes for a dramatic late summer garden feature. The young trees are *Catalpa erubescens* 'Purpurea', and the seedheads in the foreground are an *echinops* variety.
left Large perennials make an effective foreground to the natural landscape beyond the garden.

GRASSES FOR LARGER SPACES

- *Calamagrostis* x *acutiflora* 'Karl Foerster'
- *Miscanthus floridulus*
- *Miscanthus sinensis* 'Grosse Fontaine', 'Kaskade', 'Malepartus', 'Morning Light', 'Silberfeder', 'Undine'
- *Molinia caerulea* subsp. arundinacea 'Karl Foerster', 'Transparent', 'Windspiel'
- *Stipa gigantea*

suitable. Piet is particularly fond of using cultivars of *Miscanthus sinensis*, which range from 60 cm–3 m (2–10 ft) high. Used on their own or as focal points amongst other plants, they are extremely effective in the latter half of the year for their reed-like elegance.

You can also use smaller species with a very distinct habit as focal points. Try the upright *Calamagrostis* x *acutiflora* 'Karl Foerster', a particular favourite of Piet's because "it is unique and reliable, looking good for many months, and makes a punctuation point in the border". Species with fine, see-through stems are more ethereal because they respond to the slightest breeze. *Stipa gigantea* is a good example, with tall, narrow stems which support open clusters of tiny, delicate flowers and, later, seeds.

Lighting is crucial to success with many of the medium-sized and larger grasses, which is why conventional borders often do not suit them. Unlike most flowering plants, they need surrounding space so that they can be back-lit, rather than being lit from the front. The flower and seed heads of *Stipa gigantea*, *Panicum virgatum* and *Molinia caerulea* are magically transformed by being back-lit against a distant, darker background, while *Miscanthus sinensis* will glow silver in low winter sunlight.

The range of ornamental grasses that is commercially available is rapidly changing. Many selections from well-established and reliable species are being brought onto the market as well as some that are completely new. It is best to test out the latter on a small scale before committing yourself to large scale planting.

above *Stipa gigantea* is wonderful at catching every little shaft of sunlight at the end of the day; it is best seen against a darker background.

GRASSES FOR SMALLER SPACES

- *Calamagrostis brachytricha*
- *Chionochloa rubra*
- *Molinia caerulea* subsp. *caerulea* 'Edith Dudszus', 'Moorflamme', 'Moorhexe', 'Variegata'
- *Panicum virgatum* cultivars
- Pennisetum
- *Spodiopogon sibiricus*
- *Stipa arundinacea*

using evergreens **JILL BILLINGTON**

Evergreens provide seasonal continuity, winter colour and a sense of permanence. Designer Jill Billington adds that they also make valuable framework plants, creating a skeleton which can then be padded out with a range of other shapes and colours.

above Evergreens provide continuity and stability to the garden, making a kind of backbone for a design.

Traditionally, many evergreens have been clipped into geometrical shapes which are especially useful as structural elements. Many gardeners, disliking what they see as rigid, classic formality, reject clipped evergreens which is a shame as it is perfectly possible to give them an air of modern sculpture and a radically contemporary feel.

Jill's favourite evergreens

◆ Bamboos They have a shrub-like bulk but won't spread too far if they are contained. Those with a reputation as "runners" (consult a reference book or buy from a specialist supplier), can be kept within bounds by using slates or paving slabs sunk vertically around them, and preferably overlapping, to a depth of 30 cm (1 ft). Unlike shrubs which suffer branch damage from heavy snowfalls, bamboos have the ability to bend under the weight and bounce back.

◆ *Cistus* x *corbariensis* – a structure plant in more informal settings, it has a fine display of white flowers in early summer. 1 x 1.5 m (3 x 5 ft). Not for shaping.

◆ *Griselinia littoralis* Jill describes this shrub's unique quality as "its pretty rare apple-

below Box, rosemary and bay are all classic evergreens, and deservedly much used in town gardens, where they look orderly and neat if well-kept.

above Even in the depths of winter, evergreens remain. This is the same garden as seen above left – note how the clipped evergreens give the garden structure even under a blanket of snow.

left Box has traditionally been used for small-scale formal features. Worries over various "box blights" have made us more aware of the need to find alternatives.

green leaves". Best in mild climates, and ideal for windy coastal locations, it will eventually form a small tree. It is sometimes seen kept clipped as a hedge.

• *Iris foetidissima* var. *citrina* an ability to grow in dry shade makes this 70 cm (2 ft) high perennial invaluable for dull corners. Jill praises its "blade-like leaves, and winter-long, bright orange fruit".

• Mexican orange blossom (*Choisya ternata*) growing from 1–2 m (3–6½ ft) high and wide, with clusters of pure white flowers in early summer, it is ideal for smaller gardens. "I almost put one in every garden," Jill says, "especially 'Aztec Pearl' with its pinkish-white flowers."

• *Viburnum tinus* a popular shrub and with good reason, with Jill going so far as to say "if in doubt, put one in". Neat, matt leaves and very early white flowers. In mild climates it can grow to 3 x 3 m (10 x 10 ft), but can be kept smaller if clipped.

seasonal planting

"Looking good right through the year" is what many people regard as the most important feature of their gardens. This is possible, but it takes organization and planning, particularly for small spaces, as well as an awareness of what plants can do when, so that we take advantage of all the features plants can offer: foliage, berries, stems, seed heads, as well as flowers. Here we look at the two main approaches to achieving year-round interest, one using permanent planting, and the other taking advantage of plants with a shorter but more spectacular lifespan.

planting for succession – permanent planting **NOEL KINGSBURY**

Gardeners invariably want their designs to look good all-year round. The smaller the garden,

the more difficult this is but here are some useful strategies.

• Provide gardens with structure to create seasonal continuity. This can be provided by: evergreens; plants with strong, distinctive shapes; small trees or shrubs with distinctive winter features, such as an elegant branching pattern; and grasses, or perennials with eye-catching winter stems and seedheads – some species look good for three-quarters of the year.

• Stop thinking about flowers and consider plants with interesting leaves.

• Use woody plants clipped into geometric shapes as they are invaluable for spring and winter interest.

• Combine containers with permanent plants. Fill the containers with seasonal plants and move them around to bring life to areas that are temporarily dull.

• Use bulbs to provide more intense patches of colour than perennials and shrubs.

right Many gardens in spring are quite "flat" in feel, especially if they depend on perennials for their main interest. Bulbs – daffodils especially – are very useful for interplanting and introducing a splash of colour.

above Late summer is the time for enjoying large perennials. Here are pink *Eupatorium fistulosum*, yellow *Coreopsis tripteris* and blue *Aster puniceus*. The large leaves are *Paulownia tomentosa* (rear) and *Salix magnifica* (left).

- Many bulbs give colour from late winter to early summer, and even longer if you use summer lilies. The bulbs can often be shoehorned in amongst other plants.
- Pay attention to what plants look like out of season, the important kind of information many reference books don't supply. Also note that many shrubs look dull and perennials untidy after they have finished flowering, but some do continue to look smart, many evergreen shrubs such as hollies, osmanthus and choisya are useful in this respect. And some perennials have attractive leaf colours and/or shapes as they emerge in spring, such as peonies. Keep an eye out for good examples when visiting gardens.
- Use plants with two seasons, for example shrubs with attractive flowers and berries, such as ornamental apples (*malus* species).
- Try to plant under and around shrubs and trees as much as possible. Note that:
  - bulbs will usually flourish beneath deciduous species
  - ground-cover plants with evergreen foliage are especially useful
  - where dry soil is a problem beneath trees, you should seek advice on suitable plants
  - just how bad the problem is is closely related to rainfall and soil moisture, so local knowledge is invaluable – try talking to a local nursery owner or experienced gardener.
  - autumn-flowering bulbs and tubers, such as autumn crocuses (actually colchicums) and cyclamen, have good surprise value.
- Try to interweave early summer-flowering perennials, such as geraniums, with late summer/autumn-flowering ones (e.g. asters).

above Early summer is when many gardens are at their best. Here is a variety of geranium species with the distinctive foliage of *Aralia cachemeriana* (right).

top Hedges do not have to be cut in straight lines! Interesting cuts are a useful "continuity feature", as good in winter as in summer. This is yew, which, if well-fed on a fertile soil, will grow 30 cm (12 in) a year.

above The Hindu god Shiva dances the cosmos into existence at the head of a small pool in the author's garden. The yellow flower is kingcup, *Caltha palustris*.

• Buy climbers as they offer colour and interest in vertical, space-saving situations. This particularly applies to town gardens. Also note that large shrubs can have small climbers growing through or over them, to flower after the shrub has finished. And that free-standing supports for climbers, such as obelisks, can keep a border looking attractive for months being winter features in their own right, and summer supports for clematis, etc.

• Have a range of plants to keep the show going for as long as possible. The problem with concentrating on the early summer period is that the garden can look lacklustre later on, or downright untidy if there are a lot of early-flowering perennials. Later-flowering perennials invariably continue to look neat (cutting down on maintenance) until they flower.

• Features such as sculptures and archways are particularly valuable during winter, especially if they are painted. Moveable features are especially useful; try them in different positions.

Using a planting calendar

A planting calendar is a simple aid for combining plants. It consists of a vertical list of plants down one side of a piece of paper, with a grid going across representing the months of the year (see example opposite). Use a reference book or nursery catalogue to indicate with symbols or letters the time of year when the plants flower. You can now see at a glance which times of year are the most colourful, and which might need more plants. By using a colour for the horizontal line, you can work out possible combinations for different times, and indicate other points of interest such as autumn tints or fruit. Evergreens are represented by a continuous line in an appropriate colour.

The easiest way to make a planting calendar is on a computer; the endless chopping and changing is much easier than when using paper and crayons. A little ingenuity can go a long way, with your own letters and symbols used to describe particular plant features.

Name	late winter	early spring	mid spring	late spring	early summer	mid summer	late summer	early autumn	mid autumn	late autumn	early winter	notes
Shrubs												
Amelanchier canadensis			white						berries			1
Elaeagnus pungens 'Maculata'	▓	▓	▓	▓	▓	▓	▓	▓	▓	▓	▓	2
Malus 'Cowichan'			▓					fruit	fruit	fruit	fruit	1
Sorbus vilmorinii			white					berries	berries	berries	berries	1
Viburnum carlesii				white								
Perennials												
Alchemilla mollis		▓	▓		▓	▓	▓					3
Aster turbinellus									▓	▓		
Aster x frikartii 'Moench'							▓	▓	▓			
Astrantia 'Hadspen Blood'					▓	▓	▓					
Ballota acetabulosa	▓	▓	▓	▓	▓	▓	▓	▓	▓	▓	▓	4
Eryngium alpinum					▓	▓						
Geranium endressii					▓	▓		▓				5
Geranium pratense					▓	messy	messy	messy	messy			6
Geranium 'Rozanne'						▓	▓					
Helianthus 'Lemon Queen'												
Helleborus orientalis hybrids	▓	various	colours	▓	▓	▓	▓	▓	▓	▓	▓	7
Kniphofia 'Maid of Orleans'												
Pulmonaria mollis		▓	▓	▓								
Solidago rugosa								▓				
Grasses												
Carex testacea	▓	▓	▓	▓	▓	▓	▓	▓	▓	▓	▓	2
Pennisetum alopecuroides							texture	texture	texture	texture		8
Miscanthus yakushimensis							texture	texture	texture	texture		8
Dwarf Shrubs												
Buxus sempervirens	▓	▓	▓	▓	▓	▓	▓	▓	▓	▓	▓	9
Hebe 'E.A.Bowles'	▓	▓	▓	▓	▓	▓	▓	▓	▓	▓	▓	9
Lavandula 'Hidcote'	▓	▓	▓	▓	▓	▓	▓	▓	▓	▓	▓	4
Bulbs												
Colchicum autumnale								▓				
Narcissus 'Actaea'				white								
Narcissus 'February Gold'			▓									
Narcissus 'Thalia'			white									
Scilla sibirica			▓									

notes:

1 = Fruit/berries in autumn
2 = Coloured evergreen foliage
3 = Attractive early year foliage
4 = Silver/grey foliage
5 = Repeat flowers
6 = Looks messy after flowering
7 = Various flower colours
8 = Grass grown for form/texture
9 = Evergreen

planting for succession – temporary planting NORI AND SANDRA POPE

The borders at Hadspen Garden and Nursery, in Somerset, are designed to look their best for as long as possible. Nori and Sandra Pope achieve this by what they call "intensive management". The idea is to leave as few gaps as possible, with one plant performing adjacent to another which is just finishing.

above *Clematis* 'Caroline' with *Achillea* 'Salmon Beauty'.

At Hadspen, bulbs are used extensively in spring, with plenty of tulips (available in a huge colour range) providing a succession of colour from early spring to early summer. Later, annuals are used, if necessary, to provide gap-filling colour before the perennials expand, with the Popes treating them as "a colour wash through the border" (they do not grow them in blocks). Self-sowing annuals are particularly useful as they dot themselves around, creating precisely this effect. Sandra is especially fond of *Atriplex hortensis* 'Rubra' which

below *Papaver* 'Saffron' with the foliage of *Euphorbia griffithii* in early summer.

above Annuals, such as these opium poppies, *Papaver somniferum*, are immensely useful for the mid-summer period, when fewer perennials are in flower.

right The spiny flowers of *Eryngium bourgatii* have a long season.

below Dahlias are invaluable for late summer colour. They are available in a huge variety of bold colours (this is 'David Howard').

"looks good even in spring, when its red-leaved seedlings appear between other plants".

Dahlias reign supreme at the end of the summer. With their immense colour range, they are ideal for generating the type of effects that Hadspen has become famous for, while their rapid growth makes them first-rate plants at a time of year when the garden is beginning to fall apart. Most dahlias continue flowering until the first frosts. In cold, wet winter soil (i.e. clay) they will need to be dug up every autumn and re-planted in spring, but in many places they will survive over winter if covered with a thick layer of insulating material, such as straw.

AN EXAMPLE OF SUCCESSION IN THE BORDER

Papaver orientale has leaves which cover the dying tulip foliage, but which in turn die by midsummer, leaving a gap for the annual opium poppies to grow and briefly flower. Dahlias will then fill the space and flower until the frosts.

Spring	Early Summer	Mid-summer	Late Summer – Autumn
Tulips	*Papaver orientale*	*Papaver somniferum*	Dahlias

annual combinations PAUL WILLIAMS

Most gardens have a free patch of ground which can be filled with different arrangements each year by using inexpensive packets of seed. Paul Williams has worked in both public parks and private gardens, building up an unrivalled expertise in the creation of striking summer colour combinations. He is an annuals-addict because he loves "growing plants from seed and the excitement of trying new varieties."

above Castor oil plant, *Ricinus communis,* makes a large mass of dramatic foliage.

Annuals give you the whole plant in one year, unlike shrubs or perennials which might take several years to reach an appreciable size and start producing flowers. They can also be extremely colourful as they tend to produce far more flowers in proportion to leaves than perennials. Increasingly, seed companies now offer more new annual species and new seed strains of well-known ones too, offering an ever-expanding range of colours and colour-shape combinations. The foliage is often equally attractive, with deep tones of red, purple and bronze being especially common, some species of *Amaranthus* even having near fluorescent tones.

below Spider plant, *Cleome hassleriana,* is one of the larger annuals.

left Annuals can be used to create whole borders, but their season will be limited to summer and autumn. Here a few shrubs and grasses are included to lengthen the season and provide continuity. Borders planted with annuals every year will need regular feeding.

PAUL'S TOP ANNUALS FOR INTEREST IN SUMMER AND AUTUMN

- **Cerinthe major *'Purpurascens'*** glaucous foliage and small purple bracts
- ***Cleome hassleriana*** 1.2 m (4 ft) high plant with elegant foliage and flowers in a variety of colours
- ***Hibiscus trionum*** soft yellow flowers
- ***Nicandra physaloides*** shrub-like bulk with masses of small, blue-purple flowers
- ***Ricinus communis*** deep bronze colour, maple-shaped leaves, large – 1 x 1.5 m (3 x 5 ft)
- ***Cosmos sulphureus* 'Cosmic Orange' and 'Cosmic Yellow'** bright fresh colours all summer long with semi-double flowers on branching, open plants
- ***Salvia coccinea* 'Coral Nymph'** one of the most gentle and softly coloured plants. Each flower is a delightfully cool mix of white and pink, giving the plant both charm and elegance
- ***Salvia farinacea* f. *alba* or 'Silver'** with upright spikes of small flowers against grey green leaves, it is a useful shape for breaking up busy areas of pom-pom or daisy-like flowers
- ***Loasa tricolor*** "I cannot resist growing this handsome plant because not only are its flowers complex and colourful, but the whole plant is covered by stinging hairs which invariably catch out people looking to lift the nodding flowers and get a better view."

But annuals offer far more than colour. Many grow very quickly to form statuesque or bulky plants. To create the skeleton of an annual planting you need annuals with a distinct shape, such as *Ricinus communis* which has deep bronze coloured leaves and stems, and distinct lobed leaves, loved by designers since Victorian times. Wide-spreading species, such as daturas and *Nicandra physaloides*, are also "very useful for filling gaps" Paul adds, perhaps in newly planted areas as a temporary measure.

Paul is a bit sceptical, though, of creating schemes that use nothing but annuals as "they do look a bit like a parks department". Instead he prefers to combine them with perennials. The obvious perennials are those tender ones which also flower profusely in strong colours, such as *salvias* and *cupheas*. Cannas and *Melianthus* major offer colour and strong form, giving backbone to what may become an amorphous mass of annuals. Large-leaved shrubs or perennials are also good partners; if *Paulownia tomentosa* is annually coppiced as a shrub at ground level, it produces huge, tropical-looking leaves.

Key to success with annuals is understanding the difference between "hardy" ones which can be sown where they are to flower, and "half-hardy" ones which need to be grown from seed inside, in frost-free conditions, to be planted out later. The latter tend to be more exotic, but the former have a tradional cottage garden charm and if sown *en masse* can create an attractive meadowy effect.

Finally, Paul suggests that "it is well worth going through a comprehensive seed catalogue each year and picking out a few annuals that you have never heard of, and giving them a go. You'll invariably get some terrific surprises."

fading gloriously HENK GERRITSEN

"Dead plants can be beautiful," says Henk Gerritsen. "A dead garden is not such a terrible concept anymore ... I am interested not just in the growing period of plants, but also in their decay. For half the year nothing else is happening."

Henk's garden, known as The Priona Garden, is in the eastern Netherlands, where winters can be long and cold. Rather than cut back the remains of flowering perennials and annuals, he leaves them standing until late winter. Low autumn and winter sunlight illuminates the mass of stems, differentiating every subtle shade of brown and fawn. The effects can be magical – on misty days large perennial corpses become ghosts, looming out of the grey.

above Seedheads and clipped hedges make an effective contrast for autumn.

STRIKING SEED HEADS

- *Allium giganteum, A.cristophii* and other 'drumstick' alliums
- *Aruncus* 'Horatio'
- *Filipendula* species
- *Kirengeshoma palmata*
- *Lunaria rediviva*
- *monarda* species
- *Nectaroscordum sicilum*
- *Phlomis russelliana*
- *rudbeckia* species
- *Sedum spectabile*
- *solidago* species
- *sanguisorba* species
- *Stachys officinalis*
- *Veratrum californicum*
- *Veronicastrum virginicum*
- *Verbena hastata*
- umbellifers generally, i.e. members of the cow- parsley/Queen Anne's lace family

left Spider webs are often a sign that autumn is here. Gardens can be home to a huge variety of wildlife – considerably more than intensively managed farmland.

above left Bolted parsnip seedheads and leek flowers make a surprisingly decorative combination.

above right Teasel, *Dipsacus fullonum*, is a very useful plant for the winter garden, with is durable and distinctive seed heads.

Henk spends much of his life managing the garden, which he created with his late partner Anton Schlepers. From the beginning, Henk and Anton adopted an unconventional approach to gardening – most dramatically illustrated in the "vegetable garden". They had started growing vegetables when they first started gardening, and leaving some to flower had noticed how beautiful they were. Now, during the summer months, this part of the garden is a mix of annuals, such as opium poppy (*Papaver somniferum*), blue *Delphinium consolida*, and the flowers of self-sowing vegetables such as radishes, chicory, leeks and parsnips. The parsnips are particularly effective – the colour of their greeny-yellow flowers mixes well with practically any other and is reminiscent of euphorbias (which, being so widespread as a wildflower across central Europe, are a reminder of the wild spaces that were Anton and Henk's inspiration). In winter, they form

above left Seed heads offer a range of visual experience, both from afar and up close. This is *Allium christophii*.

a forest of dried stems, with the candelabra stems of mulleins (verbascum species) adding lines of crisp definition.

A garden, like anything else alive, involves a cycle of life and death. Conventional gardening had unrealistically high standards, as Henk describes "every yellow leaf was seen as an imperfection, and had to be taken out ... but now the ecology movement has encouraged people to think differently ... it is almost a religious experience. Observing nature I became aware of the fact that death is not just an ending. Being a source of food for other creatures (fungus, birds, insects) it is the beginning of something new." Anyone who shares Henk's feelings will surely be open to seeing elements of death and decay as having qualities of beauty in their own right. Think about what your garden will look like in the winter months and plant accordingly.

above right Even as seedheads decay or are eaten by snails and insects a close examination can be rewarding. This cage-like structure belongs to *Hemerocallis* 'Stafford'.

planting types

and styles

With so many plants available from nurseries the options for exciting gardening have never been better. Also, with more and more gardens open to the public, or being shown in the media, gardeners have never had so much inspiration or been more aware of different gardening styles in other countries. Adopting one particular theme or style is a good way of helping to focus – otherwise the sheer level of choice may lead rapidly to confusion! Here we look at a number of approaches which reflect some of the most dynamic and important trends in contemporary thinking.

using native plants
Isabelle Greene outlines her reasons for the use of local plants in her gardens.

planting mixed borders
The mixed border is the mainstay of many gardens – Nori and Sandra Pope present their ideas on how to make it a success.

exotics
Tim Miles explores the use of planting schemes that bring the exoticism of the tropics to temperate climes.

dry gardens
In a world where water for irrigation is in increasingly short supply, Beth Chatto's ideas for dry gardening are important.

vegetable gardens
Nori and Sandra Pope are keen to tell us how vegetables can be beautiful too.

planting for wildlife
Isabelle Van Groeningen and Gabriella Pape suggest how the garden can benefit the wider environment.

container planting
Paul Williams looks at how to pack plenty of interest into containers.

planting around water
Waterside planting offers lush opportunities, shown here by Anthony Paul.

using native plants ISABELLE GREENE

One of the great paradoxes of gardening is how gardeners have always tended to ignore the wild plants

in their own neighbourhoods. Such plants are often seen as untidy, undesirable or just too ordinary.

But, in recent years, there has been an enormous expansion of interest in using local plants because they

are known to thrive in the prevailing local conditions. They are less likely to become invasive than many

exotics and they can help support many more animal and insect species then non-native plants.

The southern Californian Isabelle Greene likes integrating native and non-native species, as well as designing gardens purely of natives. The great advantage of natives in her seasonally dry climate is that they withstand local drought conditions. But, she points out, while "xeriscape™" (i.e. gardens designed for minimum water use) is the big buzz word, people often pronounce it "zero-scape" which, she adds, is often what their gardens look like when they choose non-natives which don't suit the local conditions.

She adds, "I've learnt how native plants look and work in the wild", which has taught her to create schemes with meandering drifts of different coloured ground covers and shrubs. One very simple way in which she suggests that native plants can be sustainably used in a garden design is by "leaving as many of the existing plants as possible", rather than grubbing everything out and starting from scratch.

In a dry-climate zone shrubs generally form the bulk of the planting in a garden; some of the drought-resistant kind are also evergreen, in grey or silver, with a dense, ground-hugging habit, the "look" that is characteristic of dry-zone plants the world over.

Herbaceous plants play a more peripheral role, providing a splash of colour in the wet or cool season, but they often disappear completely in the dry.

Some dry zones also have a spectacular meadow flora composed of annuals and bulbs. Californian spring

left Native grasses, sedges and tree ferns have been used extensively used in this New Zealand garden by Ted Smyth.

above In this English garden designed by Julie Toll, a variety of native meadow wildflowers have been used to create a "mini-meadow" alongside a more conventional border.

meadows are particularly beautiful but, Isabelle points out, they are not the easiest features to incorporate in the garden "as they are dry stubble for the summer", but in larger gardens they can be incorporated into the scheme to great effect. Dry areas often have a spectacular annual flora, and increasingly these are being marketed as seed mixtures.

Choosing Habitats

Native plants always need to be understood in the context of their natural habitat. Problems will arise, though, when the conditions required by native plants are different to those which prevail in the garden, e.g. the vegetation of forest regions often fails to thrive in suburban gardens that lack tree cover. So the best advice is, do your research and choose with care.

◆ **Meadow** Being semi-natural combinations of perennial wildflowers and wild grasses,

above It is possible to combine low-growing, almost ephemeral spring-flowering plants, with ornamentals. Here *Galium odoratum* grows around the fern, *Dryopteris felix-mas*.

meadows may not look their best after midsummer, but can be kept mown after this period. They are ideal for open, sunny areas, as are prairies. Different combinations of plants (sold as seed mixtures) are suitable for different soil types.

• Prairie These diverse communities of perennial wildflowers and grasses generally have their most colourful period in late summer and autumn. Plant growth is often very high, to 2 m (6½ ft)plus, but can be kept lower with an early to midsummer cut. Seed mixtures tend to be suitable for either mesic (i.e. moist) or dry soil types. Members of the daisy family, such as *helianthus*, *rudbeckia* and aster are the major componenet, along with grasses.

• Forest floor Unlike the previous two, forest floor plant communities are not so readily established from seed, but nursery-grown plants are often available. Most species are spring-flowering, some may be summer-dormant, but a great many have attractive ever-green foliage. Shade is essential. Available species will vary greatly from place to place.

• Low-growing shrubs Areas exposed to drought or strong winds are remarkably similar although they may contain very different plants. Such vegetation has different names – maquis, chapparal, moor, etc. Small-growing shrubs with reduced or leathery leaves tend to dominate, and often have colourful flowers. One of the great advantages for gardeners is that they are generally extremely low-maintenance.

right In environments such as this, that are sensitive to disturbance and the incursion of invasive alien plants, native plants are the most appropriate species to use.

planting mixed borders **NORI AND SANDRA POPE**

The mixed border is probably the second most common garden feature after the lawn.

It evolved because it was the best way to combine plants that flowered, or looked

their best, in different seasons.

Mixing shrubs, perennials and bulbs, these borders bring together an enormous amount of decorative potential, especially if the net is cast wider to include climbers, annuals, vegetables and even small trees.

Most of the plants at Hadspen Garden and Nursery are contained within borders mainly backed by walls and, while it is a large garden, the width of the borders only varies from 2 to 4 m (6½ to 13 ft). Consequently, the conditions are much the same as those faced by domestic gardeners. And one of those problems is trying to combine shrubs and large or spreading perennials in a narrow space. The Popes don't suggest that instead of packing borders with small impulse buys you should go for potentially large plants but, they add, be prepared to be ruthless and consider these points:

• Use climbers as much as possible. Sandra points out that "there are many new small clematis varieties which flower after a lot of shrubs and roses have finished". If shrub roses are grown inside supporting structures, they will also support small climbers.

• Regenerate many large-growing shrubs and keep them small by cutting them down to the base every few years. It would be a shame to exclude such shrubs as lilac or weigela simply because of their ultimate size. Be bold.

• Take the ruthless approach further – Nori says he cuts some shrubs right back to the ground every year. While this treatment would stop most flowering species from blooming, it is very effective with those grown for their foliage, and encourages better quality leaves. At Hadspen it is used particularly for purple-, bronze-, or golden-leaved species, including some nature trees. Suitable subjects include: *Acer palmatum*, and more vigorous cultivars such as 'Sango-kaku'; *A. platanoides* 'Crimson King' and other large-leaved maples; *A. pseudoplatanus* 'Brilliantissimum'; *Cotinus coggygria*; *Physocarpus opulifolius*, e.g. 'Dart's Gold' and 'Diabolo'.

• Cut off any low branches on shrubs which obscure much more attractive ones on the same plant, for example on tree peonies. This may also improve the overall shape.

• Extend the flowering season of old-fashioned shrub roses (which, unlike most modern ones, flower for a short time) from 3-8 weeks by tying their stems to bamboo canes in late winter, and bend them down to ground level to stimulate a succession of bud-bearing side shoots.

left Grasses, bulbs, perennials, annuals, shrubs – all have their place in the mixed border.

below Roses always look better grown with other plant types than in dedicated "rose borders" which can look bare for long periods. This is *Rosa* 'Belle Amour'.

above Hollyhocks (*Alcea rosea*) and pink *Eupatorium maculatum* combine with a variety of dark foliage plants in a late-summer border.

◆ Plant low-growing, spreading perennials around the base of a rose, e.g. hardy geraniums.

◆ Place annuals in mixed borders "near to species plants which have small flowers and a loose habit," says Nori. The annuals will be able to grow up through these taller plants, with their flowers poking out of the top, intermingling as plants do in nature. Good medium to large loose annuals for late-season colour include: *Cleome hassleriana*, *Collomia grandiflora*, varieties of *Cosmos bipinnatus*, *Tagetes patula*, and *Zinnia peruviana*.

◆ Include bamboos (especially the golden-stemmed *Phyllostachys aureosulcata*) which are good border plants because they give evergreen height without being too wide. But most spread, and you must be ruthless by promptly slicing off with a spade any new growth emerging through the soil.

◆ Keep deadheading (removing dead flowers) because many perennials will then flower for longer. Or, before they flower, cut them back by half and the resulting plants will be shorter, more intensively branched with more flower buds, and later blooming.

◆ Let plants at the front of a border sprawl out, creating a relaxed, informal look. But where they spread across grass, it becomes almost impossible to mow so, to avoid the problem, edge the beds with paving slabs. This also provides a crisp edge.

◆ Try to maintain a balance between upright perennials and lower-growing, clump-forming ones, particularly towards the front of the border.

◆ Create linking themes between the front and the back of the border. For example, at Hadspen, the immensely tall perennial *Macleaya cordata* has flowers that are a subtle fawn-brown shade which is picked up by the evergreen sedge *Carex flagellifera* right at the front.

left The bold foliage of *Phormium tenax* provides year-long continuity for this mixed border. On the right is a pink *Astrantia maxima* variety. The poppy is *Papaver* 'Patty's Plum'.

exotics **TIM MILES**

One of the most exciting new garden trends is the exotic border, a concept borrowed from Victorian times when it was common to plant tender plants outside for summer. But whereas they used plants in geometric and formal bedding schemes, the 21st-century exotic border is much more relaxed and luxuriant with hints of Thailand or Brazil.

Big-leaved bananas and cannas are packed in with the brash flowers of abutilons and dahlias, which stand high above the flashy foliage of *Coleus* and *Iresine*. Ebullience and exuberance are the watchwords. So too are sunny sites with free-draining soil, and shelter for plants with big leaves to stop them being wind-flayed.

Tim Miles, gardener at an English wildlife park, is a Cornishman by birth, and so has a natural affinity for exotic-looking gardens. He says "I like a sense of adventure and showmanship in gardens, and trying to grow plants on the edge of hardiness. I like plants that say"'look at me" and entertain people." He points out that the key to exotic planting is

above Hardy palms are essential for the exotic look. This is *Trachycarpus fortunei*.

below The ornamental banana, *Musa basjoo*, is hardy in mild climate zones. Here it provides a centrepiece for a planting of dahlias.

above Dark-leaved cannas, such as 'Wyoming' are good focal-point plants for summer borders.

Left Mauve *Verbena bonariensis* (foreground) with cannas and the orange *Tithonia rotundifolia*. The former is a short-lived perennial, which can normally be relied upon to stay in gardens through self-sowing. The latter is a half-hardy annual, which needs to be raised from seed under cover in spring before planting out in early summer.

TENDER PLANTS SUITABLE FOR MILD WINTER CLIMATES

- *Canna iridiflora*
- *Cordyline australis*
- *Dicksonia antarctica*
- *Euphorbia mellifera*
- *Musa basjoo*

mixing less hardy plants with hardy, permanent ones. So, the rapidly growing, brightly coloured species, such as cannas and dahlias, planted out for the summer only, complement the hardy elements which tend to be foliage plants like palms and bamboos.

Certain plants create such a strong effect that it is worthwhile going to considerable lengths to ensure their survival. That's why Tim loves tender banana plants because, in summer, they make a powerful impression with their vast paddle-shaped leaves that instantly evoke the tropics. How much protection they need depends on location, but they are surprisingly hardy.

Other possibilities for colder climates include certain palms, such as *Trachycarpus fortunei*, which will survive temperatures down to at least -16°C (3.2°F). Bamboos, particularly those with large leaves like species of *Indocalamus*, are also valuable for scene-setting and as a background screen.

Although Tim does create plantings which echo Victorian formality, he prefers to use plants in a more relaxed way, evoking instead a cottage garden, making surprising but effective juxtapositions with the permanent plants. So, for example, he plants out the house plant *Begonia fuchsioides* so that it can grow through the lower branches of a gnarled old apple tree over summer. Nearby he has planted a lush-looking large-leaved annual cucumber relative, *Cucurbita ficifolia*, to crawl over an evergreen cotoneaster, creating a lush tropical effect and enlivening an area which could otherwise be rather dull in summer.

Planting brightly coloured and showy flowers amongst large-leaved plants helps complete the picture. Tim says that with "strong contrasts of colour, texture and form you can't go far wrong". He is fond of using cannas, all of which have architectural presence as well as colourful flowers; some have purple-flushed foliage too, eg. the well-known 'Wyoming'. Sunny spaces between them can be filled with shorter clump-forming plants like small dahlias, diascias, sprawling verbenas (such as 'Sissinghurst'), and *Iresine herbstii* with its deep beetroot foliage. "*Gaura lindheimeri*, and salvia species which have small flowers on thin spikes, are useful," says Tim, "because their flowers come up between the cannas and create a contrasting wispy effect."

The more space and inclination you have to cosset tender plants if you have cold winters, the more you can grow. But if keeping them is impractical, Tim suggests growing the following:

• Bone-hardy plants with dramatic foliage, e.g. *Fatsia japonica* or species of *Rheum*. They will be the permanent backbone.

• Tough-leaved houseplants which can be stood outside over summer, e.g. palms and dracaenas. Give less resilient houseplants good shelter.

• Permanent hardy perennials with big flowers and bright colours, e.g. *rudbeckias* and *echinaceas*. They flower in late summer and autumn.

• Half-hardy plants that can be dug up in the autumn, their top growth being cut off and their tubers stored in a cool, dry place indoors over winter, e.g. dahlias and cannas.

The opportunities for creating exotic borders are much greater if you can grow plants from seed indoors in spring, or dig up tender shrubs, such as salvias, daturas and abutilons, and put them in pots. Bring them indoors and prune them back hard, keeping them in light, cool conditions to reduce their growth until it is time to plant them out again.

above The yellow trumpets of a datura (*brugmannsia* species). A shrub which needs to be cut back, dug up and grown under cover for the winter.

left The banana on the left is *Ensete ventricosum*, which needs winter protection, the one on the right is root-hardy *Musa basjoo*.

HARDY PLANTS WITH EXOTIC FOLIAGE

Evergreens
- *Fatsia japonica*
- *Indocalamus*
- *Magnolia grandiflora*
- *Phormium tenax*
- *Trachycarpus fortunei*
- *Yucca gloriosa*

Deciduous trees and shrubs
- *Hydrangea aspera* subsp. *sargentiana*
- *Paulownia tomentosa* (best kept coppiced, i.e. cut down to ground level every winter)
- *Populus lasiocarpa*
- *Salix magnifica*

Perennials
- *Acanthus mollis*
- *Hosta sieboldiana* 'Elegans'
- *Ligularia*
- *Macleaya cordata*
- *Miscanthus floridulus*

dry gardens BETH CHATTO

With increasing demand on scarce resources, it is likely that in the future more of us will face

restrictions on the amount of water we can use in our gardens. Yet, as Beth Chatto has

convincingly shown, we do not need to water if we choose plants that thrive in dry places,

and dry gardens can be attractive all-year round.

right The fluffy seed-heads of *Pulsatilla vulgaris* in early summer.

She explains that the foliage of drought-tolerant plants is protected against dessication "by a coating of wax or hairs", or "they avoid drought by dying back to bulbs or tubers". Furthermore, "many are evergreen or ever-grey which is of enormous value to gardeners". She also points out the small, leathery leaves which are sometimes shaped like needles or scales, and explains that "the aroma of many of these plants isn't just attractive, it helps prevent them drying out, and makes them unattractive to animals to eat."
Other key points to note:

below Ornamental garlic *Allium aflatuense* thrives on dry soils.

- Plants from dry habitats tend to flower early, giving a colourful spring and early summer.
- Choose plants that have an attractive shape and interesting leaves. Using a few plants with dramatic foliage helps create visual "lift".

above Grey or silver foliage and compact shapes are characteristic of drought-tolerant plants. Good verticals, such as *Verbascum bombyciferum,* lift the eye above bun-like shapes.

• Simplicity is a key characteristic of many dry, wild habitats. Mimic them by using lots of a few species, especially those with good foliage.

• Use small groups of plants in odd numbers.

• Bulbs, such as species tulips and alliums, are important for spring colour but leave gaps later on. These are welcome sites for autumn bulbs (eg. colchicums, true crocuses, nerines).

• Many ornamental grasses are drought-tolerant. They contrast well with clump-forming, grey foliage plants especially from late summer to winter when the grasses' foliage turns to shades of fawn and straw.

Gravel gardens

After a long, very hot and dry summer, Beth Chatto's gravel garden, which she created in 1992, was still looking good, a remarkable vindication of this style of gardening for drought-prone areas. She has ornamental grasses alternating with low-growing hummocks of grey-foliage plants, and a few taller shrubs, creating a restful composition of muted colours and subtly balanced shapes.

The gravel mulch has both practical and aesthetic functions. It helps reduce moisture loss, keeps roots cool and, to an extent, prevents weed seeds from germinating. It also

PLANTS FOR DRY GARDENS

- *Allium* spring/early summer flowering bulbs. Those with tall drumstick flowerheads are particularly striking, and often self-seed
- *Cistus* shrubs with a short spectacular season of flower, but good evergreen foliage
- *Eryngium* short species, such as E. bourgatii, are most drought-tolerant
- *Iris germanica* a wide range of cultivars
- *Lavender* silver-grey foliage
- *Oreganum* useful for late summer flowers
- *Perovskia atriplicifolia* grey foliage and striking blue summer flowers
- *Rosemarinus officinalis* evergreen shrub with blue flowers
- **Thyme** good for ground cover. Profuse
- **Yucca** rosettes of spiky foliage. Good focal points
- *Zauschneria californica* fiery scarlet flowers open late in the year on a low-spreading plant

makes an attractive foil for plants, and helps provide a sense of visual continuity which is important as dry habitat planting is often quite sparse and gappy. Beth used a 8 cm (3 in) layer of gravel; it is important that this does not get mixed up with soil or compost during subsequent plantings.

Gravel gardens are very different to most other garden styles which rely on a strict distinction between areas for planting and walking on. So, with the gravel being used for paths and borders, the boundaries between the two are blurred. This works particularly well in contemporary settings.

Most plants suitable for dry environments grow well in light soils. Not all parts of the country are suitable to make a gravel garden. Where there is good loam and adequate rainfall, many plants adapted to drought will grow out of character, become lax and leggy, or lose their pale grey coats. A gravel garden is appropriate in areas of low rainfall, albeit in a variety of soils, but especially in sandy/gravelly soils.

Self-seeding can create a very attractive look, adding an element of natural spontaneity to the garden, but can become too much of a good thing. Plants such as euphorbias or verbascums can become weeds in the wrong place if found thrusting through small bulbs. While alliums and opium poppies need to be dead-headed well before they have dropped their seeds.

She recommends using local gravel otherwise the result can be quite alien. Beth created her gravel garden by planting first and then applying the stones around the plants in the second year, being careful not to cover smaller plants.

left The spire shape of *Juniperus communis* 'Hibernica' and the rosette of *Agave americana* 'Marginata' add interest to the otherwise more rounded shapes prevalent in this planting.

right The Judas Tree, *Cercis siliquastrum*, with a variety of flowering and low-growing foliage plants suitable for small gardens in areas of low rainfall.

vegetable gardens **NORI AND SANDRA POPE**

"For too long," says Sandra Pope, "vegetables have been hidden at the bottom of the garden behind a hedge." But no more. Inspired by the approach seen spectacularly at Chateau Villandry, on the River Loire, gardeners and designers have increasingly seen them as decorative areas.

By choosing vegetables for the colour of their flowers, leaves and fruit, the seed companies have responded by marketing a wider range, encouraging the preservation of old varieties and the breeding of new.

below Cane frameworks for climbing beans have their own decorative interest.

Nori and Sandra Pope have an extensive vegetable garden at Hadspen, where plants are grown in blocks, 1 m wide by 3 m (3 x 10 ft). This is a much simpler style than the traditional French potager, whose elaborate and detailed planting patterns are completely ruined when the vegetables are harvested or a snail passes through. It is quite a challenge to plan it every year, and Nori describes how "we have to juxtapose and link colours to those of plants in the borders on the other side of the path to establish continuity. And at the same time we have to rotate the vegetables so that one type does not occupy the same patch for more than one year in three, to stop the soil from building up disease."

Starting off

The vegetable garden is started in early spring when there is little to see beyond neat rows of seedlings, cloches and frameworks for climbing beans. The sense of "barracks-like order" appeals to him, "as a contrast with our much more relaxed border planting style". Nori recommends initially growing most vegetables in small pots so that you can accurately position them in the ground. He plants each one a hand's width apart, with individual plants being staggered from one row to another. The vegetables are thinned out if needed or harvested alternately, so that large gaps do not occur.

"You've also got to consider the texture of the vegetables and their three colour groups," he adds. "they are blue-greens (for example onions, leeks, and some cabbages), reds (red lettuces, beetroots and ruby chard), and the bright greens

right Vegetables with distinct leaf colours stand out amidst their green counterparts: ruby chard (foreground) and a bronze lettuce (background).

(lettuces and celeriac foliage)." The fact that many vegetables have attractive flowers (such as beans), or fruit (squashes), is an added bonus. At Hadspen vegetables are incorporated with flowers in a variety of ways; winter squash runs through the whole border with a variety of flowering plants selected to attract insects for pollination and pest control: mauve *Verbena bonariensis*, orange *Zinnia peruviana* and yellow English marigold (*Calendula officianalis*). Sandra adds that "the vertical tomatoes, beans on poles and sweet corn add an upright dimension, and utilize the space more effectively."

Beside the colourful vegetable garden, the Popes take an experimental approach to adding vegetables to their border schemes. The dark red beetroot foliage looks striking with the almost black 'Queen of Night' tulips, and the long-lasting red 'Bijou' lettuce can be sown in almost any gap for its striking red foliage.

While conventional vegetable gardeners are horrified by the idea of plants "going to seed", usually seen as a sign of neglect, the Popes sometimes deliberately encourage this. Parsnips bought from the greengrocer are planted in the border so that their delicate heads of yellow-green poke out amongst flowering perennials, and carrots are grown for their filigree grey-white flowerheads and ball-like seedheads in autumn. And leeks left in the ground are just as much fun as drumstick alliums.

below left As this detail shows, ruby chard is a strikingly attractive vegetable and is easy to grow.

below right 'Golden Teepee' is a yellow climbing bean variety.

VEGETABLE COLOURWAYS

Red/Bronze Vegetables

- **Basil** (the purple-leaved kind, such as 'Dark Opal')
- **Beetroot** 'Bull's Blood'
- **Cabbage, red** (e.g. 'Red Jewel')
- **Chard** 'Ruby chard'
- **Chicory/radicchio** (e.g. 'Augusto')
- **Kale 'Redbor'**
- **Lettuce** (red-leaved varieties, e.g. 'Bijou' and 'Lollo Rossa')
- **Sweet Corn 'Sugar Dot'** (with burgundy stems)

Yellow/Orange Vegetables

- **Bean, climbing** (varieties with yellow beans, e.g. 'Golden Teepee')
- **Chard 'Bright yellow'**
- **Courgette** (e.g. 'Sunburst')
- **Squash** (e.g. 'Kuri')
- **Tomato 'Golden Sunrise'**

Blue-Green Foliage

- **Cabbage**
- **Kale 'Nero di Toscana'**
- **Leeks**

left The red tones of ruby chard are picked up by the red of the ornamental poppies.

planting for wildlife

ISABELLE VAN GROENINGEN and GABRIELLA PAPE

Gardens are extremely important for wildlife because intensive agriculture is depriving so much wildlife of its habitats.

Designer Isabelle van Groeningen stresses that the first rule for making a garden wildlife-friendly is that it should have rich, diverse planting. "It needs plenty of species whose flowers attract pollinating insects; sterile forms, like many plants with double flowers, are not a food source," she says. And while we may not notice most garden insects, the birds do because they eat them.

Autumn and winter are the most crucial times for the survival of garden wildlife. Isabelle recommends that seedheads are left on plants for as long as possible because they feed birds and often harbour a variety of hibernating insects, many of which end up by being eaten by birds. Some seedheads are visually striking, such as teasels (*Dipsacus fullonum*) and stand up well to wet and stormy weather; also include as many as you can of these plants to perk up the late-season border.

"I tend to plant in layers," she adds, "because it's aesthetically attractive, and achieves two results. It incorporates plants which give interest through the seasons, and it provides a range of diverse habitats." Trees are essential for birds to nest in, spiny ones like hollies and berberis providing protection against cats.

above Berries are a vital winter food source for birds. This is *Malus transitoria*.

right Seedheads (this is *Phlomis fruticosa*) can be decorative as well as being avian food sources.

opposite In low autumn light, the straw tones of the dying garden have a beauty of their own. This dense planting offers plenty of shelter and hibernation locations for wildlife.

above Some seedheads (this is a verbascum species) are durable enough to last for several months.

right Seedheads of *Tanacetum macrophyllum* stand out in silhouette.

GOOD SPECIES FOR WILDLIFE

- *Berberis darwini* early season flowers which are useful for insects, followed by berries
- *Buddleia* all are good for butterflies and moths
- **Crab apple *(Malus transitoria)*** tiny apples stay until January, a valuable late food source for birds
- *Eryngium* flowers for butterflies
- **Evening primrose *(Oenothera)*** for seed and pollinating insects
- *Iris sibirica* for its statuesque seedheads
- **Purple fennel *(Foeniculum vulgare 'Purpurascens')*** for seed and pollinating insects
- **Species roses** such as *Rosa glauca* and *R. moyesii*, for their hips
- *Sedium* flowers for butterflies
- **Teasel *(Dipsacus fullonum)*** has seedheads which attract bees

container planting PAUL WILLIAMS

"Plants always grow better in the ground, but if you haven't got a garden what else are you going to do?" asks Paul Williams. He says that containers have lots of advantages as "they provide a chance to experiment on a small scale, are portable, and let you take a close look at plants, enabling you to see them in detail."

Paul stresses that the first rule of selecting plants for containers is appreciating how they will grow. "They assume a different character in a pot, which I see as an advantage. Plants which you might reject in the garden – and with me it's tulips – have a different character when confined in a pot and you actually end up liking them." Putting something in a pot is an inherently artificial exercise – so perhaps it suits inherently "unnatural"-looking flowers.

Containers and hanging baskets are also a good way of using plants with a trailing or rather pendant habit, but for more upright plants it is advisable to know how tall they will grow, and whether they are going to fill out, because the tall and gawky can make an arrangement look unbalanced. "Balance is all important," he adds, "and the plants must be in the right proportion to the container (at least double its height) and to the other plants." The advantage of low containers is that they can be placed in corners and you can see the plants from above.

He also argues that "less is more" should be a rule of thumb. Keep down the numbers of plants, and certainly restrict the range of colours and plant shapes to ensure

above A fine-leaved yucca-like plant, *Dasylirion wheeleri*, makes a good focal-point for this container planting.

right and far right Succulents (these include species of *echeveria* and *kalanchoe*) are good plants for containers as they are relatively tolerant of occasional neglect, as well as looking good all year round.

above A *Canna* with red *Dahlia* 'Bishop of Llandaff' in the larger pot and an arctotis hybrid in the smaller. These are all half-hardy plants, but with winter protection can be kept from year-to-year, the dahlia and canna as easy to store tubers, the arctotis as a pot plant in a conservatory.

left Variegated plants often have a slower rate of growth than "normal" ones, which makes them more suitable as container plants. Here silver-leaved *Liriope muscari* 'Variegata' (front), with *Carex* 'Silver Sceptre' (middle) and *Phormium tenax* 'Variegata' (rear).

left *Echeverias* make good pot plants, and if kept dry will even survive light frosts. Their orange flowers, borne in summer, are an extra bonus.

a sophisticated look. Repeating a combination in a group of containers, or amongst several containers scattered around a garden, also achieves this effect.

Containers give you the chance to combine plants from all sorts of different habitats and sites around the garden. Why not, for example, mix young shrubs, tender perennials, ornamental grasses and annuals for a few months? In this respect, such temporary plantings have more in common with flower arranging than garden design. However, semi- or permanent combinations need to be well thought through; make sure they all enjoy the same soil and watering regime, the same conditions (sun or shade), and avoid any which are too rampant.

Containers also need to be given the right position. Grand settings clearly need imposing containers and plants, while more inventive containers can be used in cottage gardens. In fact, anything that will hold soil for a few months and has drainage holes will suffice. You can even use old olive oil cans or discarded industrial containers. He recommends "exploring the non-ferrous metals section of scrapyards … to find things like parts from old heating systems, especially if they are copper and covered in verdigris". And finally, note that many containers on the market are relatively poor quality, but if they are durable enough for your purposes, and the growth will largely hide the pot, why spend more?

GOOD FOLIAGE PLANTS FOR CONTAINERS

- *Begonia rex* its varieties are usually regarded as houseplants, but they also make extremely useful summer container plants. Many have interesting foliage and compact shapes making them ideal plants for mixing with more conventional container plants.
- *Heucheras* excellent, low clump-forming herbaceous plants in a huge range of leaf colours. In mild winters they are more or less evergreen a sophisticated look.
- *Phormiums* striking for their outwardly thrust, sword-shaped leaves. Small variegated varieties are best. Though all *phormiums* are potentially tall plants, growing them in a container keeps them at a manageable size for several years.
- Ornamental grasses good container plants, often lasting several years. *Stipa arundinacea* is exceptionally good as the orange-bronze tones of its arching leaves last long into winter, making a wonderful backdrop for warm-toned flowers and foliage. Many of the small, evergreen species of *Carex* are also very successful, and 'Frosted Curls' which has long trailing leaves that look a bit of a mess in the garden but are superb when spilling out of a tall container.
- Periwinkle (*Vinca*) tough evergreen trailers available in dark green, silver or gold-variegated forms. Fills the spaces between other plants and trails down the pot sides.

planting around water

ANTHONY PAUL

"We can never copy nature," declares designer Anthony Paul, "but it is a good

starting point." And that's why he suggests that anyone wanting water in their

garden should observe how wild plants grow next to natural ponds and lakes.

They are always surrounded by very distinctive wetland vegetation including reeds, willows and large-leaved marginal plants. He adds, "I like merging water with terra firma so that you can't see an obvious line between the two."

He also loves using architectural shapes, choosing from the many large-leaved water plants, and those with dramatic or elegant shapes. Since the damp conditions encourage lush and vigorous growth, many species soar above anything similar on dry land. Anthony therefore recommends that that you "keep the planting simple. I like to plant in great blocks and use eye-catching plants like *Gunnera*. Most are very vigorous and don't need weeding."

above *Petasities japonicus* is a dramatic waterside perennial, but only suitable for large gardens as it can be very invasive.

left Purple loosestrife (*Lythrum salicaria*) is a very colourful European waterside plant – but it has unfortunately become invasive in North America.

Above *Cyperus longus*, like most waterside plants, is very vigorous – which makes appropriate plant selection for the smaller garden pond a difficult issue. Rapidly growing plants are however very useful for stabilising banks.

left Waterlilies are amazingly minimal maintenance plants, but again, it is important that their size is appropriate to the size of pond they are being introduced into.

Since small ponds may, however, be overwhelmed by such large plants (*Gunnera* can rapidly grow to 2 x 3 m (6½ x 10 ft)!), it is important that final sizes are known before the plants are selected. If they are too big, go for a smaller cultivar or similar, related species from a specialist nursery. The spread of large species may also be limited by growing them in containers plunged in the water.

Miscanthus grasses are popular for waterside planting because they resemble reeds. Though they do not like being immersed in water, they can be grown in ordinary garden soil to create the illusion of a reedy marsh.

STRIKING PLANTS FOR WATERSIDE PLANTING

- *Equisetum hiemale*
- *Darmera peltata*
- *Gunnera manicata or G.tinctoria* (which is half the size)
- *Juncus effusus*
- *Petasites japonicus* potentially very invasive but can be prevented from spreading by growing it in a concealed, bottomless container
- *Pontederia cordata*
- *Thalia dealbata* not hardy
- *Typha angustifolia*

designer biographies

Karena Batstone Since establishing her practise in 1992, Karena has designed everything from small urban courtyards to major commercial landscapes, many in collaboration with colleague Helen Tindale, giving a very distinctive contemporary stamp to each project. She has taught design at the English Gardening School, and written for the gardening press. In June 2002 her work was featured in the BBC's Curious Gardeners series and the accompanying book *Six Elements of Garden Design*.

Susan Berger ran a successful knitwear business for fifteen years, giving her a good grounding in colour combination and texture which influenced her planting style. **Helen Phillips** has a BA in 3D Construction from the Faculty of Art and Design, Bristol. She is a talented illustrator and is able to inspire clients by bringing the design to life on paper. Both she and Sue took a correspondence course in garden design with The English Gardening School. They formed a partnership in 1996.

Jill Billington trained as a sculptor, before turning to garden design in 1980. Her work is noted for its subtle use of formal features, combined with a creative use of plants. She prides herself on her ability to think laterally (with much of her work in London, she often has to create gardens in oddly-shaped spaces). She has designed several gardens for the Chelsea Flower Show, and is a member of numerous judging panels for garden shows in Britain and abroad.

John Brookes MBE is one of the world's most respected garden designers, and has played a major role in the development of garden design as a professional discipline. He started his career working as an assistant for Brenda Colvin and Sylvia Crowe, who were major names in mid-twentieth century British landscape architecture. John has created gardens and landscapes in many different countries and climates. He runs a design school in Buenos Aires and continues to lecture and offer design courses both in England and abroad.

George Carter studied Fine Art at university, specialising in sculpture. He has been a garden designer since 1988, having previously worked as primarily a museum and exhibition designer. His many private gardens in Europe and the USA have ranged in scale from large parks to small town gardens and concentrate on a formal approach to both hard and soft landscaping. Previous experience in exhibition design has lead to a theatrical attitude to gardens and he often uses the illusionism of the stage.

Beth Chatto has lived all her life in Essex, Britain's driest county. Inspired and helped by her late husband, Andrew, who had an expert amateur knowledge of plant ecology, she started gardening in 1960, with a strategy which seems obvious now, but which at the time was quite revolutionary in Britain, that of selecting plants on the basis of matching their environmental preferences with soil and microclimate conditions. An involvement with the flower arranging movement helped spark an interest in species plants and "unusuals", which were then sold from her garden nursery, a pioneer of its kind.

Henk Gerritsen, was born in The Netherlands and studied history and politics at university before studying art, and making a living as a painter and illustrator. With his late partner Anton Schlepers he began to create The Priona Garden in the eastern Netherlands in the late 1970s, which is now regularly open to the public. Managing the garden is central to Henk's working life; he also designs gardens and has collaborated on several books with Piet Oudolf.

Isabelle Greene is a native of California, originally trained in botany and fine art. She created her first garden design in 1964 and has gone on to be involved with over 500 more innovative designs, mostly in the western US. She has been made a fellow of the American Institute of Architecture, a rare distinction for a landscape architect. Deeply committed to sustainable practices she is involved with a variety of environmental committees, and is a founding member of The Green Building Alliance.

Catherine Heatherington was born and brought up in East Anglia, and she thinks that "the legacy of a landscape of vast skies and distant horizons is evident in my gardens". Following a first degree in Mathematics, Catherine studied garden design, setting up practice in London. She is increasingly known for designs both urban and rural, which take contemporary ideas into settings where they link with both architecture and the wider landscape. Catherine writes regularly for garden design publications.

Carol Klein taught art in London, before moving to rural Devon where she created a garden and set up a nursery business. Her stands at flower shows are renowned for their colour combinations – she has won a gold medal at The Chelsea Flower Show six times (although she isn't sure – "I've never counted properly"). She is a frequent contributor to garden magazines and to television programmes.

Steve Martino is a native of Phoenix, Arizona, from where he runs his landscape architecture practice, renowned for its integration of desert plants and a desert aesthetic in drought-prone climates. Steve studied art and architecture at Arizona State University; and the integration of landscape and building is one of the most distinctive aspects of his work. The architect Franklin D. Israel has been a particular influence, along with local landscapes and natural ecological processes. His work includes public and private commissions and public art.

Julie Moir Messervy practices as a garden and landscape designer in northeast USA, using a highly distinctive style which involves a close liaison with clients. Her studies in Japan, under a renowned garden design master in Kyoto, have clearly influenced her style. She creates gardens for private and public spaces (both commercial and institutional), with The Toronto Music Garden on the Toronto waterfront a recent example of the latter. She writes and lectures widely, and is particularly committed to the teaching side of her career.

Tim Miles was born and bred in Cornwall and carried his love of exotic plants through his working life, which has included working in a therapeutic community, as gardens manager at London Zoo, at the Lost Gardens of Heligan in Cornwall, and now at the Cotswold Wildlife Park. He also writes, broadcasts and sits on a Royal Horticultural Society committee. He is a great believer in showmanship in the garden and in always challenging received wisdom.

Piet Oudolf has practised as a garden designer practically all his life in his native Netherlands. Initially very influenced by the architectural style of the Bauhaus-trained Dutch designer Mien Ruys, he developed a more plant-focused style in the 1980s, influenced by British and German gardens. In 1982 he and his wife Anja set up their own nursery, primarily to provide plants for his projects, but it has turned out to have become a very successful retail business in its own right, with many new introductions. Piet's work is increasingly for public landscapes, although he also undertakes private work.

Anthony Paul has practised as a landscape designer for some 30 years, and has always been known for his strongly contemporary work, often with a Japanese influence. He has worked in New Zealand, France, Switzerland and elsewhere, as well as the UK, on both private garden and corporate landscape projects. His garden in Surrey, England, was created in conjunction with his wife Hannah Peschar, who runs it as a sculpture garden.

Dan Pearson studied horticulture at RHS Wisley and Kew. He has completed a wide range of private and public sector commissions in Britain and also in Italy, Egypt and Japan. Amongst his best-known works are the re-landscaping of the grounds of Althorp House and the surroundings of the Millennium Dome. His travels in wild landscapes, and a love of natural plant communities has played a major role in informing his work, which is strongly naturalistic. He has presented several British gardening TV series.

Nori and Sandra Pope come from Vancouver Island in Canada, where they worked as designers and ran a nursery. In 1987 though they fell in love with the garden at Hadspen in England, moving over soon afterwards to start work there, creating what has become one of the most talked about gardens of modern times, with colour harmonies the dominant theme. As well as managing Hadspen the couple also lecture widely, and offer their services as consultants.

Lesley Rosser has a degree in botany, and worked in research, moving on to her own garden design-and-build practice in 1983. The garden at The Urn Cottage is her own rural retreat although has opened regularly to the public. Lesley is Course Director for Horticulture at The English Gardening School and lectures also on planting design at London's Inchbald School of Design and for the John Brookes Garden Design Course based at East Lambrook Manor in Somerset.

Ted Smyth is New Zealand's premier garden designer, having been creating gardens since the 1960s. Originally trained in art (painting and sculpture) he still creates sculptural pieces for his gardens. He has consciously tried to avoid "influences" and draws his inspiration primarily from the New Zealand landscape, but also from twentieth century art. He has never left his native land, simply feeling that it offers everything he needs.

Julie Toll trained in horticulture (nursery production) but soon moved into garden design. She is known primarily for her work with British native wildflowers, but in fact she is involved with a very wide range of projects, including work with developers and corporate landscapes. She also has an office on the island of Nevis in the Caribbean. Her wildflower show gardens at the Chelsea Flower Show have done much to raise public consciousness about wild flora.

Isabelle Van Groeningen was born in Belgium, and came to Britain to study horticulture at the Royal Botanic Gardens Kew, followed by a PhD in Conservation Studies at York University. She is an established garden historian, designer and consultant, with a particular interest in herbaceous planting schemes, both traditional border planting and a more relaxed naturalistic style. In 1992 she founded the practice Land Art Ltd, with **Gabriella Pape**. The company specialises in the creation of new schemes in historically sensitive settings. Gabriella Pape was born in Hamburg, starting her career apprenticed to the German tree nursery Von Ehren. She then moved to England to take a degree in Biodynamic agriculture before going to Kew to do the Kew Diploma in Horticulture. Gabriella has been gardening organically all her life, and is very keen on creating gardens that are environmentally sensitive and which enhance biodiversity.

James van Sweden trained originally as an architect, but then found himself more interested in "the spaces between buildings", and went on to study landscape architecture in the Netherlands. In 1975 he formed the partnership with German-trained horticulturalist and landscape architect Wolfgang Oehme which revolutionised the way people in the US look at landscape through a number of high-profile schemes for private, public and corporate clients on the US east coast. The two men have now brought younger partners Sheila Brady, Lisa Delplace and Eric Groft into their practice and the company style continues to evolve.

Paul Williams started his working life in a council parks department, before moving to a series of jobs as head gardener, culminating with 18 years at Bourton House in the Cotswolds, where he was able to perfect his highly creative plant-focused style. Since 1999 he has worked as a garden designer and freelance writer. He has a regular "phone-in" local radio programme and also teaches on plants and gardens in schools.

contacts

Karena Batstone
21, Somerset Street
Bristol
BS2 8LZ
United Kingdom
info@karenabatstone.com
www.karenabatstone.com

Sue Berger and Helen Phillips
69, Kingsdown Parade
Bristol
BS6 5UG
United Kingdom
sue@gardenberger.freeserve.co.uk

Jill Billington
100, Fox Lane
London
N13 4AX
United Kingdom
jill.billington@btinternet.com

John Brookes
Denmans, Fontwell
Arundel
BN19 0SU
United Kingdom
denmans@denmans-garden.co.uk
www.denmans-garden.co.uk

George Carter
Silverstone Farm
North Elmham
Norfolk
NR20 5EX
United Kingdom
grcarter@easynet.co.uk

Beth Chatto
Beth Chatto Gardens
Elmstead Market
Essex
CO7 7DB
United Kingdom

Henk Gerritsen
Schuineslootweg, 13
7777RE Schuinesloot
Netherlands
henk@prionatuinen.com
www.prionatuinen.com

Isabelle Greene Associates
2613 Del Vina St.
Santa Barbara
93105 California
USA
iga@isabellegreene.com

Catherine Heatherington
9, Cecil Road
London
N10 2BU
United Kingdom
www.chdesigns.co.uk

Noel Kingsbury
Landscape Solutions
Sugnall Business Centre
Sugnall, Stafford
ST21 6NF
United Kingdom
www.landsol.com

Carol Klein
Glebe Cottage Plants
Pixie Lane
Warkleigh
Devon EX37 9DH
United Kingdom
www.glebecottageplants.co.uk

Steve Martino
3336N, 32nd St.
Suite 115
Phoenix, Arizona
USA
steve@stevemartino.net
www.stevemartino.net

Julie Moir Messervy
PO Box 629
Saxtons River, VT 05154
USA
www.juliemoirmesservy.com

Tim Miles
Cotswold Wildlife Park
Burford
OX18 4JW
United Kingdom
tim@cotswoldwildlifepark.co.uk

Piet Oudolf
Broekstraat 17
Hummelo 6999 DE
Netherlands
info@oudolf.com
www.oudolf.com

Anthony Paul
Black & White Cottage
Standon Lane
Ockley
Surrey
RH5 5QR
United Kingdom

Dan Pearson Studio
80c Battersea Rise
London
SW11 1EH
United Kingdom
www.danpearsonstudio.com

Nori and Sandra Pope
Hadspen Garden
Castle Cary
BA7 7NG
United Kingdom
pope@hadspengarden.co.uk

Lesley Rosser BSc, PhD,
MI Hort, MSGD
The Urn Cottage, Station Road
Charfield, Wotton-under-Edge
GLOS GL12 8SY
United Kingdom
www.lesleyrossergardens.co.uk

Ted Smyth
95, McEntee Rd
Waitakere
New Zealand

Julie Toll
Landscape and Garden Design
Business and Technology Centre
Bessemer Drive, Stevenage
SG1 2DX
United Kingdom
info@julietoll.co.uk

**Isabelle Van Groeningen and
Gabriella Pape**
Land Art Ltd
The Old Carpenters Yard
Coleshill nr. Swindon
SN6 7PR2
United Kingdom
office@land-art.co.uk
www.land-art.co.uk

**Oehme, van Sweden &
Associates**
800 G Street, SE
Washington DC 20003, USA
www.ovsla.com

Paul Williams
Keepers Cottage
Station Road
Blockley, Moreton in the Marsh
GL56 9DZ
United Kingdom
pw@mitochondria.freeserve.co.uk

bibliography

Karena Batstone
A Handbook for Garden Designers (with Rosemary Alexander) Ward Lock, 1994

Jill Billington
Colour Your Garden Quadrille, 2002

New Formal Gardens: Formality Updated for Today's Gardens Quadrille, 2002

Really Small Gardens: A Practical Guide to Gardening in a Truly Small Space Quadrille, 2002

Architectural Foliage Cassell Illustrated, 1991

Using Foliage Plants in the Garden Cassell Illustrated, 1994

John Brookes (a selection)
John Brookes' The New Garden Dorling Kindersley (Macmillan in US), 1998

Natural Landscapes Dorling Kindersley (MacMillan in US), 1998

John Brookes' Garden Design Book Dorling Kindersley, 2001

John Brookes' Garden Masterclass Dorling Kindersley, 2002

George Carter
The New London Garden Mitchell Beazley, 2000

Living with Plants Mitchell Beazley, 2000

Containers (Gardening Workbooks) Ryland Peters & Small (Stewart, Tabori, & Chang in US/Canada), 1997

Herbs (Gardening Workbooks) Ryland Peters & Small (Stewart, Tabori, & Chang in US/Canada), 1997

Garden Spaces, Simple Solutions for Planning and Design Mitchell Beazley, 2005

Beth Chatto
Beth Chatto's Woodland Garden: Shade-loving Plants Cassell 2002

The Dry Garden Orion, 1998

Beth Chatto's Gravel Garden Frances Lincoln, 2000

The Green Tapestry: Perennial Plants for the Garden Collins, 1989

Beth Chatto's Garden Notebook Phoenix, 1993

The Damp Garden Sagapress, 1996

Henk Gerritsen (with Piet Oudolf)
Planting the Natural Garden Timber Press, 2003

Dream Plants for the Natural Garden Timber Press, 2000

Catherine Heatherington
A New Naturalism (with Juliet Sargeant) Packard Publishing, 2005

Noel Kingsbury (a selection)
The New Perennial Garden Frances Lincoln, 1996

Dramatic Effects with Architectural Plants Mitchell Beazley, 1996

Designing with Plants (with Piet Oudolf) Conran Octopus (Timber Press in US/Canada), 1999

Bold Leaved Plants Ryland, Peters and Small, 2000

Grasses and Bamboos Ryland, Peters and Small, 2000

Natural Gardening for Small Spaces Frances Lincoln (Timber Press in US/Canada), 2003

Planting on Roofs and Walls (with Nigel Dunnett), Timber Press, 2004

VISTA: the culture and politics of the garden (a collection of essays co-edited with Tim Richardson) Frances Lincoln, 2005

Carol Klein
Plant Personalities, Cassell, 2004

Julie Moir Messervy
The Inward Garden: Creating a Place of Beauty and Meaning Little Brown & Company, 1995

The Magic Land: Designing Your Own Enchanted Garden Hungry Minds Inc., 1998

Contemplative Gardens Howell Press, 1990

Tim Miles
The New Cornish Garden (with David Rowe) Truran (UK), 2003

Piet Oudolf
Planting the Natural Garden (with Henk Gerritsen) Timber Press, 2003

Designing with Plants (with Noel Kingsbury) Conran Octopus (Timber Press in US/Canada),1999

Dream Plants for the Natural Garden (with Henk Gerritsen) Frances Lincoln, 2000

Gardening with Grasses (with Michael King) Frances Lincoln, 1998

Anthony Paul
The Water Garden (with Yvonne Rees) Frances Lincoln, 2001

The Garden Design Book (with Yvonne Rees) Harper Collins 1994

Designing with Trees (with Yvonne Rees) Windward, 1989

Dan Pearson
The Garden, A Year At Home Farm Ebury Press, 2001

The Essential Garden Book (with Terence Conran) Conran Octopus, 1998

Garden Doctors (with Steven Bradley) Boxtree Press, 1995

Nori and Sandra Pope
Colour by Design: Planting Effects for the Contemporary Garden Conran Octopus, 1998

Julie Toll
The Small Garden (The Royal Horticultural Society Collection) Conran Octopus, 1995

James van Sweden
Architecture in the Garden Frances Lincoln (Random House in US), 2003

Bold Romantic Gardens: The New World Landscapes of Oehme and van Sweden (with Wolfgang Oehme) Acropolis Books Ltd, 1990

Gardening with Nature Random House, 1997

Gardening with Water Random House, 1995

Paul Williams
Creative Containers Conran Octopus, 2002

Creative Climbers Conran Octopus (Trafalgar Square in US), 1999

Garden Colour Palette Conran Octopus, 2000

Digging Deeper – understanding how your garden works Conran Octopus, 2003

Container Gardening Dorling Kindersley, 2004

gardens to visit

This is just a handful of the gardens it is possible to visit. For UK gardens, opening times may be found in either the annual *National Garden Scheme Handbook* (the "yellow book") or the *Good Gardens Guide*, published annually by Frances Lincoln. Some gardens are not open regularly, or may be accessible by appointment only. It is advisable to ring ahead. Details often change, so where full addresses have not been included, try visiting *www.ngs.org.uk* where information on open gardens is regularly updated.

Jill Billington
Weir House
Hampshire, UK

John Brookes
The English Garden in the Chicago
Botanical Garden
1000 Lake Cook Road
Glencoe, Illinois, USA
www.chicagobotanic.org

Ecclesden Manor
West Sussex, UK (open occasionally)

George Carter
Columbine Hall
Stowupland, Stowmarket
Suffolk, IP14 4AT, UK

Burghley House Garden of Surprises
Lincolnshire, UK
www.burghley.co.uk

Holkham Hall, Wells-next-the-Sea
Norfolk, NR23 1AB, UK
01328 710227
www.holkham.co.uk

Beth Chatto
Beth Chatto Gardens
Elmstead Market, Colchester
Essex, CO7 7DB, UK
01206 822007
www.bethchatto.co.uk

Henk Gerritsen
Priona Gardens
Schuineslootweg 13
7777 RE Schuinesloot
Netherlands
0031 523 681734

Isabelle Greene
Sadako Peace Garden
La Casa de Maria, 800 El Bosque Road
Santa Barbara, CA 93108, USA
www.wagingpeace.org

Noel Kingsbury
A number of public park and highway
plantings in Bristol, UK

Carol Klein
Dairy Lawn Borders
Tapeley Park Gardens
Devon, UK

Glebe Cottage
Devon, UK

Steve Martino
Display at Arid Zone Trees Nursery
9750 E Germann Road Mesa
Phoenix AZ, USA
www.aridzonetrees.com

WaterWorks at Arizona Falls
G R Herberger Park
56th Street and Indian School Road
Phoenix, Arizona, USA

Julie Moir Messervy
The Toronto Music Garden
475 Queens Quay West
Toronto ON, Canada

Spruce Knoll
Mount Aubern Cemetery
Cambridge MA, USA

Tim Miles
Cotswold Wildlife Park and Gardens
Burford, Oxfordshire
OX18 4JW, UK
01993 823006

Piet Oudolf
Bury Court
Surrey, UK

Pensthorpe Waterfowl Park
Fakenham, Norfolk
NR21 0LN, UK
01328 851465

RHS Garden, Wisley
Woking, Surrey
GU23 6QB, UK
01483 224234

Uithof Botanic Gardens
Fort Hoofddijk
Budapestlaan 17
Utrecht, Netherlands
(+31) 030 253 5455

The Battery Park (South of Broadway),
New York, USA

The Millenium Park
222 N Columbus Drive
Chicago, USA
(in conjunction with Kathryn Gustafson)

Anthony Paul
Hannah Peschar Sculpture Garden
Black and White Cottage
Standon Lane
Ockley, Surrey
RH5 5QR, UK
01306 627269

Dan Pearson
Althorp House
Northampton, NN7 4HQ, UK
www.althorp.com

Rooftop Gardens
Roppongi Hills, Tokyo, Japan
www.roppongihills.com

Worthing Hospital Arts Project
Lyndhurst Road
Worthing, Sussex
BN11 2DH, UK
01903 285186

British Council, Cairo
4 El Minya Street
Heliopolis, Cairo, Egypt

Nori and Sandra Pope
Hadspen Gardens
Castle Cary, Somerset
BA7 7NG, UK
01749 813707

The University of Oxford Botanic
Garden (late-season border)
Rose Lane, Oxford, OX1 4AZ, UK
01865 286690
www.botanic-garden.ox.ac.uk

Lesley Rosser
The Urn Cottage, Station Road
Charfield, Wotton-under-Edge
Gloucestershire, GL12 8SY, UK

Julie Toll
Jenningsbury (open occasionally)
Hertford, UK

**Isabelle Van Groeningen and
Gabriella Pape**
Tha Ammonite Garden
London Wetland Centre
Queen Elizabeth's Walk, Barnes
London, SW13 9WT, UK
www.wwt.org.uk

South Moat Border/Woodland Garden
Eltham Palace, Court Yard, Eltham
London, SE9 5QE, UK
020 8294 2548

The Secret Garden, Cliveden, Taplow
Berkshire, SL6 0JF, UK
(National Trust)
www.clivedenhouse.co.uk

Paradise Garden/Vegetable Kingdom/
Vegetable Inspiration Gardens
Ryton Organic Garden
Coventry
CV8 3LG, UK
(Henry Doubleday Research
Association)
020 7630 3517

James van Sweden
German-American Friendship Garden
Constitution Avenue, 16th Street NW
Washington DC, USA

Work in Chicago Botanical Garden
1000 Lake Cook Road, Glencoe
Illinois, USA
www.chicagobotanic.org

Work in Red Butte Garden &
Arboretum
300 Wakara Way, Salt Lake City
UT 84108, USA
www.redbuttegarden.org

Paul Williams
The Cotswold House Hotel
Chipping Campden
Gloucestershire, GL55 6AN, UK
01386 840330
www.cotswoldhouse.com

Bourton House
Gloucestershire, UK
www.bourtonhouse.com

index

Page numbers in *italics* refer to captions.

acknowledgements

Unless credited below, all pictures depict gardens by the featured designer.

2: Isabelle Greene
3 top left: Ross Palmer
3 top right: Steve Martino
3 bottom left: Catherine Heatherington
4 top: James van Sweden
4 middle: Steve Martino
6 left: Noel Kingsbury
6-7 middle: Nori and Sandra Pope
7: Piet Oudolf
8-9: Noel Kingsbury
10-11: James van Sweden
12: James van Sweden
13 top: James van Sweden
13 bottom: Ross Palmer
14 bottom: Helen Dooley, Petersham House
15: Parc Citroen
16: Ross Palmer
17: Lesley Rosser
18 top: Ross Palmer
18 bottom: Jinny Blom
19 top: no attributable designer
19 bottom: Pietro Porcinai
32: Julie Moir Messervy
33 top: Dan Pearson
33 bottom: Julie Moir Messervy
35: Steve Martino
51 left: Julie Toll
54: Dan Pearson
55 top: Sue Berger & Helen Phillips
55 bottom: Dan Pearson
62 top: Donald McIntyre & Jane Lipington
70: Lesley Rosser
71 left and right: Lesley Rosser
74 top: Kathryn Gustafson, Terrasson
74 bottom: John Brookes
75: Ross Palmer
76: Naila Green
77 John Brookes
84-85: Steve Martino
86: Ted Smyth
87: Karena Batstone

100 top: Naila Green
100 bottom: Lesley Rosser
101 left: Isabelle Greene
101 right: Lesley Rosser
110: Ted Smyth
111 top: Kathryn Gustafson
111 bottom: Ted Smyth
118 bottom: Kathryn Gustafson, Terrasson
119 right: Lesley Rosser
126: Dan Pearson
127 bottom: Sandra & Nori Pope, Hadspen
128 bottom: Piet Oudolf
129 bottom: Isabelle Greene
130 top: Sandra & Nori Pope, Hadspen
130 bottom: Donald McIntyre & Jane Lipington
136 top and bottom: Sandra & Nori Pope, Hadspen
137 top: Sandra & Nori Pope, Hadspen
139: Sandra & Nori Pope, Hadspen
140 middle: Christopher Lloyd, Great Dixter
149: Beth Chatto
150: Piet Oudolf
151 top: Piet Oudolf
151 bottom: George Carter
164 top: Dan Pearson
165 top: Dan Pearson
166: Noel Kingsbury
167 top: Paul Williams
167 bottom: Henk Gerritsen
178 left: Priona
179 left: Dan Pearson
180: Beth Chatto
181 top: Isabelle Greene
181 bottom: Steve Martino
182: Ted Smyth
183: Julie Toll
184: Dan Pearson
206 top: Ross Palmer
206 bottom: Isabelle Greene
207: Isabelle Greene
210: Dan Pearson
212: Dan Pearson
213: Dan Pearson

First published in North America in 2005 by Timber Press, Inc.
The Haseltine Building
133 S.W. Second Avenue, Suite 450
Portland, Oregon 97204-3527, U.S.A.

www.timberpress.com

First published in the United Kingdom by Pavilion Books, an imprint of Chrysalis Books Group plc

Text © Noel Kingsbury, 2005
Photography © Nicola Browne, 2005
Design and layout © Pavilion Books, 2005

The moral right of the author has been asserted.

A CIP catalogue record for this book is available from the Library of Congress.

ISBN 0-88192-741-4

EDITOR: Emily Preece-Morrison
DESIGNER: Ruth Hope
PHOTOGRAPHER: Nicola Browne
ILLUSTRATOR: Paul Williams
COPY EDITOR: Richard Rosenfeld
INDEXER: Helen Snaith

Printed in China by SNP Leefung Printers Ltd.
Reproduction by Mission Productions Ltd.

10 9 8 7 6 5 4 3 2 1

author's acknowledgements

I'd like to thank all the designers who so generously gave me their time and often supplied additional material. I have very much enjoyed working with photographer Nicola Browne, whose stunning images have given this project its immediate impact, with editor Emily Preece-Morrison and again with designer Ruth Hope. Commissioning editor Stuart Cooper deserves recognition and thanks for the bold concept of the book and getting it accepted. I'd also like to thank my agent, Fiona Lindsay, without whose efforts this book would probably never have happened. Finally I'd like to thank my ever-supportive partner, Jo Eliot, with whom I am lucky enough to be able to share the more enjoyable aspects of my work.

Poems to Learn by Heart

CAROLINE KENNEDY

Poems to Learn by Heart

PAINTINGS BY

JON J MUTH

𝒟ISNEY · HYPERION BOOKS

NEW YORK

Contents

I Dreamed I Had to Pick a Mother Out

and other poems about family 36

I'm Expecting You!

and other poems about friendship and love 52

I Met a Little Elf-Man, Once

and other poems about fairies, ogres, and witches 70

Where Can a Man Buy a Cap for His Knee?

and other nonsensical poems 84

It Is the Duty of the Student
and other poems about school 98

We Dance Round in a Ring and Suppose
and other poems about sports and games 114

Four Score and Seven Years Ago
and other poems about war 130

The World Is So Full of a Number of Things
and other poems about nature 152

Extra Credit 166

Last Poem Catch a Little Rhyme • *Eve Merriam* 182

Introduction

People often ask me why they should learn a poem by heart. In today's world, where it is so easy to look things up, we discount the value of memorization. For example, kids don't see the point of learning the multiplication tables when they have a calculator. But it makes us feel empowered to know that we have the knowledge to solve a problem, rather than having to depend on a device to do the work for us. It's the same with words. Poets distill life's lessons into the fewest possible words. But those tiny packages of thought contain worlds of images and experiences and feeling. If our circumstances change and things seem to be falling apart, we can recall a poem that reassures us. If we find ourselves in unfamiliar or frightening surroundings, a poem can remind us that others have journeyed far and returned safely home. If we learn poems by heart, we will always have their wisdom to draw on, and we gain understanding that no one can take away.

The best time to start memorizing is when we are young and remember things easily. Children can recite their favorite books by heart, and through repetition, even exhausted parents will learn them eventually. In my house, we can all recite *The Poky Little Puppy*, *Caps for Sale*, and *The Owl and the Pussycat*, as well as the rhymes, prayers, and songs that are the incantations of childhood.

Poems are no more difficult. In fact, they are written to be remembered and recited aloud. Although we recollect without conscious effort, memorizing is more like sports practice—the more you do it, the more skilled and confident you become. If we learn a poem by heart, it is ours forever—and better still, we can share it with others, yet not have to give it away.

In the ancient world, when there were no books or printed material, people had to memorize the information they needed, for navigating, farming, trading, entertainment, and civic life. Epic and heroic poems were composed to transmit values and the collective memory of a civilization. These were recited in gatherings, competitions, and religious festivals, and passed down from one generation to the next. A testament to the importance of memory in ancient times is that the goddess Memory, known as Mnemosyne, was a Titan, a daughter of the first ruler of the universe. Her gift was the gift of reason; she is considered the first philosopher, and it was her responsibility to name everything on earth.

In contemporary life, we cannot imagine memorizing anything as long as *The Odyssey*, but the ancient Greeks and Romans invented helpful techniques to make it easier. First, they suggested imagining a building, preferably one with many rooms. In ancient times, there were enormous temples, public baths, and stadiums. Private houses often had colonnaded courtyards opening onto rooms decorated with statues, tables, and altars. Today, you can use a museum, a part of a city that you know well, or even a mall. The next step is to imagine objects that remind you of the images in the poem and mentally place them around the building, or down the street. Make sure you remember exactly where you have put everything so that later, when you recite the poem, you can picture yourself walking through the building or the city, pausing in front of each object and calling to mind the section of the poem. Using this method, Seneca, an ancient Roman teacher of rhetoric and memorization, was able to recite two thousand names in order, and when his two hundred students each recited a line of poetry in class, he could recite them all backward.

When my mother was a child, she and her classmates had to memorize Bible verses and poetry to recite at morning assembly. A generation later, when I was growing up, memorization was rarely required, but the eighth grade poetry contest was still a major event for the entire school. Since that time, the study and memorization of poetry has fallen out of favor in most schools. However, over the past few years, thanks to the explosion of urban poetry slams, open-mic competitions, and spoken-word festivals, poetry recitation is making a comeback. Poetry has come out of solitary confinement to become an agent of empowerment and social change. The solitary acts of reading and composing are complemented by teamwork, performance, and audience participation.

For some people, standing up in front of others is a frightening prospect. But if you look above their heads and focus your mind on the images in the poem, rather than your friends' faces, it isn't as scary. And after you do it a few times, you might even begin to enjoy it.

In my work with the New York City public schools, I have gotten to know a few young poets. They attend DreamYard Prep, a small high school with an arts-based curriculum that opened in the Bronx in 2006. From the 1970s through the 1990s, Bronx schools suffered the tragedies of poverty, AIDS, violence, and neglect. The neighborhood became one of the most dangerous in the city. School attendance rates were dismal, and only 12.5 percent of the ninth grade graduated from high school four years later. Over the past few years, the school land-scape has been transformed. Large failing schools have been closed and new small high schools like DreamYard Prep have been opened in their place. Attendance rates are up, and seniors are graduating at rates of 60–80 percent, with many becoming the first in their families to attend college.

I was so impressed with the work of these talented students that I asked a few of them to help select poems for this book. I was curious whether they would enjoy reading great poems of the past or whether the language and imagery would seem old-fashioned and disconnected from their lives. I was not surprised that funny poems and poems about friendship and love were the most accessible to them. But I was intrigued to see how the students came to appreciate more complex traditional poems. When I was growing up, the emphasis was on reading and imitating the style of literary masters. By contrast, today's students are more likely to write about their own lives and challenges, and through that process, they become more interested in how past poets have explored the same issues.

I continue to be inspired by my assistants—their enthusiasm and ability to memorize and perform long poetic compositions, their love of words and language, and their passionate desire to express themselves. I hope that other young writers will use this book as a starting point for their own memory-palaces of poems—and once they learn them by heart, they won't even need this book.

First Poem

The First Book
Rita Dove

Open it.

Go ahead, it won't bite.
Well . . . maybe a little.

More a nip, like. A tingle.
It's pleasurable, really.

You see, it keeps on opening.
You may fall in.

Sure, it's hard to get started;
Remember learning to use

knife and fork? Dig in:
You'll never reach the bottom.

It's not like it's the end of the world—
just the world as you think

you know it.

Here I Am

and other poems about the self

Poetry announces us. It is the most personal and direct expression of who we are and how we are feeling. In a world where it sometimes seems that no one is listening, poetry can help us find our own voice and be heard. Growing up is hard, but poems can protect, guide, and connect us to others. If we learn them by heart, the emotion, the wisdom, and the power they contain can bring joy to our lives and sustain us through difficult times.

The poems in this section explore complicated questions of identity and ways of being. The first poem, by Gertrude Stein, is a forceful presentation of self to the world. Other poems, like "Crying" by Galway Kinnell or "Bad Morning" by Langston Hughes, reveal fears or emotions that the poet is struggling to overcome. Poems can also help us keep going when we feel like giving up. Sometimes a short poem like "Don't Worry if Your Job Is Small," or a verse from "It Couldn't Be Done" by Edgar Albert Guest, can make us smile and persevere. Rudyard Kipling's famous poem "If—" sets forth a moral code of conduct to guide us. Two other poems in the section, an excerpt from *A Drama of Exile* by Elizabeth Barrett Browning and "Between What I See and What I Say . . ." by Octavio Paz, address essential elements in a meaningful life—service to others, and creativity.

Poetry can help us resist the pulls and tugs of life, and stay true to what we believe. As the great poet Wallace Stevens wrote, "[Poetry] is the imagination pressing back against the pressure of reality. It seems, in the last analysis, to have something to do with our self-preservation; and that, no doubt, is why the expression of it, the sound of its words, helps us to live our lives."

from *The World is Round*

Gertrude Stein

Here I am.
When I wish a dish
I wish a dish of ham.
When I wish a little wish
I wish that I was where I am.

I Am Cherry Alive
Delmore Schwartz

"I am cherry alive," the little girl sang,
"Each morning I am something new:
I am apple, I am plum, I am just as excited
As the boys who made the Hallowe'en bang:
I am tree, I am cat, I am blossom too:
When I like, if I like, I can be someone new,
Someone very old, a witch in a zoo:
I can be someone else whenever I think who,
And I want to be everything sometimes too:
And the peach has a pit and I know that too,
And I put it in along with everything
To make the grown-ups laugh whenever I sing:
And I sing: *It is true; It is untrue;*
I know, I know, the true is untrue,
The peach has a pit,
The pit has a peach:
And both may be wrong
When I sing my song,
But I don't tell the grown-ups; because it is sad,
And I want them to laugh just like I do
Because they grew up
And forgot what they knew
And they are sure
I will forget it some day too.
They are wrong. They are wrong.
When I sang my song, I knew, I knew!
I am red, I am gold,
I am green, I am blue,
I will always be me,
I will always be new!"

My Shadow
Robert Louis Stevenson

I have a little shadow that goes in and out with me,
And what can be the use of him is more than I can see.
He is very, very like me from the heels up to the head;
And I see him jump before me, when I jump into my bed.

The funniest thing about him is the way he likes to grow—
Not at all like proper children, which is always very slow;
For he sometimes shoots up taller like an India-rubber ball,
And he sometimes gets so little that there's none of him at all.

He hasn't got a notion of how children ought to play,
And can only make a fool of me in every sort of way.
He stays so close beside me, he's a coward you can see;
I'd think shame to stick to nursie as that shadow sticks to me!

One morning, very early, before the sun was up,
I rose and found the shining dew on every buttercup;
But my lazy little shadow, like an arrant sleepyhead,
Had stayed at home behind me and was fast asleep in bed.

Crying

Galway Kinnell

Crying only a little bit
is no use. You must cry
until your pillow is soaked!
Then you can get up and laugh.
Then you can jump in the shower
and splash–splash–splash!
Then you can throw open your window
and, "Ha ha! ha ha!"
And if people say, "Hey,
what's going on up there?"
"Ha ha!" sing back, "Happiness
was hiding in the last tear!
I wept it! Ha ha!"

O dear! How disgusting is life!
Edward Lear

O dear! How disgusting is life!
To improve it O what can we do?
Most disgusting is hustle and strife,
and of all things an ill-fitting shoe—
shoe,
O bother an ill-fitting shoe!

Bad Morning
Langston Hughes

Here I sit
With my shoes mismated.
Lawdy-mercy!
I's frustrated!

Ode to Pablo's Tennis Shoes
Gary Soto

They wait under Pablo's bed,
Rain-beaten, sun-beaten,
A scuff of green
At their tips
From when he fell
In the school yard.
He fell leaping for a football
That sailed his way.
But Pablo fell and got up,
Green on his shoes,
With the football
Out of reach.

Now it's night.
Pablo is in bed listening
To his mother laughing
to the Mexican *novelas* on TV.
His shoes, twin pets
That snuggle his toes,
Are under the bed.

He should have bathed,
But he didn't.
(Dirt rolls from his palm,

Blades of grass
Tumble from his hair.)
He wants to be
Like his shoes,
A little dirty
From the road,
A little worn
From racing to the drinking fountain
A hundred times in one day.

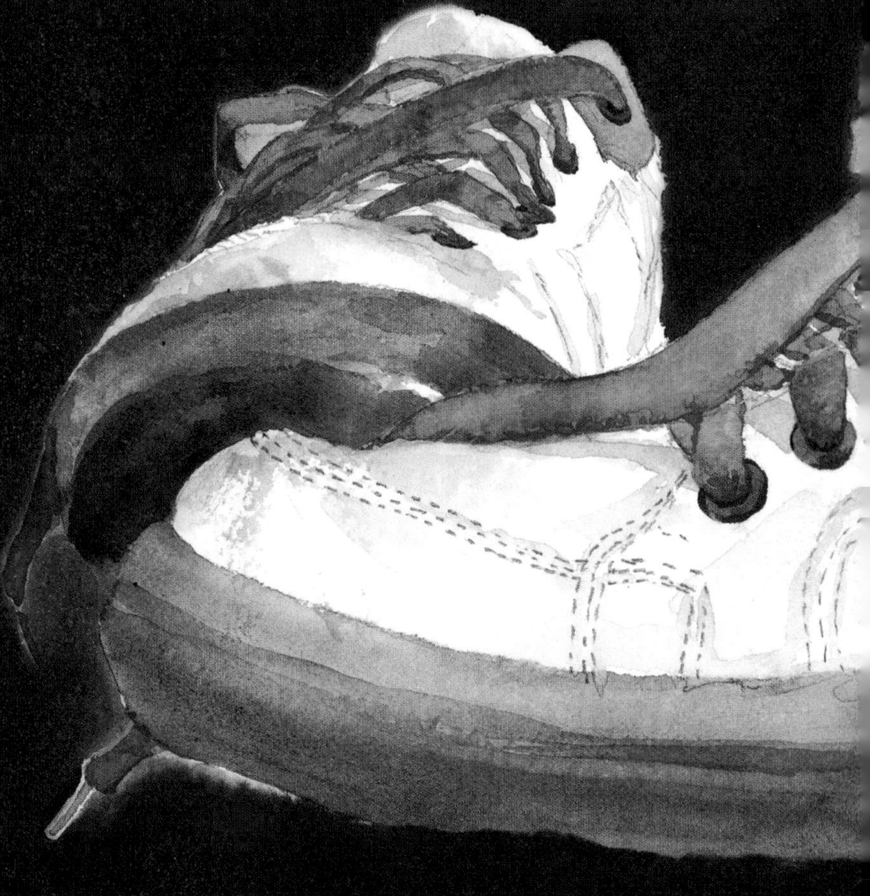

It takes water
To make him go,
And his shoes to get him
There. He loves his shoes,

Cloth like a sail,
Rubber like
A lifeboat on rough sea.

Pablo is tired,
Sinking into the mattress.
His eyes sting from
Grass and long words in books.
He needs eight hours
Of sleep
To cool his shoes,
The tongues hanging
Out, exhausted.

Don't Worry if Your Job Is Small

Anonymous

Don't worry if your job is small,
And your rewards are few.
Remember that the mighty oak,
Was once a nut like you.

It Couldn't Be Done

Edgar Albert Guest

Somebody said that it couldn't be done
    But he with a chuckle replied
That "maybe it couldn't," but he would be one
    Who wouldn't say so till he tried.
So he buckled right in with the trace of a grin
    On his face. If he worried he hid it.
He started to sing as he tackled the thing
    That couldn't be done, and he did it!

Somebody scoffed: "Oh, you'll never do that;
    At least no one ever has done it;"
But he took off his coat and he took off his hat
    And the first thing we knew he'd begun it.
With a lift of his chin and a bit of a grin,
    Without any doubting or quiddit,
He started to sing as he tackled the thing
    That couldn't be done, and he did it.
There are thousands to tell you it cannot be done,
    There are thousands to prophesy failure,
There are thousands to point out to you one by one,
    The dangers that wait to assail you.
But just buckle in with a bit of a grin,
    Just take off your coat and go to it;
Just start in to sing as you tackle the thing
    That "cannot be done," and you'll do it.

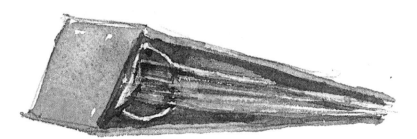

Personal
Langston Hughes

In an envelope marked:
    Personal
God addressed me a letter.
In an envelope marked:
    Personal
I have given my answer.

A man said
Stephen Crane

A man said to the universe:
"Sir, I exist!"
"However," replied the universe,
"The fact has not created in me
A sense of obligation."

Sonnet 94

William Shakespeare

They that have pow'r to hurt, and will do none,
That do not do the thing they most do show,
Who, moving others, are themselves as stone,
Unmovèd, cold, and to temptation slow—
They rightly do inherit heaven's graces,
And husband nature's riches from expense;
They are the lords and owners of their faces,
Others but stewards of their excellence.
The summer's flow'r is to the summer sweet,
Though to itself it only live and die,
But if that flow'r with base infection meet,
The basest weed outbraves his dignity:
    For sweetest things turn sourest by their deeds;
    Lilies that fester smell far worse than weeds.

Dust of Snow
Robert Frost

The way a crow
Shook down on me
The dust of snow
From a hemlock tree

Has given my heart
A change of mood
And saved some part
Of a day I had rued.

30

If—

Rudyard Kipling

If you can keep your head when all about you
      Are losing theirs and blaming it on you;
If you can trust yourself when all men doubt you,
      But make allowance for their doubting too;
If you can wait and not be tired by waiting,
      Or, being lied about, don't deal in lies,
Or, being hated, don't give way to hating,
      And yet don't look too good, nor talk too wise;

If you can dream—and not make dreams your master;
      If you can think—and not make thoughts your aim;
If you can meet with triumph and disaster
      And treat those two imposters just the same;
If you can bear to hear the truth you've spoken
      Twisted by knaves to make a trap for fools,
Or watch the things you gave your life to broken,
      And stoop and build 'em up with worn-out tools;

If you can make one heap of all your winnings
      And risk it on one turn of pitch-and-toss,
And lose, and start again at your beginnings
      And never breathe a word about your loss;
If you can force your heart and nerve and sinew
      To serve your turn long after they are gone,
And so hold on when there is nothing in you
      Except the Will which says to them: "Hold on!"

If you can talk with crowds and keep your virtue,
      Or walk with kings—nor lose the common touch;
If neither foes nor loving friends can hurt you;
      If all men count with you, but none too much;
If you can fill the unforgiving minute
      With sixty seconds' worth of distance run,
Yours is the Earth and everything that's in it,
      And—which is more—you'll be a Man, my son!

from *A Drama of Exile*

Elizabeth Barrett Browning

Thy love
Shall chant itself its own beatitudes,
After its own life-working. A child's kiss,
Set on thy sighing lips, shall make thee glad:
A poor man, served by thee, shall make thee rich;
An old man, helped by thee, shall make thee strong;
Thou shalt be served thyself by every sense
Of service which thou renderest.

Between What I See and What I Say . . .

Octavio Paz

(1)
Between what I see and what I say,
   between what I say and what I keep
     silent,
   between what I keep silent and what I
    dream,
   between what I dream and what I forget:
poetry.
     It slips
between yes and no,
         says
what I keep silent,
        keeps silent
what I say,
      dreams
what I forget.
      It is not speech:
it is an act.
      It is an act
of speech.
     Poetry
speaks and listens:
       it is real.
And as soon as I say
       it is real,
it vanishes.
      Is it then more real?

(2)
Tangible idea,
      intangible
word:
   poetry
comes and goes
       between what is
and what is not.
      It weaves
and unweaves reflections.
        Poetry
scatters eyes on a page,
scatters words on our eyes.
Eyes speak,
      words look,
looks think.
     To hear
thoughts,
     see
what we say.
     Touch
the body of an idea.
       Eyes close,
the words open.

Micah 6:8

He has showed you, O man, what is good.
And what does the LORD require of you?
To act justly and to love mercy
And to walk humbly with your God.

I Dreamed I Had to Pick a Mother Out

and other poems about family

When we begin writing poetry, we are often told to write about what we know best. For most of us, that subject is our family. Poems move effortlessly between the unique and the universal, so that while individual poets may be writing about their particular families, great poems are also about all families. There are many funny poems about brothers and sisters, their squabbles and their shared experiences, while poems about parents tend to be more poignant and emotional. Often, these are written from the parents' point of view—reflecting back on the feelings of childhood after the authors have had children of their own. However, since this book is intended for those who are still growing up (including those for whom that is a lifelong challenge), I chose poems written from the child's point of view.

One of my favorite poems to learn by heart is "Disobedience" by A. A. Milne. I always liked the fact that as the child sees it, the mother is the irresponsible member of the family—the opposite of the usual child-to-parent refrain, "When I grow up, I am going to give my children all the candy they want and let them stay up late, not be mean like you!"

Other poems are more serious. When I served as a judge for a national poetry recitation contest, one of the most frequently memorized poems was the heartbreaking "Ballad of Birmingham," which describes a mother's effort to protect her child. The dialogue and the rhyme make this poem seem simple, yet it describes a complex tragedy of both personal and national significance. The section finishes with Elizabeth Bishop's poem "Manners," which is affectionate and wise, as grandparents tend to be.

Disobedience

A. A. Milne

James James
Morrison Morrison
Weatherby George Dupree
Took great
Care of his Mother,
Though he was only three.
James James
Said to his Mother,
"Mother," he said, said he;
"You must never go down to the end of the town,
 if you don't go down with me."

James James
Morrison's Mother
Put on a golden gown,
James James
Morrison's Mother
Drove to the end of the town.
James James
Morrison's Mother
Said to herself, said she:
"I can get right down to the end of the town
 and be back in time for tea."

King John
Put up a notice,
"LOST or STOLEN or STRAYED!
JAMES JAMES
MORRISON'S MOTHER
SEEMS TO HAVE BEEN MISLAID.
LAST SEEN
WANDERING VAGUELY:
QUITE OF HER OWN ACCORD,
SHE TRIED TO GET DOWN TO THE END OF THE TOWN—
 FORTY SHILLINGS REWARD!"

James James
Morrison Morrison
(Commonly known as Jim)
Told his
Other relations
Not to go blaming *him*.
James James
Said to his Mother,
"Mother," he said, said he:
"You must *never* go down to the end of the town
    without consulting me."

James James
Morrison's mother
Hasn't been heard of since.
King John
Said he was sorry,
So did the Queen and Prince.
King John
(Somebody told me)
Said to a man he knew:
"If people go down to the end of the town, well,
    what can *anyone do*?"

(*Now then, very softly*)
J. J.
M. M.
W. G. Du P.
Took great
C/o his M*****
Though he was only 3.
J. J.
Said to his M*****
"M*****," he said, said he:
"You-must-never-go-down-to-the-end-of-the-town-
    if-you-don't-go-down-with ME!"

Brother

Mary Ann Hoberman

I had a little brother
And I brought him to my mother
And I said I want another
Little brother for a change.

But she said don't be a bother
So I took him to my father
And I said this little bother
Of a brother's very strange.

But he said one little brother
Is exactly like another
And every little brother
Misbehaves a bit, he said.

So I took the little bother
From my mother and my father
And I put the little bother
Of a brother back to bed.

Brother and Sister

Lewis Carroll

"Sister, sister go to bed!
Go and rest your weary head."
Thus the prudent brother said.

"Do you want a battered hide,
Or scratches to your face applied?"
Thus his sister calm replied.

"Sister, do not raise my wrath,
I'd make you into mutton broth
As easily as kill a moth!"

The sister raised her beaming eye
And looked on him indignantly
And sternly answered, "Only try!"

Off to the cook he quickly ran.
"Dear Cook, please lend a frying-pan
To me as quickly as you can."

"And wherefore should I lend it to you?"

"The reason, Cook, is plain to view.
I wish to make an Irish stew."

"What meat is in that stew to go?"

"My sister'll be the contents!"
   "Oh!"

"You'll lend the pan to me, Cook?"
   "No!"

Moral: Never stew your sister.

If Little Red Riding Hood . . .

Jeff Moss

If Little Red Riding Hood had a dad,
Perhaps things wouldn't have turned out so bad.
He'd have taught her the useful things a dad can teach you,
Like the difference between Grandma and a wolf who'll eat you.
He'd have brought her two photographs to let her see
How completely different two things can be.
He'd show her a picture of his kindly old mother,
And say, "Grandma's one thing. A wolf is another.
Grandma wants to hug you and give you a kiss.
A wolf wants to eat you, and he looks like this—
Big teeth, big ears, and plenty of fur.
Now look at your grandma, does a wolf look like her?
Your report card was great, I know you're smart,
So it shouldn't be hard to tell them apart.
Now, please get to Grandma's before it gets dark,
Don't go through the forest, stay out of the park,
Don't stop to talk to any wolves you meet,
And don't wear that red thing when you walk down the street."

Andre

Gwendolyn Brooks

I had a dream last night. I dreamed
I had to pick a Mother out.
I had to choose a Father too.
At first, I wondered what to do,
There were so many there, it seemed,
Short and tall and thin and stout.

But just before I sprang awake,
I knew what parents I had to take.

And this surprised me and made me glad:
They were the ones I always had!

The Parent
Ogden Nash

Children aren't happy with nothing to ignore,

And that's what parents were created for.

Bilingual/*Bilingüe*
Rhina P. Espaillat

My father liked them separate, one there,
one here (*allá y aquí*), as if aware

that words might cut in two his daughter's heart
(*el corazón*) and lock the alien part

to what he was—his memory, his name
(*su nombre*)—with a key he could not claim.

"English outside this door, Spanish inside,"
he said, "*y basta.*" But who can divide

the world, the word (*mundo y palabra*) from
any child? I knew how to be dumb

and stubborn (*testaruda*); late, in bed,
I hoarded secret syllables I read

until my tongue (*mi lengua*) learned to run
where his stumbled. And still the heart was one.

I like to think he knew that, even when,
proud (*orgulloso*) of his daughter's pen,

he stood outside *mis versos*, half in fear
of words he loved but wanted not to hear.

Ballad of Birmingham

(On the bombing of a church in Birmingham, Alabama, 1963)
Dudley Randall

"Mother dear, may I go downtown
Instead of out to play,
And march the streets of Birmingham
In a Freedom March today?"

"No, baby, no, you may not go,
For the dogs are fierce and wild,
And clubs and hoses, guns and jails
Aren't good for a little child."

"But, mother, I won't be alone.
Other children will go with me,
And march the streets of Birmingham
To make our country free."

"No, baby, no, you may not go,
For I fear those guns will fire.
But you may go to church instead
And sing in the children's choir."

She has combed and brushed her night-dark hair,
And bathed rose petal sweet,
And drawn white gloves on her small brown hands,
And white shoes on her feet.

The mother smiled to know her child
Was in the sacred place,
But that smile was the last smile
To come upon her face.

For when she heard the explosion,
Her eyes grew wet and wild.
She raced through the streets of Birmingham
Calling for her child.

Manners

For a Child of 1918
Elizabeth Bishop

My grandfather said to me
as we sat on the wagon seat,
"Be sure to remember to always
speak to everyone you meet."

We met a stranger on foot.
My grandfather's whip tapped his hat.
"Good day, sir. Good day. A fine day."
And I said it and bowed where I sat.

Then we overtook a boy we knew
with his big pet crow on his shoulder.
"Always offer everyone a ride;
don't forget that when you get older,"

my grandfather said. So Willy
climbed up with us, but the crow
gave a "Caw!" and flew off. I was worried.
How would he know where to go?

But he flew a little way at a time
from fence post to fence post, ahead;
and when Willy whistled he answered.
"A fine bird," my grandfather said,

"and he's well brought up. See, he answers
nicely when he's spoken to.
Man or beast, that's good manners.
Be sure that you both always do."

When automobiles went by,
the dust hid the people's faces,
but we shouted "Good day! Good day!
Fine day!" at the top of our voices.

When we came to Hustler Hill,
he said that the mare was tired,
so we all got down and walked,
as our good manners required.

I'm Expecting You!

and other poems about friendship and love

Relationships are at the heart of poetry. Love, friendship, sacrifice, anger, jealousy, longing, and joy are all easy to find in the simplest poems as well as the most complex. Emily Dickinson's whimsical poem "Bee! I'm expecting you!" is about looking forward to seeing a friend after a long separation and all the things you are going to do together. In "Evil," Langston Hughes describes being so cranky that the only way to make yourself feel better is to make someone else feel worse. Countee Cullen explores deeper aspects of friendship in "Tableau," where he captures the profound impact of an interracial friendship at the dawn of the civil rights era. Love and longing are palpable for the poet in Paul Laurence Dunbar's "Invitation to Love," in which the poet waits for his beloved; whereas in Henry van Dyke's poem "For Katrina's Sun-Dial," time ceases to exist.

One of my favorite poems in the book is "Voices Rising" by the young poets of DreamYard Prep who worked with me on this book. The poem transforms anger into hope, words into action, and holds the reader accountable. In our networked, connected, and collaborative world some of the most interesting poetry is composed not by one poet but by groups of poets working, writing, and performing together, showing us how poetry reflects the society around it.

Bee! I'm expecting you!

Emily Dickinson

Bee! I'm expecting you!
Was saying Yesterday
To Somebody you know
That you were due—

The Frogs got Home last Week—
Are settled, and at work—
Birds, mostly back—
The Clover warm and thick—

You'll get my Letter by
The seventeenth; Reply
Or better, be with me—
Yours, Fly.

Vade Mecum

Billy Collins

I want the scissors to be sharp
and the table to be perfectly level
when you cut me out of my life
and paste me in that book you always carry.

Evil

Langston Hughes

Looks like what drives me crazy
Don't have no effect on you—
But I'm gonna keep on at it
Till it drives you crazy, too.

A Poison Tree
William Blake

I was angry with my friend:
I told my wrath, my wrath did end.
I was angry with my foe:
I told it not, my wrath did grow;

And I water'd it in fears,
Night & morning with my tears;
And I sunned it with my smiles,
And with soft deceitful wiles.

And it grew both day and night,
Till it bore an apple bright,
And my foe beheld it shine,
And he knew that it was mine,

And into my garden stole,
When the night had veil'd the pole;
In the morning glad I see
My foe outstretch'd beneath the tree.

Tableau
Countee Cullen

For Donald Duff

Locked arm in arm they cross the way,
The black boy and the white,
The golden splendor of the day,
The sable pride of night.

From lowered blinds the dark folk stare,
And here the fair folk talk,
Indignant that these two should dare
In unison to walk.

Oblivious to look and word
They pass, and see no wonder
That lightning brilliant as a sword
Should blaze the path of thunder.

57

Voices Rising

DreamYard Prep Slam Team
Jesica Blandon, Destiny Campbell, Miosoty Castillo,
Denisse Cotto, and Chris Taylor
arranged by Renée Watson

They say,
"Life and Death are in the power of the tongue."
And if this is so,
Our words are oxygen.

Listen.

Let your ears breathe deeply. Take in our *palabras*.
What we're about to say will save you. Listen.

Do you hear that sound?
That is the sound of a million voices rising.

Our voices rise
For Oscar Grant.
For the Black Friday massacre.
For my *abuelo y abuela*.
For little girls and boys.
For my mother. My uncle.
For the aborted and abandoned.

We speak for the ones who have been silenced by fear.
By choice. By ignorance.
Shame. Death.
Listen.

Oscar Grant,
My voice rises for the fight you never put up.
Tell that burning steel, "You don't belong here beneath my flesh.
Leave. Go. Don't come back.
My skin is not a crime."

Is it just that some things can't be changed?
How many times can the red blood of black and brown men
be spilled on gray cement and be called an accident?

Listen.

My voice rises for the Black Friday massacre.
A modern day Guérnica.

Our voices rise for the tragedies that don't make the 5 o'clock news.
My voice rises for the children in third world countries.
No education. Little food.
Their struggles taken out of the newspaper
and replaced by articles reporting A-Rod's scandal with steroids.
By celebrity weight gains and break-ups.

Listen.
I know you have problems of your own,
But will you listen?

Will you be different from the thousands of others
who cast us aside because we are young?

Listen.

My voice rises for the girls trapped in four walls with men who think they're sexy.
My voice rises for the times when little girls aren't given the chance to speak for
themselves.

(continued)

Little girls, my voice rises over your screams
of broken innocence.
Like glass bits in the wind,
your screams pierce my lungs.

And I know these words aren't easy on the ears.
Medicine doesn't always taste good going down,
But I promise you—
I-PROMISE-YOU
If you hear this, you will get better.

You will get better once you listen to the sound of hope,
of change.
It's manifestation came in a man and a mantra, "Yes we can."
But hope was birthed through
Me and Me
and Us.
Poets have been pregnant with change for centuries.
We push out revolutions in prose and poems.
Planted word-seeds sowed a long time ago
are just now coming into harvest.

So listen.

This is for the future.
For tomorrow.
Our very breath is the ink that will write future history books.
Our vignettes collect voices of today so tomorrow can survive the future.

Listen.
Can you spare me your eardrum?
Keep your change.
I don't want your money.
Just your heart.

Just want your ears.
Just want you to listen.

Listen and speak.
Speak your story.
Tell someone else's.

And if you can't find enough words to plant,
Sow these.
Nurture these words
and bring them back to me in a million quotes
so I know you were listening.

Bring them back to me fully bloomed
and my voice will rise to Langston and tell him
those dreams deferred are paid in full.

Listen.
Can you hear us now?
Our voices are rising.

Listen.
Put away the distractions:
The iPods, the games.
The reality tv shows,
text messaging and cell phones.

Listen.

Can you hear us now?
Our voices are rising.

Can you hear us now El Barrio?
Can you hear us now New York City?

Or has Sprint dropped this poem?

61

He Wishes for the Cloths of Heaven
William Butler Yeats

Had I the heavens' embroidered cloths,
Enwrought with golden and silver light,
The blue and the dim and the dark cloths
Of night and light and the half light,
I would spread the cloths under your feet:
But I, being poor, have only my dreams;
I have spread my dreams under your feet;
Tread softly because you tread on my dreams.

The Dream Keeper

Langston Hughes

Bring me all of your dreams
You dreamers,
Bring me all of your
Heart melodies
That I may wrap them
In a blue cloud-cloth
Away from the too-rough fingers
Of the world.

A Blessing

James Wright

Just off the highway to Rochester, Minnesota,
Twilight bounds softly forth on the grass.
And the eyes of those two Indian ponies
Darken with kindness.
They have come gladly out of the willows
To welcome my friend and me.
We step over the barbed wire into the pasture
Where they have been grazing all day, alone.
They ripple tensely, they can hardly contain their happiness
That we have come.
They bow shyly as wet swans. They love each other.
There is no loneliness like theirs.
At home once more,
They begin munching the young tufts of spring in the darkness.
I would like to hold the slenderer one in my arms,
For she has walked over to me
And nuzzled my left hand.
She is black and white,
Her mane falls wild on her forehead,
And the light breeze moves me to caress her long ear
That is delicate as the skin over a girl's wrist.
Suddenly I realize
That if I stepped out of my body I would break
Into blossom.

Invitation to Love
Paul Laurence Dunbar

Come when the nights are bright with stars
Or come when the moon is mellow;
Come when the sun his golden bars
Drops on the hay-field yellow.
Come in the twilight soft and gray,
Come in the night or come in the day,
Come, O love, whene'er you may,
And you are welcome, welcome.

You are sweet, O Love, dear Love,
You are soft as the nesting dove.
Come to my heart and bring it to rest
As the bird flies home to its welcome nest.

Come when my heart is full of grief
Or when my heart is merry;
Come with the falling of the leaf
Or with the redd'ning cherry.
Come when the year's first blossom blows,
Come when the summer gleams and glows,
Come with the winter's drifting snows,
And you are welcome, welcome.

1 Corinthians 13:1-8
Saint Paul

Though I speak with the tongues of men and of angels, but have not love, I have become sounding brass or clanging cymbal. And though I have the gift of prophecy, and understand all mysteries and all knowledge, and though I have all faith, so that I could remove mountains, but have not love, I am nothing. And though I bestow all my goods to feed the poor, and though I give my body to be burned, but have not love, it profits me nothing.

Love suffers long and is kind; love does not envy; love does not parade itself, is not puffed up; does not behave rudely, does not seek its own, is not provoked, thinks no evil; does not rejoice in iniquity, but rejoices in the truth; bears all things, believes all things, hopes all things, endures all things.

Love never fails.

For Katrina's Sun-Dial

Henry van Dyke

Hours fly,
  Flowers die:
New days,
New ways:
Pass by!
Love stays.

Time is
Too Slow for those who Wait,
Too Swift for those who Fear,
Too Long for those who Grieve,
Too Short for those who Rejoice,
  But for those who Love,
    Time is not.

Liberty
Janet S. Wong

I pledge acceptance
of the views,
so different,
that make us America

To listen, to look,
to think, and to learn

One people
sharing the earth
responsible
for liberty
and justice
for all.

I Met a Little Elf-Man, Once
and other poems about fairies, ogres, and witches

In today's world of standardized images, all elves wear little green jackets and make toys in Santa's Workshop, and all fairies look like Tinker Bell. But it wasn't always so.

In times past, when people lived closer to nature, the powerful forces of the natural world often took human form. The gods and goddesses of ancient Greek mythology assumed both human and natural forms to interfere with individual destiny. The leprechauns of Ireland added a similar shot of unpredictability and chaos into human society, often playing tricks on unsuspecting souls. Today, we turn to science, technology, and logic to combat crime or explain accidents. But in premodern societies, fairies, gnomes, trolls, and ogres were often blamed for terrible things, like luring children away from their homes, kidnapping them for years at a time, and even poisoning them.

In contemporary poems, elves and fairies may have become increasingly diminutive, but they remain as popular as ever. Rose Fyleman and Robert Graves capture our fascination in their poems "The Fairies" and "I'd Love to Be a Fairy's Child." These poems use the power of imagination to create another world—a power that lies within us all.

The Little Elf
John Kendrick Bangs

I met a little Elf-man, once,
    Down where the lilies blow.
I asked him why he was so small
    And why he didn't grow.

He slightly frowned, and with his eye
    He looked me through and through.
"I'm quite as big for me," said he,
    "As you are big for you."

The Fairies
Rose Fyleman

There are fairies at the bottom of our garden!
  It's not so very, very far away;
You pass the gardener's shed and you just keep straight ahead,
  I do so hope they've really come to stay.
There's a little wood, with moss in it and beetles,
  And a little stream that quietly runs through;
You wouldn't think they'd dare to come merry-making there.
    Well, they do.

There are fairies at the bottom of our garden!
  They often have a dance on summer nights;
The butterflies and bees make a lovely little breeze,
  And the rabbits stand about and hold the lights.
Did you know that they could sit upon the moonbeams
  And pick a little star to make a fan,
And dance away up there in the middle of the air?
    Well, they can.

There are fairies at the bottom of our garden!
  You cannot think how beautiful they are;
They stand up and sing when the Fairy Queen and King
  Come gently floating down upon their car.
The King is very proud and very handsome;
  The Queen—now can you guess who that could be
(She's a little girl all day, but at night she steals away)?
    Well—it's me!

I'd Love to Be a Fairy's Child

Robert Graves

Children born of fairy stock
Never need for shirt or frock,
Never want for food or fire,
Always get their heart's desire:
Jingle pockets full of gold,
Marry when they're seven years old.
Every fairy child may keep
Two strong ponies and ten sheep;
All have houses, each his own,
Built of brick or granite stone;
They live on cherries, they run wild—
I'd love to be a Fairy's child.

Some One
Walter de la Mare

Some one came knocking
    At my wee, small door;
Some one came knocking,
    I'm sure—sure—sure;
I listened, I opened,
    I looked to left and right,
But nought there was a-stirring
    In the still dark night;
Only the busy beetle
    Tap-tapping in the wall,
Only from the forest
    The screech-owl's call,
Only the cricket whistling
    While the dewdrops fall,
So I know not who came knocking,
    At all, at all, at all.

Under the Bed
Penny Trzynka

There's a terrible green monster
Who lives beneath my bed.
I hear his long white teeth click.
He's waiting to be fed.
I shiver underneath my sheets
And squeeze my eyes up tight.
Maybe if I lie real still
He won't eat me up tonight . . .
He taps me on the shoulder.
I don't know what to do.
He looks at me and says, "I'm scared!
Can I get in with you?"

What's That?

Florence Parry Heide

What's that?
Who's there?
There's a great huge horrible *horrible*
creeping up the stair!
A huge big terrible *terrible*
with creepy crawly hair!
There's a ghastly grisly *ghastly*
with seven slimy eyes!
And flabby grabby tentacles
of a gigantic size!
He's crept into my room now,
he's leaning over me.
I wonder if he's thinking
how delicious I will be.

from *The Masque of Queens*
Ben Jonson

*These eleven witches beginning to dance (which is a usual
ceremony at their convents or meetings, where sometimes
also they are vizarded and masked), on the sudden one of
them missed their chief, and interrupted the rest with this
speech:*

The owl is abroad, the bat and the toad,
    And so is the cat-a-mountain;
The ant and the mole both sit in a hole,
    And frog peeps out of the fountain;
The dogs they do bay and the timbrels play,
    The spindle is now a-turning;
The moon it is red, and the stars are fled,
    But all the sky is a-burning:
The ditch is made, and our nails the spade,
With pictures full, of wax and wool,
Their livers I stick with needles quick,
There lacks but the blood to make up the flood.
    Quickly, Dame, then, bring your part in,
    Spur, spur upon little Martin,
    Merrily, merrily make him sail,
    A worm in his mouth and a thorn in his tail,
    Fire above and fire below,
    With a whip in your hand to make him go.
    Oh, now she's come!
    Let all be dumb.

*At this the Dame entered to them, naked-armed, barefooted,
her frock tucked, her hair knotted and folded with vipers;
in her hand a torch made of a dead man's arm, lighted,
girded with a snake.*

Song of the Ogres

W. H. Auden

Little fellow, you're amusing,
Stop before you end up losing
    Your shirt:
Run along to Mother, Gus,
Those who interfere with us
    Get hurt.

Honest Virtue, old wives prattle,
Always wins the final battle,
    Dear, Dear!
Life's exactly what it looks,
Love may triumph in the books,
    Not here.

We're not joking, we assure you:
Those who rode this way before you
    Died hard.
What? Still spoiling for a fight?
Well, you asked for it all right:
    On guard!

Always hopeful, aren't you? Don't be.
Night is falling and it won't be
    Long now:
You will never see the dawn,
You will wish you'd not been born,
    And how!

The Splendour Falls on Castle Walls

Alfred, Lord Tennyson

The splendour falls on castle walls
    And snowy summits old in story:
The long light shakes across the lakes,
    And the wild cataract leaps in glory.
Blow, bugle, blow, set the wild echoes flying,
Blow, bugle; answer, echoes, dying, dying, dying.

O hark, O hear! how thin and clear,
    And thinner, clearer, farther going!
O sweet and far from cliff and scar
    The horns of Elfland faintly blowing!
Blow, let us hear the purple glens replying:
Blow, bugle; answer, echoes, dying, dying, dying.

O love, they die in yon rich sky,
    They faint on hill or field or river:
Our echoes roll from soul to soul,
    And grow for ever and for ever.
Blow, bugle, blow, set the wild echoes flying,
And answer, echoes, answer, dying, dying, dying.

Where Can a Man Buy a Cap for His Knee?

and other nonsensical poems

The first poems we learn by heart are usually limericks like Edward Lear's "There was an old Person whose habits" or rhyming poems like Tweedledum and Tweedledee's argument from Lewis Carroll's *Through the Looking-Glass*. These poems encourage younger children to learn vocabulary and explore language. There is something about the way the sounds and the words, the rhyme and the meter go together that makes these poems easy to remember. As we grow older, we learn the words and melodies to songs. Although we don't always think of poems as songs, in fact, poetry used to be sung because melody made the stories easier to remember and recite, as well as to understand.

The poems in this section help make us more aware of words and how we use them—a serious business that lies underneath silly questions like "Where can a man buy a cap for his knee?" Richard Wilbur, a former United States poet laureate, plays similar tricks in his poem "Some Words Inside of Words." "The Toys Talk of the World" by Katharine Pyle explores nighttime in the nursery when toys come to life. Children who say that their toys can talk are usually told that they are imagining things. But they keep saying it, so how do we really know?

Foolish Questions

American Folk Rhyme
adapted by William Cole

Where can a man buy a cap for his knee?
Or a key for the lock of his hair?
And can his eyes be called a school?
I would think—there are pupils there!
What jewels are found in the crown of his head,
And who walks on the bridge of his nose?
Can he use, in building the roof of his mouth,
The nails on the ends of his toes?
Can the crook of his elbow be sent to jail—
If it can, well, then, what did it do?
And how does he sharpen his shoulder blades?
I'll be hanged if I know—do you?
Can he sit in the shade of the palm of his hand,
And beat time with the drum in his ear?
Can the calf of his leg eat the corn on his toe?—

There's somethin' pretty strange around here!

Way Down South
Anonymous

Way down South where bananas grow,
A grasshopper stepped on an elephant's toe.
The elephant said, with tears in his eyes,
"Pick on somebody your own size."

There was an old man in a garden
Edward Lear

There was an old man in a garden,
Who always begged every-one's pardon;
When they asked him, "What for?"—He replied "You're a bore!
And I trust you'll go out of my garden."

There was an old Person whose habits
Edward Lear

There was an old Person whose habits,
Induced him to feed upon Rabbits;
When he'd eaten eighteen, he turned perfectly green,
Upon which he relinquished those habits.

Baby Ate a Microchip

Neal Levin

Baby ate a microchip,
Then grabbed a bottle, took a sip.
He swallowed it and made a beep,
And now he's thinking pretty deep.

He's downloading his ABCs
And calculating 1-2-3s.
He's memorizing useless facts
While doing Daddy's income tax.

He's processing, and now he thrives
On feeding his internal drives.
He's throwing fits, and now he fights
With ruthless bits and toothless bytes.

He must be feeling very smug.
But hold on, Baby caught a bug.
Attempting to reboot in haste,
He accidentally got erased!

from *Through the Looking-Glass*
Lewis Carroll

Tweedledum and Tweedledee
    Agreed to have a battle;
For Tweedledum said Tweedledee
    Had spoiled his nice new rattle.

Just then flew down a monstrous crow,
    As black as a tar-barrel;
Which frightened both the heroes so,
    They quite forgot their quarrel.

Herbert Glerbett
Jack Prelutsky

Herbert Glerbett, rather round
swallowed sherbet by the pound.
fifty pounds of lemon sherbet
went inside of Herbert Glerbett.

With that glop inside his lap
Herbert Glerbett took a nap,
and as he slept, the boy dissolved,
and from the mess a thing evolved—

a thing that is a ghastly green,
a thing the world had never seen,
a puddle thing, a gooey pile
of something strange that does not smile.

Now if you're wise, and if you're sly
you'll swiftly pass this creature by,
it is no longer Herbert Glerbett,
Whatever it is, do not disturb it.

The Toys Talk of the World
Katharine Pyle

"I should like," said the vase from the china-store,
"To have seen the world a little more.

"When they carried me here I was wrapped up tight,
But they say it is really a lovely sight."

"Yes," said a little plaster bird,
"That is exactly what *I* have heard;

"There are thousands of trees, and oh, what a sight
It must be when the candles are all alight."

The fat top rolled on his other side:
"It is not in the least like that," he cried.

"Except myself and the kite and ball,
None of you know of the world at all.

"There are houses, and pavements hard and red,
And everything spins around," he said;

"Sometimes it goes slowly, and sometimes fast,
And often it stops with a bump at last."

The wooden donkey nodded his head:
"I had heard the world was like that," he said.

The kite and the ball exchanged a smile,
But they did not speak; it was not worth while.

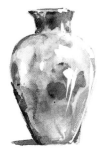

All About Boys and Girls
John Ciardi

I know all about boys, I do,
And I know all about little girls, too.
I know what they eat. I know what they drink.
I know what they like. I know what they think.

And so I'm writing this to say,
Don't let the children out to play.
It makes them sad. They'd rather go
To school or to the dentist. Oh,

I know they're bashful about saying
How much it hurts to be out playing
When they could go to school and spell
And mind their manners. They won't tell

How tired they are of games and toys.
But I know girls, and I know boys.
They like to sweep floors, chop the wood,
And practice being very good.

They'd rather sit and study hard
Than waste the whole day in the yard.
What good is fun and making noise?
That's not for girls! That's not for boys!

Some Words Inside of Words

For Children and Others

Richard Wilbur

If you've washed your clothes, and they're still wringing wet,
Don't put them on! You mustn't wear them yet!
No, hang them on the line, and you'll learn why
It's best when *laundry* ends by being *dry*.

Someone in every family photograph
Has moved his head, or blinked, or had to laugh.
Sister may be a blur, Great-Aunt a smear,
And *Uncle*, too, is frequently *unclear*.

Funambulists are acrobats who dare
To walk on tightropes high up in the air,
While we look up at them, enthralled and thrilled,
And hope that they won't tumble and be killed,
In what they do, I'm sure there's lots of *fun*,
So long as they remember how it's done.

In a flower bed, the ranks of bright-faced plants
Look like a choir that's singing hymns and chants
And psalms and Christmas carols. That's how come
We find an *anthem* in *chrysanthemum*.

When faced with anything I loathe and fear,
I try to grit my teeth and persevere,
But there's one gritty thing I just can't stand—
A *sandwich* that is halfway full of *sand*.

There seems to be a *camel* in *Camelot*.
Does it belong there? Absolutely not.
Wouldn't Sir Galahad have been a chump
To ride some desert animal with a hump?
King Arthur's knights went forth to do their deeds
Mounted exclusively on trusty steeds.

The Tale of Custard the Dragon
Ogden Nash

Belinda lived in a little white house,
With a little black kitten and a little gray mouse,
And a little yellow dog and a little red wagon,
And a realio, trulio, little pet dragon.

Now the name of the little black kitten was Ink,
And the little gray mouse, she called her Blink,
And the little yellow dog was sharp as Mustard,
But the dragon was a coward, and she called him Custard.

Custard the dragon had big sharp teeth,
And spikes on top of him and scales underneath,
Mouth like a fireplace, chimney for a nose,
And realio, trulio daggers on his toes.

Belinda was as brave as a barrel-full of bears,
And Ink and Blink chased lions down the stairs,
Mustard was as brave as a tiger in a rage,
But Custard cried for a nice safe cage.

Belinda tickled him, she tickled him unmerciful,
Ink, Blink, and Mustard, they rudely called him Percival,
They all sat laughing in the little red wagon
At the realio, trulio, cowardly dragon.

Belinda giggled till she shook the house,
And Blink said *Weeek!*, which is giggling
    for a mouse,
Ink and Mustard rudely asked his age,
When Custard cried for a nice safe cage.

Suddenly, suddenly they heard a nasty sound
And Mustard growled, and they all looked around.
Meowch! cried Ink, and Ooh! cried Belinda,
For there was a pirate, climbing in the winda.

(continued)

Pistol in his left hand, pistol in his right,
And he held in his teeth a cutlass bright;
His beard was black, one leg was wood.
It was clear that the pirate meant no good.

Belinda paled, and she cried Help! Help!
But Mustard fled with a terrified yelp,
Ink trickled down to the bottom of the household,
And little mouse Blink strategically mouseholed.

But up jumped Custard, snorting like an engine,
Clashed his tail like irons in a dungeon,
With a clatter and a clank and a jangling squirm
He went at the pirate like a robin at a worm.

The pirate gaped at Belinda's dragon,
And gulped some grog from his pocket flagon,
He fired two bullets, but they didn't hit,
And Custard gobbled him, every bit.

Belinda embraced him, Mustard licked him;
No one mourned for his pirate victim.
Ink and Blink in glee did gyrate
Around the dragon that ate the pyrate.

Belinda still lives in her little white house,
With her little black kitten and her little gray mouse,
And her little yellow dog and her little red wagon,
And her realio, trulio, little pet dragon.

Belinda is as brave as a barrel full of bears,
And Ink and Blink chase lions down the stairs,
Mustard is as brave as a tiger in a rage,
But Custard keeps crying for a nice safe cage.

It Is the Duty of the Student

and other poems about school

Kids spend much of their lives in school but, not surprisingly, there aren't all that many poems about enjoyable classroom activities. Instead, a strain of silent rebellion runs through the genre.

The villains are usually Teachers, with Moms as occasional substitutes. The subject of Homework inspires venomous perorations—most likely because Grown-Ups, a species not known for intelligence, came up with the idea. Although I am not sure if readers will want to memorize poems about school, I have attended numerous talent shows where Shel Silverstein's immortal poem "Sick" was always a crowd-pleaser, so I decided the section was worth including.

In the course of research, I came across a poem I hadn't read before—"Gnome" by Samuel Beckett. The poem seems to revolve around itself, causing us to think about familiar things in new and different ways. It's only four lines long, but it raises questions about school, about life, about learning through experience, and about how to use what we learn. Beckett grew up in Ireland and worked for William Butler Yeats before moving to Paris, where he began writing in French. He then translated his own work back into English. Perhaps that is why he can condense meaning into so few words, and still leave room for thought.

Duty of the Student
Edward Anthony

It is the duty of the student
Without exception to be prudent.
If smarter than his teacher, tact
Demands that he conceal the fact.

Gnome
Samuel Beckett

Spend the years of learning squandering
Courage for the years of wandering
Through a world politely turning
From the loutishness of learning.

Sick

Shel Silverstein

"I cannot go to school today,"
Said little Peggy Ann McKay.
"I have the measles and the mumps,
A gash, a rash and purple bumps.
My mouth is wet, my throat is dry,
I'm going blind in my right eye.
My tonsils are as big as rocks,
I've counted sixteen chicken pox
And there's one more—that's seventeen,
And don't you think my face looks green?
My leg is cut, my eyes are blue—
It might be instamatic flu.
I cough and sneeze and gasp and choke,
I'm sure that my left leg is broke—
My hip hurts when I move my chin,
My belly button's caving in,
My back is wrenched, my ankle's sprained,
My 'pendix pains each time it rains.
My nose is cold, my toes are numb,
I have a sliver in my thumb.
My neck is stiff, my voice is weak,
I hardly whisper when I speak.
My tongue is filling up my mouth,
I think my hair is falling out.
My elbow's bent, my spine ain't straight,
My temperature is one-o-eight.
My brain is shrunk, I cannot hear,
There is a hole inside my ear.
I have a hangnail, and my heart is—what?
What's that? What's that you say?
You say today is . . . Saturday?
G'bye, I'm going out to play!"

Homework

Jane Yolen

What is it about homework
That makes me want to write
My Great Aunt Myrt to thank her for
The sweater that's too tight?

What is it about homework
That makes me pick up socks
That stink from days and days of wear,
Then clean the litter box?

What is it about homework
That makes me volunteer
To take the garbage out before
The bugs and flies appear?

What is it about homework
That makes me wash my hair
And take an hour combing out
The snags and tangles there?

What is it about homework?
You know, I wish I knew,
'Cause nights when I've got homework
I've got much too much to do!

Lucky Trade
Matthew M. Fredericks

I told my mom I'd go to work
if she would to go school.
She thought that trading places once
just might be kind of cool.

So she agreed; I packed her lunch
and made her wash her face.
Then Mother said, "I wonder why
you want to take my place?"

"I wonder what you do at work.
I'd like to meet your boss.
Now hurry up and brush your teeth
and don't forget to floss.

"There's just one other thing, Mom,
that I forgot to mention:
I'll pick you up at four o'clock—
today you have detention."

Bubble Troubles

Janet S. Wong

I'm in trouble with my bubbles.
I put a double answer—
A and D—
down for #10
accidentally.
Could've been an easy fix.
It should've been an easy fix,
if I'd caught it right away,
but I'm on #36.
I'm erasing the wrong answers,
bubbling in one line below,
and I've got an awful lot of painful
bubbling left to go.
And a queasy feeling's filling up
my mouth and throat and chest.
What would happen if I happened
to vomit on the test?

How to Paint a Donkey

Naomi Shihab Nye

She said the head was too large,
the hooves too small.

I could clean my paintbrush
but I couldn't get rid of that voice.

While they watched,
I crumpled him,

let his blue body
stain my hand.

I cried when he hit the can.
She smiled. I could try again.

Maybe this is what I unfold in the dark,
deciding, for the rest of my life,
that donkey was just the right size.

The Lesson

Billy Collins

In the morning when I found History
snoring heavily on the couch,
I took down his overcoat from the rack
and placed its weight over my shoulder blades.

It would protect me on the cold walk
into the village for milk and the paper
and I figured he would not mind,
not after our long conversation the night before.

How unexpected his blustering anger
when I returned covered with icicles,
the way he rummaged through the huge pockets
making sure no major battle or English queen
had fallen out and become lost in the deep snow.

Theme for English B

Langston Hughes

The instructor said,

> Go home and write
> a page tonight.
> And let that page come out of you—
> Then, it will be true.

I wonder if it's that simple?
I am twenty-two, colored, born in Winston-Salem.
I went to school there, then Durham, then here
to this college on the hill above Harlem.
I am the only colored student in my class.
The steps from the hill lead down into Harlem
through a park, then I cross St. Nicholas,
Eighth Avenue, Seventh, and I come to the Y,
the Harlem Branch Y, where I take the elevator
up to my room, sit down, and write this page:

It's not easy to know what is true for you or me
at twenty-two, my age. But I guess I'm what
I feel and see and hear, Harlem, I hear you:
hear you, hear me—we two—you, me, talk on this page.
(I hear New York too.) Me—who?
Well, I like to eat, sleep, drink, and be in love.
I like to work, read, learn, and understand life.
I like a pipe for a Christmas present,
or records—Bessie, bop, or Bach.

I guess being colored doesn't make me NOT like
the same things other folks like who are other races.
So will my page be colored that I write?
Being me, it will not be white.
But it will be
a part of you, instructor.
You are white—
yet a part of me, as I am a part of you.
That's American.
Sometimes perhaps you don't want to be a part of me.
Nor do I often want to be a part of you.
But we are, that's true!
As I learn from you,
I guess you learn from me—
Although you're older—and white—
and somewhat more free.

This is my page for English B.

if everything happens that can't be done
E. E. Cummings

if everything happens that can't be done
(and anything's righter
than books
could plan)
the stupidest teacher will almost guess
(with a run
skip
around we go yes)
there's nothing as something as one

one hasn't a why or because or although
(and buds know better
than books
don't grow)
one's anything old being everything new
(with a what
which
around we come who)
one's everyanything so

so world is a leaf so tree is a bough
(and birds sing sweeter
than books
tell how)
so here is away and so your is a my
(with a down
up
around again fly)
forever was never till now

now i love you and you love me
(and books are shuter
than books
can be)
and deep in the high that does nothing but fall
(with a shout
each
around we go all)
there's somebody calling who's we

we're anything brighter than even the sun
(we're everything greater
than books
might mean)
we're everyanything more than believe
(with a spin
leap
alive we're alive)
we're wonderful one times one

We Dance Round in a Ring and Suppose

and other poems about sports and games

Too often poetry is reserved for "serious" pursuits, but poets can have fun too. A former New York City deputy chancellor of education also coached his son's Little League team, and credits poetry as much as practice for the team's successful seasons. At the end of every game, he would bring a poem onto the field and hand out a copy to each player for the team to discuss as a group. He could tell that the kids enjoyed sharing their ideas and reciting the poems together, because, unlike with other handouts, no one ever left a poem behind on the grass. The team favorite was "Casey at the Bat." With familiar imagery, easy rhyme, and epic drama, Casey's tragedy is perhaps the most memorized American poem of all time. Less well known and also included here is "Casey's Revenge," an attempt to make things right. The final poem in this section, which would be a good choice to memorize for Father's Day, is "May" by John Updike. It takes the poetry-sports connection to its logical end—watching baseball on TV—proving that poems can capture the joy even in the most ordinary things we do.

Games and sports teach us many different lessons. Observers have long noticed that little girls more often settle to play within a circle's embrace while boys break the enclosure, striking out with mock battles and competition. Enigmatic poems, like Robert Frost's "The Secret Sits," explore these circles and tantalize us with the mystery at the heart of the simplest things. And Nikki Giovanni telescopes time in "The Girls in the Circle," where young girls playing dress-up could also be older women playing more dangerous games.

The Secret Sits
Robert Frost

We dance round in a ring and suppose,
But the Secret sits in the middle and knows.

Hide-and-Seek, 1933
Galway Kinnell

Once when we were playing
hide-and-seek and it was time
to go home, the rest gave up
on the game before it was done
and forgot I was still hiding.
I remained hidden as a matter
of honor until the moon rose.

Block City

Robert Louis Stevenson

What are you able to build with your blocks?
Castle and palaces, temples and docks.
Rain may keep raining, and others go roam,
But I can be happy and building at home.

Let the sofa be mountains, the carpet be sea,
There I'll establish a city for me:
A church and a mill and a palace beside,
And a harbor as well where my vessels may ride.

Great is the palace with pillar and wall,
A sort of a tower on the top of it all,
And steps coming down in an orderly way
To where my toy vessels lie safe in the bay.

This one is sailing and that one is moored:
Hark to the song of the sailors on board!
And see, on the steps of my palace, the kings
Coming and going with presents and things!

Now I have done with it, down let it go!
All in a moment the town is laid low.
Block upon block lying scattered and free,
What is there left of my town by the sea?

Yet as I saw it, I see it again,
The church and the palace, the ships and the men,
And as long as I live and where'er I may be,
I'll always remember my town by the sea.

The Girls in the Circle
Nikki Giovanni

The girls in the circle
Have painted their toes

They twisted their braids
With big yellow bows

They took Grandma's face powder
And powdered each nose

And sprayed *Evening In Paris*
All over their clothes

They are amazed
At how they look
They smell good too
Mother may not be amused

The girls in the circle
Now tease and giggle

They look so grown up
With that high heel wiggle

Their pearls are flapping
Their dresses flow

They are so sorry
They have no place to go

Mother refuses to drive them
Anywhere
Looking like that

We Real Cool

Gwendolyn Brooks

The Pool Players.
Seven at the Golden Shovel.

We real cool. We
Left school. We

Lurk late. We
Strike straight. We

Sing sin. We
Thin gin. We

Jazz June. We
Die soon.

120

Slam, Dunk, & Hook
Yusef Komunyakaa

Fast breaks. Lay ups. With Mercury's
Insignia on our sneakers,
We outmaneuvered to footwork
Of bad angels. Nothing but a hot
Swish of strings like silk
Ten feet out. In the roundhouse
Labyrinth our bodies
Created, we could almost
Last forever, poised in midair
Like storybook sea monsters.
A high note hung there
A long second. Off
The rim. We'd corkscrew
Up & dunk balls that exploded
The skullcap of hope & good
Intention. Lanky, all hands
& feet . . . sprung rhythm.
We were metaphysical when girls
Cheered on the sidelines.
Tangled up in a falling,

Muscles were a bright motor
Double-flashing to the metal hoop
Nailed to our oak.
When Sonny Boy's mama died
He played nonstop all day, so hard
Our backboard splintered.
Glistening with sweat,
We rolled the ball off
Our fingertips. Trouble
Was there slapping a blackjack
Against an open palm.
Dribble, drive to the inside,
& glide like a sparrow hawk.
Lay ups. Fast breaks.
We had moves we didn't know
We had. Our bodies spun
On swivels of bone & faith,
Through a lyric slipknot
Of joy, & we knew we were
Beautiful & dangerous.

Defender
Linda Sue Park

Everyone wants to get the ball,
Run with it, and score a goal.
But when we win one–nothing,
that "nothing" means everything.

It's tough, playing for nothing.
Defense: Intense immense suspense.

Zuri at Bat

Nikki Grimes

Dear Danitra,
At the softball game last week,
smart-mouth J.T. snickered loud and said,
"What makes you think a puny girl like you can
help us win?"
"Exactly where you been?" I asked him, stepping in.
When the pitch came, I slammed the ball so far,
it ripped through the clouds and headed for a star.
I strutted 'round the bases, took my own sweet time.
My new friend, Nina, laughed and bet J.T.
he couldn't hit a ball as far as me.
He can't, and that's a fact.

Casey at the Bat

A Ballad of the Republic, Sung in the Year 1888

Ernest Lawrence Thayer

The outlook wasn't brilliant for the Mudville nine that day;
The score stood four to two but with one inning more to play.
And then when Cooney died at first, and Barrows did the same,
A sickly silence fell upon the patrons of the game.

A straggling few got up to go in deep despair. The rest
Clung to that hope which springs eternal in the human breast;
They thought if only Casey could but get a whack at that—
We'd put up even money, now, with Casey at the bat.

But Flynn preceded Casey, as did also Jimmy Blake,
And the former was a lulu and the latter was a cake;
So upon that stricken multitude grim melancholy sat,
For there seemed but little chance of Casey's getting to the bat.

But Flynn let drive a single, to the wonderment of all,
And Blake, the much despised, tore the cover off the ball;
And when the dust had lifted, and men saw what had occurred,
There was Jimmy safe at second and Flynn a-hugging third.

Then from 5,000 throats and more there rose a lusty yell;
It rumbled through the valley, it rattled in the dell;
It knocked upon the mountain and recoiled upon the flat,
For Casey, mighty Casey, was advancing to the bat.

There was ease in Casey's manner as he stepped into his place;
There was pride in Casey's bearing and a smile on Casey's face.
And when, responding to the cheers, he lightly doffed his hat,
No stranger in the crowd could doubt 'twas Casey at the bat.

Ten thousand eyes were on him as he rubbed his hands with dirt;
Five thousand tongues applauded when he wiped them on his shirt.
Then while the writhing pitcher ground the ball into his hip,
Defiance gleamed in Casey's eye, a sneer curled Casey's lip.

And now the leather-covered sphere came hurtling through the air,
And Casey stood a-watching it in haughty grandeur there.
Close by the sturdy batsman the ball unheeded sped—
"That ain't my style," said Casey. "Strike one," the umpire said.

From the benches, black with people, there went up a muffled roar,
Like the beating of the storm-waves on a stern and distant shore.
"Kill him! Kill the umpire!" shouted someone on the stand;
And it's likely they'd have killed him had not Casey raised his hand.

With a smile of Christian charity great Casey's visage shone;
He stilled the rising tumult; he bade the game go on;
He signaled to the pitcher, and once more the spheroid flew;
But Casey still ignored it, and the umpire said, "Strike two."

"Fraud!" cried the maddened thousands, and echo answered fraud;
But one scornful look from Casey and the audience was awed.
They saw his face grow stern and cold, they saw his muscles strain,
And they knew that Casey wouldn't let that ball go by again.

The sneer is gone from Casey's lip, his teeth are clinched in hate;
He pounds with cruel violence his bat upon the plate.
And now the pitcher holds the ball, and now he lets it go,
And now the air is shattered by the force of Casey's blow.

Oh, somewhere in this favored land the sun is shining bright;
The band is playing somewhere, and somewhere hearts are light,
And somewhere men are laughing, and somewhere children shout;
But there is no joy in Mudville—mighty Casey has struck out.

Casey's Revenge

Grantland Rice

There were saddened hearts in Mudville for a week or even more;
There were muttered oaths and curses—every fan in town was sore.
"Just think," said one, "how soft it looked with Casey at the bat,
And then to think he'd go and spring a bush league trick like that!"

All his past fame was forgotten—he was now a hopeless "shine."
They called him "Strike-Out Casey," from the mayor down the line;
And as he came to bat each day his bosom heaved a sigh,
While a look of hopeless fury shone in mighty Casey's eye.

He pondered in the days gone by that he had been their king,
That when he strolled up to the plate they made the welkin ring;
But now his nerve had vanished, for when he heard them hoot
He "fanned" or "popped out" daily, like some minor league recruit.

He soon began to sulk and loaf, his batting eye went lame;
No home runs on the score card now were chalked against his name;
The fans without exception gave the manager no peace,
For one and all kept clamoring for Casey's quick release.

The Mudville squad began to slump, the team was in the air;
Their playing went from bad to worse—nobody seemed to care.
"Back to the woods with Casey!" was the cry from Rooters' Row.
"Get some one who can hit the ball, and let that big dub go!"

The lane is long, some one has said, that never turns again,
And Fate, though fickle, often gives another chance to men;
And Casey smiled; his rugged face no longer wore a frown—
The pitcher who had started all the trouble came to town.

All Mudville had assembled—ten thousand fans had come
To see the twirler who had put big Casey on the bum;
And when he stepped into the box, the multitude went wild;
He doffed his cap in proud disdain, but Casey only smiled.

"Play ball!" the umpire's voice rang out, and then the game began.
But in that throng of thousands there was not a single fan
Who thought that Mudville had a chance, and with the setting sun
Their hopes sank low—the rival team was leading "four to one."

The last half of the ninth came round, with no change in the score;
But when the first man up hit safe, the crowd began to roar;
The din increased, the echo of ten thousand shouts was heard
When the pitcher hit the second and gave "four balls" to the third.

Three men on base—nobody out—three runs to tie the game!
A triple meant the highest niche in Mudville's hall of fame;
But here the rally ended and the gloom was deep as night,
When the fourth one "fouled to catcher" and the fifth "flew out to right."

A dismal groan in chorus came; a scowl was on each face
When Casey walked up, bat in hand, and slowly took his place;
His bloodshot eyes in fury gleamed, his teeth were clenched in hate;
He gave his cap a vicious hook and pounded on the plate.

But fame is fleeting as the wind and glory fades away;
There were no wild and woolly cheers, no glad acclaim this day;
They hissed and groaned and hooted as they clamored: "Strike him out!"
But Casey gave no outward sign that he had heard this shout.

(continued)

The pitcher smiled and cut one loose—across the plate it sped;
Another hiss, another groan. "Strike one!" the umpire said.
Zip! Like a shot the second curve broke just below the knee.
"Strike two!" the umpire roared aloud; but Casey made no plea.

No roasting for the umpire now—his was an easy lot;
But here the pitcher whirled again—was that a rifle shot?
A whack, a crack, and out through space the leather pellet flew,
A blot against the distant sky, a speck against the blue.

Above the fence in center field in rapid whirling flight
The sphere sailed on—the blot grew dim and then was lost to sight.
Ten thousand hats were thrown in air, ten thousand threw a fit,
But no one ever found the ball that mighty Casey hit.

O, somewhere in this favored land dark clouds may hide the sun,
And somewhere bands no longer play and children have no fun!
And somewhere over blighted lives there hangs a heavy pall,
But Mudville hearts are happy now, *for Casey hit the ball.*

May

John Updike

Now children may
    Go out of doors,
Without their coats,
    To candy stores.

The apple branches
    And the pear
May float their blossoms
    Through the air,

And Daddy may
    Get out his hoe
To plant tomatoes
    In a row,

And, afterward,
    May lazily
Look at some baseball
    On TV.

Four Score and Seven Years Ago

and other poems about war

War has inspired some of the greatest poems ever written. Poets have memorialized the bravery, the nobility, and the sacrifice of those who fight, and the suffering and loss of those who love them. Commemorating warriors is one way society can show gratitude and provide inspiration to future generations. But since the poet's role is also to speak truth to power, poets have long explored war's futility. "The Destruction of Sennacherib" by Lord Byron, and Shakespeare's Saint Crispin's Day speech from *Henry V*, concern themselves with the immortality of the hero and his glorious deeds. Modern poetry, like Nabokov's "When he was small, when he would fall," more often focuses on the soldier as an ordinary person, or the moral dilemmas faced in wartime.

One of the most powerful antiwar poems is "Charge of the Light Brigade," by Alfred, Lord Tennyson. Writing about a Crimean War battle in which the British suffered needless and disastrous losses, Tennyson condemns the officers who ordered the charge, while honoring the bravery of the soldiers who carried it out. We want to believe that such sacrifice is always for a noble cause, but the poem reminds us that questioning authority in order to save lives is another way to honor the fallen. Memorizing and recalling such poems can give us comfort and resolve when we need it most.

This section also includes a soldier's poem about coming home—"Ukase" by World War II Private First Class C. G. Tiggas—as well as a poem by Pastor Martin Niemöller, who was sent to Dachau for opposing the Nazi takeover of German churches.

Seamus Heaney grew up in Northern Ireland during a time of great violence between Catholics and Protestants. In 1995, when he was awarded the Nobel Prize for Literature, he told the story of a minibus full of workers who were held up at gunpoint. The masked hijackers ordered everyone off the bus, and asked if anybody was Catholic. All but one of the workers were Protestant, and the Catholic man had to decide whether to identify himself and face certain death, or stay silent. The Protestant man next to him squeezed his hand in a gesture of sympathy, suggesting that no one would turn him in if he chose silence. But the Catholic man stepped forward, bearing witness to his faith, only to hear the sound of gunfire massacring his companions.

Heaney elevates this hand squeeze into a gesture of brotherhood. This simple act demonstrates that by recognizing our common humanity, individuals can bring about a better future, in spite of the overwhelming violence around us. The duty of the citizen is to stay engaged in the world, and to stand against brutality wherever we find it. We must believe that each act of courage will inspire others—and, as Heaney suggests, that those individual acts will combine to prove "once in a lifetime / That justice can rise up / And hope and history rhyme."

Will, lost in a sea of trouble

Archilochos
translated by Kenneth Rexroth

Will, lost in a sea of trouble,
Rise, save yourself from the whirlpool
Of the enemies of willing.
Courage exposes ambushes.
Steadfastness destroys enemies.
Keep your victories hidden.
Do not sulk over defeat.
Accept good. Bend before evil.
Learn the rhythm which binds all men.

The Destruction of Sennacherib

George Gordon, Lord Byron

The Assyrian came down like the wolf on the fold,
And his cohorts were gleaming in purple and gold;
And the sheen of their spears was like stars on the sea,
When the blue wave rolls nightly on deep Galilee.

Like the leaves of the forest when Summer is green,
That host with their banners at sunset were seen:
Like the leaves of the forest when Autumn hath flown,
That host on the morrow lay withered and strown.

For the Angel of Death spread his wings on the blast,
And breathed in the face of the foe as he passed;
And the eyes of the sleepers waxed deadly and chill,
And their hearts but once heaved, and forever grew still.

And there lay the steed with his nostrils all wide,
But through it there rolled not the breath of his pride;
And the foam of his gasping lay white on the turf,
And cold as the spray of the rock-beating surf.

And there lay the rider distorted and pale,
With the dew on his brow, and the rust on his mail;
And the tents were all silent, the banners alone,
The lances unlifted, the trumpet unblown.

And the widows of Ashur are loud in their wail,
And the idols are broke in the temple of Baal;
And the might of the Gentile, unsmote by the sword,
Hath melted like snow in the glance of the Lord!

Ozymandias

Percy Bysshe Shelley

I met a traveler from an antique land
Who said: Two vast and trunkless legs of stone
Stand in the desert. Near them, on the sand,
Half sunk, a shattered visage lies, whose frown
And wrinkled lip and sneer of cold command
Tell that its sculptor well those passions read
Which yet survive, stamped on these lifeless things,
The hand that mocked them and the heart that fed;
And on the pedestal these words appear:
"My name is Ozymandias, king of kings:
Look on my works, ye Mighty, and despair!"
Nothing beside remains. Round the decay
Of that colossal wreck, boundless and bare,
The lone and level sands stretch far away.

from *Henry V*, IV, iii, 56–67

William Shakespeare

This story shall the good man teach his son;
And Crispin Crispian shall ne'er go by,
From this day to the ending of the world,
But we in it shall be remembered;
We few, we happy few, we band of brothers;
For he to-day that sheds his blood with me
Shall be my brother; be he ne'er so vile
This day shall gentle his condition:
And gentlemen in England now a-bed
Shall think themselves accurs'd they were not here,
And hold their manhoods cheap whiles any speaks
That fought with us upon Saint Crispin's day.

Shiloh

A Requiem
(April, 1862)
Herman Melville

Skimming lightly, wheeling still,
　　The swallows fly low
Over the field in clouded days,
　　The forest-field of Shiloh—
Over the field where April rain
Solaced the parched ones stretched in pain
Through the pause of night
That followed the Sunday fight
　　Around the church of Shiloh—
The church so lone, the log-built one,
That echoed to many a parting groan
　　　　And natural prayer
　　Of dying foemen mingled there—
Foemen at morn, but friends at eve—
　　Fame or country least their care:
(What like a bullet can undeceive!)
　　But now they lie low,
While over them the swallows skim,
　　And all is hushed at Shiloh.

Gettysburg Address

Abraham Lincoln

Four score and seven years ago
our fathers brought forth on this continent
a new nation, conceived in liberty,
and dedicated to the proposition that all men are created equal.

Now we are engaged in a great civil war,
testing whether that nation,
or any nation so conceived and so dedicated,
can long endure.

We are met on a great battlefield of that war.
We have come to dedicate a portion of that field
as a final resting-place for those who here gave their lives
that that nation might live.
It is altogether fitting and proper that we should do this.

But, in a larger sense, we cannot dedicate—
we cannot consecrate—we cannot hallow—this ground.
The brave men, living and dead, who struggle here,
have consecrated it far above our poor power to add or detract.

The world will little note, nor long remember, what we say here,
but it can never forget what they did here.

It is for us, the living, rather, to be dedicated here
to the unfinished work which they who fought here
have thus far so nobly advanced.

It is rather for us to be here dedicated
to the great task remaining before us—
that from these honored dead we take increased devotion
to that cause for which they gave the last full measure of devotion—
that we here highly resolve
that these dead shall not have died in vain—
that this nation, under God, shall have a new birth of freedom—
and that government of the people, by the people, for the people,
shall not perish from the earth.

Charge of the Light Brigade

Alfred, Lord Tennyson

Half a league, half a league,
Half a league onward,
All in the valley of Death
　　Rode the six hundred.
"Forward, the Light Brigade!
Charge for the guns!" he said:
Into the valley of Death
　　Rode the six hundred.

"Forward, the Light Brigade!"
Was there a man dismay'd?
Not tho' the soldiers knew
　　Someone had blunder'd:
Theirs not to make reply,
Theirs not to reason why,
Theirs but to do and die:
Into the valley of Death
　　Rode the six hundred.

Cannon to right of them,
Cannon to left of them,
Cannon in front of them
　　Volley'd and thunder'd;
Storm'd at with shot and shell,
Boldly they rode and well,
Into the jaws of Death,
Into the mouth of Hell,
　　Rode the six hundred.

Flash'd all their sabres bare,
Flash'd as they turned in air,
Sabring the gunners there,
Charging an army, while
　　All the world wonder'd:
Plunged in the battery smoke,
Right thro' the line they broke;
Cossack and Russian
Reel'd from the sabre-stroke
　　Shatter'd and sunder'd.
Then they rode back, but not—
　　Not the six hundred.

Cannon to the right of them,
Cannon to left of them,
Cannon behind them
　　Volley'd and thunder'd;
Stormed at with shot and shell,
While horse and hero fell,
They that had fought so well
Came thro' the jaws of Death,
Back from the mouth of Hell,
All that was left of them
　　Left of six hundred.

When can their glory fade?
O the wild charge they made!
　　All the world wonder'd.
Honour the charge they made!
Honour the Light Brigade,
　　Noble six hundred!

Ukase

Private First Class C. G. Tiggas

When this is over
And we come home again,
Forget the band
And the cheers from the stand,
Just have the things
Well in hand—
The things we fought for.
Understand?

When he was small, when he would fall
Vladimir Nabokov

When he was small, when he would fall,
on sand or carpet he would lie
quite flat and still until he knew
what he would do: get up or cry.

After the battle, flat and still
upon a hillside now he lies—
but there is nothing to decide,
for he can neither cry nor rise.

The Unknown Soldier

Billy Rose

There's a graveyard near the White House
    Where the Unknown Soldier lies,
And the flowers there are sprinkled
    With the tears from mother's eyes.

I stood there not so long ago
    With roses for the brave,
And suddenly I heard a voice
    Speak from out the grave:

"I am the Unkown Soldier,"
    The spirit voice began,
"And I think I have the right
    To ask some questions man to man.

"Are my buddies taken care of?
    Was their victory so sweet?
Is that big reward you offered
    Selling pencils on the street?

"Did they really win the freedom
    They battled to achieve?
Do you still respect that Croix de Guerre
    Above the empty sleeve?

"Does a gold star in the window
    Now mean anything at all?
I wonder how my old girl feels
    When she hears a bugle call.

"And that baby who sang
        'Hello, Central, give me no man's land'—
Can they replace her daddy
        With a military band?

"I wonder if the profiteers
        Have satisfied their greed?
I wonder if a soldier's mother
        Ever is in need?

"I wonder if the kings, who planned it all
        Are really satisfied?
They played their game of checkers
        And eleven million died.

"I am the Unknown Soldier
        And maybe I died in vain,
But if I were alive and my country called,
        I'd do it all over again."

First They Came for the Jews
Martin Niemöller

First they came for the Jews
and I did not speak out—
because I was not a Jew.
Then they came for the communists
and I did not speak out—
because I was not a communist.
Then they came for the trade unionists
and I did not speak out—
because I was not a trade unionist.
Then they came for me—
and there was no one left
to speak out for me.

from "Voices from Lemnos"

Seamus Heaney

Human beings suffer,
They torture one another,
They get hurt and get hard.
No poem or play or song
Can fully right a wrong
Inflicted and endured.

History says, Don't hope
On this side of the grave
But then, once in a lifetime
The longed-for tidal wave
Of justice can rise up,
And hope and history rhyme.

So hope for a great sea-change
On the far side of revenge.
Believe that a farther shore
Is reachable from here.
Believe in miracles
And cures and healing wells.

Call miracle self-healing:
The utter self-revealing
Double-take of feeling.
If there's fire on the mountain
And lightning and storm
And a god speaks from the sky

That means someone is hearing
The outcry and the birth-cry
Of new life at its term.
It means once in a lifetime
That justice can rise up
And hope and history rhyme.

Peace

Gerard Manley Hopkins

When will you ever, Peace, wild wooddove, shy wings shut,
Your round me roaming end, and under be my boughs?
When, when, Peace, will you, Peace? I'll not play hypocrite
To own my heart: I yield you do come sometimes; but
That piecemeal peace is poor peace. What pure peace allows
Alarms of wars, the daunting wars, the death of it?

O surely, reaving Peace, my Lord should leave in lieu
Some good! And so he does leave Patience exquisite,
That plumes to Peace thereafter. And when Peace here does house
He comes with work to do, he does not come to coo,
    He comes to brood and sit.

The World Is So Full of a Number of Things

and other poems about nature

Robert Louis Stevenson's couplet "The world is so full of a number of things, / I'm sure we should all be as happy as kings" captures the inquisitive, celebratory spirit at the heart of poetry.

The mysteries of morning, of the seasons, and of our place in the world are all questions that have occupied children and poets throughout the ages. My son's favorite poem is Wallace Stevens's "Anecdote of the Jar," which he memorized so that he could stay connected to the natural world while confined in the classroom.

Likewise, the Navajo song "In beauty may I walk" expresses the harmony of nature. The last poem in this section, which my daughter translated for me for Christmas, is from Ovid's *Metamorphoses*. It is an ancient text that brings us back to the beginning, which seems like a good place to end.

from "Auguries of Innocence"
William Blake

To see a World in a Grain of Sand
And a Heaven in a Wild Flower,
Hold Infinity in the palm of your hand
And Eternity in an hour.

Happy Thought
Robert Louis Stevenson

The world is so full of a number of things,
I'm sure we should all be as happy as kings.

What Are Heavy?
Christina Rossetti

What are heavy? sea-sand and sorrow:
What are brief? today and tomorrow:
What are frail? spring blossoms and youth:
What are deep? the ocean and truth.

Devotion
Robert Frost

The heart can think of no devotion
Greater than being shore to the ocean—
Holding the curve of one position,
Counting an endless repetition.

Will there really be a "Morning"?

Emily Dickinson

Will there really be a "Morning"?
Is there such a thing as "Day"?
Could I see it from the mountains
If I were as tall as they?

Has it feet like Water lilies?
Has it feathers like a Bird?
Is it brought from famous countries
Of which I have never heard?

Oh some Scholar! Oh some Sailor!
Oh some Wise Man from the skies!
Please to tell a little Pilgrim
Where the place called "Morning" lies!

Ballad of the Morning Streets

Amiri Baraka

The magic of the day is the morning
I want to say the day is morning high
and sweet, good
morning.

The ballad of the morning streets, sweet
voices turns
of cool warm weather
high around the early windows grey to blue
and down again amongst the kids and
broken signs, is pure love magic, sweet day
come into me, let me live with you
and dig your blazing

who are you, little i

E. E. Cummings

who are you, little i

(five or six years old)
peering from some high

window; at the gold
of november sunset

(and feeling that: if day
has to become night

this is a beautiful way)

In beauty may I walk

From the Navajo
translated by Jerome K. Rothenberg

In beauty	may I walk
All day long	may I walk
Through the returning seasons	may I walk

Beautifully will I possess again
Beautifully birds
Beautifully joyful birds

On the trail marked with pollen	may I walk
With grasshoppers about my feet	may I walk
With dew about my feet	may I walk
With beauty	may I walk
With beauty before me	may I walk
With beauty behind me	may I walk
With beauty above me	may I walk
With beauty all around me	may I walk

In old age, wandering on a trail of beauty,
                                lively, may I walk
In old age, wandering on a trail of beauty,
                        living again, may I walk

It is finished in beauty
It is finished in beauty

Tommy
Gwendolyn Brooks

I put a seed into the ground
And said, "I'll watch it grow."
I watered it and cared for it
As well as I could know.
One day I walked in my back yard,
And oh, what did I see!
My seed had popped itself right out,
Without consulting me.

from *As You Like It*, II, v, 5–12; 18–25
William Shakespeare

    Under the greenwood tree
    Who loves to lie with me,
    And tune his merry note
    Unto the sweet bird's throat—
Come hither, come hither, come hither!
    Here shall he see
    No enemy
But winter and rough weather.

    Who doth ambition shun
    And loves to live i' the sun,
    Seeking the food he eats
    And pleased with what he gets—
Come hither, come hither, come hither!
    Here shall he see
    No enemy
But winter and rough weather.

Anecdote of the Jar
Wallace Stevens

I placed a jar in Tennessee,
And round it was, upon a hill.
It made the slovenly wilderness
Surround that hill.

The wilderness rose up to it,
And sprawled around, no longer wild.
The jar was round upon the ground
And tall and of a port in air.

It took dominion everywhere.
The jar was gray and bare.
It did not give of bird or bush,
Like nothing else in Tennessee.

The Snow Man

Wallace Stevens

One must have a mind of winter
To regard the frost and the boughs
Of the pine-trees crusted with snow;

And have been cold a long time
To behold the junipers shagged with ice,
The spruces rough in the distant glitter

Of the January sun; and not to think
Of any misery in the sound of the wind,
In the sound of a few leaves,

Which is the sound of the land
Full of the same wind
That is blowing in the same bare place

For the listener, who listens in the snow,
And, nothing himself, beholds
Nothing that is not there and the nothing that is.

Winter Trees

William Carlos Williams

All the complicated details

of the attiring and

the disattiring are completed!

A liquid moon

moves gently among

the long branches.

Thus having prepared their buds

against a sure winter

the wise trees

stand sleeping in the cold.

Scarcely had the Creator separated all things into their finite bands,

When the stars began to blaze in the whole sky, which had been for so long buried in blind darkness;

And so that no realm of the universe would lack life, he made the firmament to hold the bright constellations and the gods and goddesses.

The waves gleamed with swimming fish, the earth had its wild beasts, the gusty air its birds.

A holier animal with a mind capable of loftier things and who could be a master over all the other creatures was still absent:

So man was born, either the Creator of all things made him from divine stock, so as to found a better world,

or else perhaps the new made earth, so recently separated from the heavens, kept some essences of the familiar sky.

That earth, sprung from the Creator, mixed with rainwater, was molded by Prometheus into the appearance of the gods who govern all things,

And while all the other animals look down upon the earth, he made the face of man to look upon the heavens, and to hold his face up toward the stars,

And so the earth, which once was crude and without form, took on the unknown shape of humankind.

The World
William Brighty Rands

Great, wide, beautiful, wonderful World,
With the wonderful water round you curled,
And the wonderful grass upon your breast—
World, you are beautifully drest.

The wonderful air is over me,
And the wonderful wind is shaking the tree,
It walks on the water, and whirls the mills,
And talks to itself on the tops of the hills.

You friendly Earth, how far do you go,
With the wheatfields that nod and the rivers that flow,
With the cities and gardens, and cliffs, and isles,
And people upon you for thousands of miles?

Ah, you are so great, and I am so small,
I tremble to think of you, World, at all;
And yet, when I said my prayers today,
A whisper inside me seemed to say,
"You are more than the Earth, though you are such a dot:
You can love and think, and the Earth cannot."

Extra Credit

There are people who can memorize just about anything—baseball statistics, state capitals, the presidents, and even the vice presidents. They do it for their own satisfaction, or to impress their friends, but you never know what may come of this unusual talent. In fact, the art of memorization begins with a dramatic story.

In ancient Greece, a rich nobleman hired the famous poet Simonides to compose and recite a poem praising him at a banquet. Although most of the poem was about the wonderful host, in the middle of the poem, Simonides also briefly praised two Greek gods—Castor and Pollux. The host was furious that the poem was not only and entirely about him. He refused to pay half of what he had promised, telling Simonides to get the rest from Castor and Pollux. A little while later, a messenger came in to dinner to say that there were two young men outside who wished to see Simonides. Some said they looked like Castor and Pollux. While the poet stepped out of the room, the roof of the banquet hall collapsed, killing everyone inside. The bodies were mangled beyond recognition. Fortunately, Simonides was able to remember where each guest had been sitting and thereby identify the bodies. Ever since, Simonides has been credited with inventing the rules of memory.

So for all those for whom no poem is long enough, here is a selection of poems that carry us along on the backs of plot, rhyme, melody, and images. Mostly they are old chestnuts that have fallen out of favor, but the feats of memory required to master them will impress even the most modern audiences. Go ahead and give them a try. You won't be graded—it's just for extra credit.

from *The Canterbury Tales*, General Prologue

Geoffrey Chaucer

Whan that Aprill with his shoures soote
The droghte of March hath perced to the roote,
And bathed every veyne in swich licour
Of which vertu engendred is the flour;
Whan Zephirus eek with his sweete breeth
Inspired hath in every holt and heeth
The tendre croppes, and the yonge sonne
Hath in the Ram his halve cours yronne,
And smale foweles maken melodye,
That slepen al the nyght with open ye
(So priketh hem nature in hir corages);
Thanne longen folk to goon on pilgrimages,
And palmeres for to seken straunge strondes,
To ferne halwes, kowthe in sondry londes;
And specially from every shires ende
Of Engelond, to Caunterbury they wende,
The hooly blisful martir for to seke,
That hem hath holpen whan that they were seeke.

Young Lochinvar

Sir Walter Scott

Oh, young Lochinvar is come out of the West,—
Through all the wide Border his steed was the best,
And save his good broadsword he weapons had none,—
He rode all unarm'd, and he rode all alone.
So faithful in love, and so dauntless in war,
There never was knight like the young Lochinvar.

He stay'd not for brake, and he stopp'd not for stone,
He swam the Esk river where ford there was none,
But ere he alighted at Netherby gate,
The bride had consented, the gallant came late;
For a laggard in love, and a dastard in war
Was to wed the fair Ellen of brave Lochinvar.

So boldly he enter'd the Netherby hall,
'Mong bridesmen and kinsmen and brothers and all.
Then spoke the bride's father, his hand on his sword
(For the poor craven bridegroom said never a word)
"Oh, come ye in peace here, or come ye in war,
Or to dance at our bridal, young Lord Lochinvar?"

"I long woo'd your daughter,—my suit you denied;
Love swells like the Solway, but ebbs like its tide;
And now am I come, with this lost love of mine
To lead but one measure, drink one cup of wine.
There are maidens in Scotland more lovely, by far,
That would gladly be bride to the young Lochinvar."

The bride kissed the goblet, the knight took it up,
He quaff'd off the wine and he threw down the cup.
She look'd down to blush, and she look'd up to sigh,
With a smile on her lips and a tear in her eye.
He took her soft hand ere her mother could bar:
"Now tread we a measure!" said young Lochinvar.

So stately his form, and so lovely her face,
That never a hall such a galliard did grace,
While her mother did fret, and her father did fume,
And the bridegroom stood dangling his bonnet and plume,
And the bridesmaids whisper'd, "'Twere better by far,
To have match'd our fair cousin with young Lochinvar."

One touch to her hand, and one word in her ear,
When they reach'd the hall-door, and the charger stood near;
So light to the croup the fair lady he swung,
So light to the saddle before her he sprung!
"She is won! we are gone, over bank, bush, and scaur;
They'll have fleet steeds that follow," quoth young Lochinvar.

There was mounting 'mong Graemes of the Netherby clan;
Forsters, Fenwicks, and Musgraves, they rode and they ran;
There was racing and chasing on Cannobie Lee,
But the lost bride of Netherby ne'er did they see.
So daring in love, and so dauntless in war,
Have ye e'er heard of gallant like young Lochinvar?

The Cremation of Sam McGee

Robert Service

There are strange things done in the midnight sun
  By the men who moil for gold;
The Arctic trails have their secret tales
  That would make your blood run cold;
The Northern Lights have seen queer sights,
  But the queerest they ever did see
Was that night on the marge of Lake Lebarge
  I cremated Sam McGee.

Now Sam McGee was from Tennessee, where the cotton blooms and blows.
Why he left his home in the South to roam 'round the Pole, God only knows.
He was always cold, but the land of gold seemed to hold him like a spell;
Though he'd often say in his homely way that "he'd sooner live in hell."

On a Christmas Day we were mushing our way over the Dawson trail.
Talk of your cold! through the parka's fold it stabbed like a driven nail.
If our eyes we'd close, then the lashes froze till sometimes we couldn't see;
It wasn't much fun, but the only one to whimper was Sam McGee.

And that very night, as we lay packed tight in our robes beneath the snow,
And the dogs were fed, and the stars o'erhead were dancing heel and toe,
He turned to me, and "Cap," says he, "I'll cash in this trip, I guess;
And if I do, I'm asking that you won't refuse my last request."

Well, he seemed so low that I couldn't say no; then he says with a sort of moan:
"It's the cursed cold, and it's got right hold till I'm chilled clean through to the bone.
Yet 'tain't being dead—it's my awful dread of the icy grave that pains;
So I want you to swear that, foul or fair, you'll cremate my last remains."

A pal's last need is a thing to heed, so I swore I would not fail;
And we started on at the streak of dawn; but God! he looked ghastly pale.
He crouched on the sleigh, and he raved all day of his home in Tennessee;
And before nightfall a corpse was all that was left of Sam McGee.

(continued)

There wasn't a breath in that land of death, and I hurried, horror-driven,
With a corpse half hid that I couldn't get rid, because of a promise given;
It was lashed to the sleigh, and it seemed to say: "You may tax your brawn and brains,
But you promised true, and it's up to you, to cremate those last remains."

Now a promise made is a debt unpaid, and the trail has its own stern code.
In the days to come, though my lips were dumb, in my heart how I cursed that load.
In the long, long night, by the lone firelight, while the huskies, round in a ring,
Howled out their woes to the homeless snows—Oh God! how I loathed the thing.

And every day that quiet clay seemed to heavy and heavier grow;
And on I went, though the dogs were spent and the grub was getting low;
The trail was bad, and I felt half mad, but I swore I would not give in;
And I'd often sing to the hateful thing, and it hearkened with a grin.

Till I came to the marge of Lake Lebarge, and a derelict there lay;
It was jammed in the ice, but I saw in a trice it was called the "Alice May."
And I looked at it, and I thought a bit, and I looked at my frozen chum;
Then "Here," said I, with a sudden cry, "is my cre-ma-tor-eum."

Some planks I tore from the cabin floor, and I lit the boiler fire;
Some coal I found that was lying around, and I heaped the fuel higher;
The flames just soared, and the furnace roared—such a blaze you seldom see;
And I burrowed a hole in the glowing coal, and I stuffed in Sam McGee.

Then I made a hike, for I didn't like to hear him sizzle so;
And the heavens scowled, and the huskies howled, and the wind began to blow.
It was icy cold, but the hot sweat rolled down my cheeks, and I don't know why;
And the greasy smoke in an inky cloak went streaking down the sky.

I do not know how long in the snow I wrestled with grisly fear;
But the stars came out and they danced about ere again I ventured near;
I was sick with dread, but I bravely said: "I'll just take a peep inside.
I guess he's cooked, and it's time I looked"; . . . then the door I opened wide.

And there sat Sam, looking cool and calm, in the heart of the furnace roar;
And he wore a smile you could see a mile, and said: "Please close that door.
It's fine in here, but I greatly fear, you'll let in the cold and storm—
Since I left Plumtree, down in Tennessee, it's the first time I've been warm."

There are strange things done in the midnight sun
    By the men who moil for gold;
The Arctic trails have their secret tales
    That would make your blood run cold;
The Northern Lights have seen queer sights,
    But the queerest they ever did see
Was that night on the marge of Lake Lebarge
    I cremated Sam McGee.

Paul Revere's Ride

Henry Wadsworth Longfellow

Listen, my children, and you shall hear
Of the midnight ride of Paul Revere
On the eighteenth of April, in Seventy-five;
Hardly a man is now alive
Who remembers that famous day and year.

He said to his friend, "If the British march
By land or sea from the town to-night,
Hang a lantern aloft in the belfry arch
Of the North Church tower as a signal light—
One, if by land, and two, if by sea;
And I on the opposite shore will be,
Ready to ride and spread the alarm
Through every Middlesex village and farm,
For the country folk to be up and to arm."

Then he said "Good-night," and with muffled oar
Silently row'd to the Charlestown shore,
Just as the moon rose over the bay,
Where swinging wide at her moorings lay
The Somerset, British man-of-war;
A phantom ship, with each mast and spar
Across the moon like a prison bar,
And a huge black hulk, that was magnified
By its own reflection in the tide.

Meanwhile his friend, through alley and street,
Wanders and watches with eager ears,
Till in the silence around him he hears
The muster of men at the barrack-door,
The sound of arms, and the tramp of feet,
And the measured tread of the grenadiers,
Marching down to their boats on the shore.

Then he climb'd the tower of the Old North Church,
By the wooden stairs, with stealthy tread,
To the belfry-chamber overhead,
And started the pigeons from their perch
On the sombre rafters, that round him made

Masses and moving shapes of shade,—
By the trembling ladder, steep and tall,
To the highest window in the wall,
Where he paused to listen and look down
A moment on the roofs of the town
And the moonlight flowing over all.

Beneath, in the churchyard, lay the dead,
In their night-encampment on the hill,
Wrapp'd in silence so deep and still
That he could hear, like a sentinel's tread,
The watchful night-wind, as it went
Creeping along from tent to tent,
And seeming to whisper, "All is well!"
A moment only he feels the spell
Of the place and the hour, and the secret dread
Of the lonely belfry and the dead;
For suddenly all his thoughts are bent
On a shadowy something far away,
Where the river widens to meet the bay,—
A line of black that bends and floats
On the rising tide like a bridge of boats.
Meanwhile, impatient to mount and ride,
Booted and spurr'd, with a heavy stride
On the opposite shore walk'd Paul Revere.
Now he patted his horse's side,
Now he gazed at the landscape far and near,
Then, impetuous, stamp'd the earth,

(continued)

And turn'd and tighten'd his saddle-girth;
But mostly he watched with eager search
The belfry-tower of the Old North Church,
As it rose above the graves on the hill,
Lonely and spectral and sombre and still.
And lo! as he looks, on the belfry's height
A glimmer, and then a gleam of light!
He springs to the saddle, the bridle he turns,
But lingers and gazes, till full on his sight
A second lamp in the belfry burns.

A hurry of hoofs in a village street,
A shape in the moonlight, a bulk in the dark,
And beneath, from the pebbles, in passing,
    a spark
Struck out by a steed flying fearless and fleet:
That was all; and yet, through the gloom and the light,
The fate of a nation was riding that night;
And the spark struck out by that steed, in his flight
Kindled the land into flame with its heat.

He has left the village and mounted the steep,
And beneath him, tranquil and broad and deep,
Is the Mystic, meeting the ocean tides,
And under the alders that skirt its edge,
Now soft on the sand, now loud on the ledge,
Is heard the tramp of his steed as he rides.

It was twelve by the village clock
When he cross'd the bridge into Medford town.
He heard the crowing of the cock,
And the barking of the farmer's dog,
And felt the damp of the river fog,
That rises after the sun goes down.

It was one by the village clock
When he galloped into Lexington.
He saw the gilded weathercock
Swim in the moonlight as he pass'd,
And the meeting-house windows, black and bare,
Gaze at him with a spectral glare,
As if they already stood aghast
At the bloody work they would look upon.

It was two by the village clock
When he came to the bridge in Concord town.
He heard the bleating of the flock,
And the twitter of birds among the trees,
And felt the breath of the morning breeze
Blowing over the meadow brown.
And one was safe and asleep in his bed
Who at the bridge would be first to fall,
Who that day would be lying dead,
Pierced by a British musket-ball.

You know the rest; in the books you have read
How the British Regulars fired and fled,—
How the farmers gave them ball for ball,
From behind each fence and farmyard wall,
Chasing the redcoats down the lane,
Then crossing the fields to emerge again
Under the trees at the turn of the road,
And only pausing to fire and load.
So through the night rode Paul Revere,
And so through the night went his cry of alarm
To every Middlesex village and farm,—
A cry of defiance, and not of fear,
A voice in the darkness, a knock at the door,
And a word that shall echo for evermore!
For, borne on the night-wind of the Past,
Through all our history, to the last,
In the hour of darkness, and peril, and need,
The people will waken and listen to hear
The hurrying hoof-beats of that steed,
And the midnight message of Paul Revere.

Kubla Khan

Or a Vision in a Dream. A Fragment
Samuel Taylor Coleridge

In Xanadu did Kubla Khan
A stately pleasure dome decree:
Where Alph, the sacred river, ran
Through caverns measureless to man
    Down to a sunless sea.
So twice five miles of fertile ground
With walls and towers were girdled round:
And there were gardens bright with sinuous rills,
Where blossomed many an incense-bearing tree;
And here were forests ancient as the hills,
Enfolding sunny spots of greenery.

But oh! that deep romantic chasm which slanted
Down the green hill athwart a cedarn cover!
A savage place! as holy and enchanted
As e'er beneath a waning moon was haunted
By woman wailing for her demon lover!
And from this chasm, with ceaseless turmoil seething
As if this earth in fast thick pants were breathing,
A mighty fountain momently was forced:
Amid whose swift half-intermitted burst
Huge fragments vaulted like rebounding hail,
Or chaffy grain beneath the thresher's flail:
And 'mid these dancing rocks at once and ever
It flung up momently the sacred river.
Five miles meandering with a mazy motion
Through wood and dale the sacred river ran,
Then reached the caverns measureless to man,

And sank in tumult to a lifeless ocean:
And 'mid this tumult Kubla heard from far
Ancestral voices prophesying war!

The shadow of the dome of pleasure
Floated midway on the waves;
Where was heard the mingled measure
From the fountains and the caves.
It was a miracle of rare device,
A sunny pleasure dome with caves of ice!

A damsel with a dulcimer
In a vision once I saw:
It was an Abyssinian maid,
And on her dulcimer she played,
Singing of Mount Abora.
Could I revive within me
Her symphony and song,
To such a deep delight 'twould win me,
That with music loud and long,
I would build that dome in air,
That sunny dome! those caves of ice!
And all who heard should see them there,
And all should cry, Beware! Beware!
His flashing eyes, his floating hair!
Weave a circle round him thrice,
And close your eyes with holy dread,
For he on honey-dew hath fed,
And drunk the milk of Paradise.

Last Poem

Catch a Little Rhyme

Eve Merriam

Once upon a time
I caught a little rhyme

I set it on the floor
but it ran right out the door

I chased it on my bicycle
but it melted to an icicle

I scooped it up in my hat
but it turned into a cat

I caught it by the tail
but it stretched into a whale

I followed it in a boat
but it changed into a goat

When I fed it tin and paper
it became a tall skyscraper

Then it grew into a kite
and flew far out of sight . . .

Index of First Lines

Index by Author Last Name

Acknowledgments

This book is dedicated to my friends who sent me the poems they remember best—and to the DreamYard poets and all the poems they are going to write.
—CK

For Molly, Caroline, Alex, and Leo, my inspiration and enthusiasm for the paintings in this book. They modeled often and effortlessly and outgrew their clothes many times during its making.

With thanks to Caroline and Gretchen, my elegant partners.
—JJM

Acknowledgments:

I would like to thank Jon Muth for his dedication to this project over many years, and his astonishing illustrations that add meaning, depth, and freshness to the poems. Applause to Gretchen Young, who believed in this book and made sure it was beautiful. I would also like to thank all the people at Disney·Hyperion who have been involved— especially Rotem Moscovich, Abby Ranger, Tanya Ross-Hughes, and Stephanie Lurie. And cheers for Esther Newberg and all the poems she has memorized. I would also like to thank Lauren Lipani and Sally McCartin for their invaluable help. Most of all, I would like to thank the young poets of DreamYard who helped select the poems for this book, especially Denisse Cotto and Destiny Campbell, as well as their amazing teachers Ellen Hagan and Renee Watson who bring poetry to life in their own work, and into the lives of so many talented students in the Bronx.
—CK

The painter would like to thank: Allen Spiegel, Abby Ranger, Sylas Ranger Lyon, Rotem Moscovich, Tanya Ross-Hughes, Joann Hill, Stephanie Lurie, and everyone at Disney·Hyperion Books for Children. And Bonnie, my beautiful, perfect wife, for patience beyond measure.
—JJM

For information address Disney·Hyperion Books, 114 Fifth Avenue, New York, New York 10011-5690.

First Edition

1 3 5 7 9 10 8 6 4 2

Printed in the United States of America

Designed by Tanya Ross-Hughes

Library of Congress Cataloging-in-Publication Data
Poems to learn by heart / [selected by] Caroline Kennedy ;
paintings by Jon J Muth.
p. cm.
ISBN-13: 978-1-4231-0805-4
ISBN-10: 1-4231-0805-1
1. American poetry. 2. English poetry. I. Kennedy, Caroline, 1957–
PS586.P575 2012
821.008—dc23

Reinforced binding

Visit www.disneyhyperionbooks.com